Weimar Radicals

Monographs in German History

The complexities and peculiarities of German history present challenges on various levels, not least on that of historiography. This series offers a platform for historians who, in response to the challenges, produce important and stimulating contributions to the various debates that take place within the discipline.

For full volume listing, please see pages 215 and 216

WEIMAR RADICALS

Nazis and Communists
between Authenticity and Performance

Timothy S. Brown

berghahn
NEW YORK · OXFORD
www.berghahnbooks.com

Published in 2009 by
Berghahn Books
www.berghahnbooks.com

Library of Congress Cataloging-in-Publication Data

Brown, Timothy Scott.
   Weimar radicals : Nazis and communists between authenticity and performance /
Timothy S. Brown.
      p. cm. — (Monographs in German history ; v. 28)
   Includes bibliographical references.
   ISBN 978-1-84545-564-4 (hardback) — ISBN 978-1-78533-336-1 (paperback) —
ISBN 978-1-84545-908-6 (ebook)
   1. Radicalism—Germany—History—20th century. 2. National Socialism—
Germany—History—20th century. 3. Communism—Germany—History—20th
century. 4. Authenticity (Philosophy)—Case studies. 5. Group identity—Case studies.
6. Militarism—Germany—History—20th century. 7. Youth movements—Germany—
History—20th century. 8. Working class—Germany—Political activity—History—20th
century. 9. Masculinity—Political aspects—Germany—History—20th century.
10. Germany—Politics and government–1918–1933. I. Title.

HN460.R3B77 2009
324.243'023809042—dc22   2008053760

British Library Cataloguing in Publication Data

A catalogue record for this book is available from the British Library

ISBN: 978-1-84545-564-4 hardback
ISBN: 978-1-78533-336-1 paperback
ISBN: 978-1-84545-908-6 ebook

To Donna
To my parents
To Gerry

CONTENTS

FIGURES

ACKNOWLEDGEMENTS

For their help in reading and commenting on the manuscript or portions of the material contained therein I wish to thank Gerald Feldman, Margaret Anderson, Victoria Bonnell, Diethelm Prowe, John Connelly, Pamela Swett, Richard Bessel, James Ward, and Nicholas Wolfinger. I also wish to express my gratitude to my colleagues in the Boston German History Workshop: Jonathan Zatlin, David Ciarlo, Daniel Ziblatt, Devin Pendas, Allison Frank, Thomas Kühne, and Uta Poiger. Further thanks is due to Verdinal and Eloise Mckean. Finally, a sincere thank you is in order to my friend and research assistant extraordinaire Alexander Holmig, without whom so much would have been impossible.

ABBREVIATIONS

Archives and Document Collections

BA   Bundesarchiv (Berlin)

BHStA   Bayerisches Hauptstaatsarchiv

BLHA   Brandenburgisches Landeshauptarchiv

GStA PK   Geheimes Staatsarchiv preußischer Kulturbesitz (Berlin-Dahlem)

HA   Hauptarchiv (Nazi party main archive)

IfZ   Institut für Zeitgeschichte (Munich)

NWHStA   Nordrhein-Westfälisches Hauptstaatsarchiv

SAPMO   Stiftung Archiv der Parteien und Massenorganisationen der DDR

Sopade   *Deutschland-Bericht der* Sopade, 2 vols., (Frankfurt am Main, 1980).

WaH   *Widerstand als "Hochverrat." Die Verfahren gegen deutsche Reichsangehörige vor dem Reichsgericht, dem Volksgerichtshof und dem Reichskriegsgericht,* (Munich, 1998).

Political Parties and Other Organizations

BVG   Berlin Transportation Company

DNVP   *Deutschnationale Volkspartei*

Gestapo   Geheime Staatspolizei

GSRN   Group of Social Revolutionary Nationalists

HJ   *Hitlerjugend* (Hitler Youth)

KgdF   *Kampfbund gegen den Faschismus*

KGRNS   *Kampfgemeinschaft Revolutionäre Nationalsozialisten*

KJVD   Communist Youth Association of Germany

KPD   *Kommunistische Partei Deutschlands* (Communist party)

NSBO	*Nationalsozialistische Betriebszellenorganization*
NSDAP	*Nationalsozialistische Deutsche Arbeiterpartei* (Nazi party)
NSKD	*Nationalsozialistische Kampfbewegung Deutschlands*
RFB	*Rotfrontkämpferbund* (Red Front Fighter's League)
RFS	*Reichsführerschule*
SA	*Sturmabteilung*
SAJ	Socialist Worker Youth
SAPD	Socialist Workers Party
SD	*Sicherheitsdienst*
Sopade	Social Democratic Party in exile
SPD	*Sozialdemokratische Partei Deutschlands* (Social Democratic Party)
SS	*Schutzstaffel*

Official Titles

IM	Interior Minister
OP	*Oberpräsident*
PD	Police department
PP	*Polizeipräsident*
RP	*Regierungspräsident*

Chapter 1

THE REVOLT OF THE MASSES
Populist Radicalism and the Discontents of Modernity

❈

*I*n June 1931, in the midst of Hitler's drive to power in Germany, an official of the Nazi paramilitary wing (the *Sturmabteilung* or SA) wrote to party headquarters in Munich to report a worrying incident.[1] A crude antiparty newspaper—*Der Freiheitskämpfer* (The Freedom Fighter)—had appeared in Düsseldorf. The product of a self-styled "Opposition" within the SA, this invective-laced sheet lambasted local party leaders for corruption and challenged the overall direction of the Nazi movement. The paper complained of the watering down of Nazism's revolutionary goals, a charge it leveled in particular against Adolf Hitler.[2] Such charges were not uncommon in a Nazi movement struggling to walk the tightrope between bourgeois respectability and revolutionary élan, even if critics usually stopped short of blaming the *Führer* himself; but particularly worrying in this case was that *Der Freiheitskämpfer* had been distributed in a local SA barracks by a uniformed *Sturmführer* (the equivalent of a platoon leader), the very rank responsible for overseeing the discipline and political reliability of the rank and file. The incident seemed to underline just how serious had become the rot within the SA, a formation that had played a major role establishing the presence of National Socialism on the political stage. Only a year previously, open rebellion had broken out in Berlin around the regional SA leader, Walther Stennes, and the rebel group led by Stennes and the former party leader Otto Strasser—a self-styled proponent of the "socialism" in National Socialism—continued to agitate and canvas for followers.[3] The official took it for granted that *Der Freiheitskämpfer* was a product of the Stennes-Strasser group; but in arriving at the obvious conclusion, he failed to take account of the evidence presented in his own letter.

The *Sturmführer* who distributed the paper, he wrote, had been seen afterward in the company of another SA man entering a Communist printing house. This proved, he wrote, that the man was a "scoundrel." But there was something more at work, for the two stormtroopers were actually (in the parlance of the times) "Beefsteaks"—Nazis who were "brown on the outside and red on the inside."[4] Indeed, the *Sturmführer*—who, after being expelled from the SA as a result of this incident, became a star performer at Communist meetings organized to win over Nazi militants to Communism—was by no means the only Beefsteak at work in the SA, either before or after January 1933.[5] But how did Communists come to

Figure 1.1 *Der Freiheitskämpfer,* no. 2, May 1931. NSDAP Hauptarchiv, Hoover Institution Microfilm Collection.

join the Nazi stormtroopers? And how did the Communist Party of Germany (KPD)—a party that staked its very existence on its intransigent opposition to fascism—come to produce a "Nazi" newspaper complete with bloodthirsty rhetoric and anti-Semitic stereotypes?[6]

If *Der Freiheitskämpfer* were to appear in any of the existing works on the relationship between Nazism and Communism in the Weimar Republic, these questions would probably be answered as follows: the production of *Zersetzungsschriften* (subversion papers) and the activity of Communist agents in enemy uniform was but an extreme expression of the KPD's effort to combat the growing influence of the Nazi Party (NSDAP) in the latter years of the Weimar Republic.[7] Carried out by a secret department within the party charged with undermining both the armed forces of the state and the mass paramilitary formations of the radical right, it was part of a broader campaign of subversion aimed at dissolving from within the organizational cohesiveness of Communism's opponents.[8] Characterized by semiotic trickery and deliberate blurring of ideological boundaries that mirrored similarities in ideology and tactics at the party level,[9] this campaign was carried out in the context of a shared "culture of radicalism" between rank-and-file militants at the neighborhood level.[10] This hypothetical analysis of *Der Freiheitskämpfer*'s significance would be correct as far as it goes—as we will see, such papers were indeed part of a Communist campaign of subversion.[11] But in folding this most striking incident back into a narrative emphasizing the ideological and organizational coherence of "left" and "right," such an analysis would risk closing down inquiry at precisely the point at which it should be opened up. For this artificially constructed point of convergence between the radical extremes—one that resonated, as we will see, with the suspicions, fears, or hopes of contemporaries—represents more than a piece of tactical ephemera in a clandestine struggle between two extremist movements; it offers us a challenging point of departure for a fresh appraisal of the radical politics of the Weimar Republic.

Der Freiheitskämpfer is a fictive intervention at the juncture of two competing radicalisms; but it is also a signpost pointing toward a little-known world of espionage and infiltration in which two mass movements watched, interacted with, and attempted to influence each other, right down to the individual level. The sphere within which it was produced, distributed, and received represents a concrete location of overlap between two extremist movements; the sources with which it is imbedded—the little-exploited files of the secret Communist spy apparatus that produced it, the reports of police and Nazi counterspies who observed it, the propaganda of rebel Nazis and other radical groups that competed against it—cast a new light on seldom-analyzed aspects of the relationship between Nazism and Communism. The idea of the Beefsteak—as both social myth and reality—is one of these, as is the phenomenon of "side-switching" between one party and the other.[12] In this book's final chapter, in particular, these sources—especially the little-exploited reports of Communist spies within the Nazi mass organizations—cast a new light on the process of *Gleichschaltung* (coordination) through which the Nazi regime consolidated its hold on power after 30 January 1933.

But sources such as *Der Freiheitskämpfer* function on a second level as well, for they represent the attempt of one extremist movement to *perform* the other, to quote, to mimic its opponent. In this respect they offer indirect evidence about rank-and-file Nazi ideology by suggesting what Communists—who, as recent scholarship has demonstrated, frequently lived in intimate physical and cultural proximity to their Nazi opponents—knew about Nazi grievances and motivations.[13] They also tell us something about the Communist Party itself, for the attempt to divert rank-and-file Nazi radicalism in a class conscious direction can be seen as an extension of the practice of speaking in the voice of the masses that characterized the party's relationship with workers in general.[14] But the real importance of this mimetic element is that it suggests the way that in quoting each other, extremist movements played with a set of ideas and terms—"socialism," "nationalism," "revolution," among others—that, whatever their differing valence from situation to situation, made up part of a discourse that extended across organizational boundaries and allowed radicals of differing stripes to talk to each other. The ideas and terms of this discourse, to which we will refer, after the contemporary social philosopher Helmuth Plessner, as a discourse of *social radicalism,* supplied the basis for a wide-ranging discussion about the nature of the ideal revolution and the ideal qualities of the revolutionary.[15] It also supplied the basis for appeals, by turns emotive and rationalist, aimed at "enlightening" or converting opponents. This emphasis on argument, moral persuasion, and "conversion" is at least as important to our understanding of the relationship between the radical extremes in the Weimar Republic as the political violence that has so often been emphasized.[16] One aim of this study, therefore, is to emphasize the importance of this many-sided conversation—a conversation that took place across the various National Socialist and *Völkisch* splinter groups; the individuals and grouplets of the "National Bolshevik" scene; the manifold formations of the youth movement—and to situate the relationship between Nazism and Communism as mass movements within it.[17]

This approach differs significantly from what has come before, not only in its empirical focus—it is one of the very few studies, since the work of Schüddekopf in the 1960s, to pay much attention to the interplay between the mass movements and the smaller groups around them, and the first to explore in any detail the KPD's subversive work in and around the NSDAP—but in its theoretical and methodological approach.[18] Whereas previous studies have emphasized the political history of the relationship between the two movements—largely through the lens of the KPD's defensive response to insurgent Nazism—or examined radical culture in highly local and essentially social-historical terms, this study is concerned with culture in its performative aspect; that is, while acknowledging the concrete importance of factors such as class, gender, and generation (as they appear, for example, in the recent work of Pamela Swett), it is more concerned with the symbolic function of these qualities, not only in the formation of radical identities from below—that is, in the self-understanding of radicals—but also in the depiction of those identities from above. The study breaks new ground in examining how the two mass movements attempted to shape and direct the radicalism of their followers and in demonstrating how this shaping and directing was central, not only to the self-constitution of the two movements but also to their relationship with each other. It traces this struggle to shape and direct into the early years of the regime, when the multisided debate over the meaning of revolution continued, contributing to the revolutionary ferment that helped solidify the Nazi hold on power.

Both Nazism and Communism tried to embody a form of populist anti-authoritarianism, the former under the rubric of race and nation (embodied in the idea of the *Volksgemeinschaft* or "people's community"), the latter under the rubric of class.[19] At a purely formal level, these conceptions were diametrically opposed—one was nationalist, the other internationalist; one mystical-vitalist, the other materialist; one racist, the other universalist. In practice, however, these competing rubrics tended to lose their clear delineation and in places even to overlap, as Conan Fischer has demonstrated.[20] This overlap occurred in particular, it will be argued here, where one movement tried to *stage* elements of the radicalism associated with the other—that is, in cases where (for example) the Nazis played with symbols and rhetoric of class (i.e., "working class-ness"), or where the Communists played with the symbolism and rhetoric of the nation.[21] In doing so, both contributed to the discourse of social radicalism in which a range of ideas traditionally associated with "left" and "right" were in play. Characteristically, however—and here we come to a central contention of this study—the staging that movements attempted to enact for their own followers became entwined with the mimetic staging that they enacted for purposes of prosyletization or subversion of their competitor. In this light, the relationship between Communism and Nazism in the Weimar Republic becomes not simply a matter of two discrete mass organizations (two competing "totalitarianisms") trying to outmuscle each other in a struggle for power, but a matter of the dovetailing of two sorts of staging—that *within* movements and that *between* movements.[22]

This approach requires a fresh way of looking at radical politics, one that can be usefully developed with the help of three spatial metaphors. The first of these involves looking at Nazism and Communism not as two movements occupying opposite ends of a political "spectrum," but rather as two *poles* around which coalesce particular constellations of force. Such a scheme does not involve jettisoning the terms "left" and "right," which retain a heuristic usefulness in capturing broad affective orientations—the former suggesting Marxism, workers, the primacy of class; the latter the authority, order, the primacy of nation—but it does entail recognizing these orientations to be contingent, nominal, only partly coherent; and it entails recognizing the same about the parties that claimed to embody these qualities. We may think of the latter, indeed, to function much like poles in the magnetic sense—"polarized" and thus mutually influencing each other—which possess a greater or lesser degree of attractive power. This attractive power has many sources; ideology is only one of them, and not always the most important. Others may be more prosaic—the desire for sociability and comradeship; the need (in a time of desperate unemployment and poverty like the late Weimar Republic) for help with food, clothing, and accommodation. Even more important—and lying, in some ways, at the intersection of strictly ideological and more practical concerns—is the desire to live out deeply held cultural values even more important than official ideology (comradeship, solidarity, manliness, etc.), a point to which we will return below.

The metaphor of the poles has one important practical consequence: it allows us to avoid the confusion inherent in referring to the space "between" the radical extremes where, under the "spectrum" metaphor, should lie the political middle. But there are other, more profound analytical consequences. One of these is that it allows us to conceptualize a space around and between the two poles in which radicals operating *within* organizational boundaries (party members, paramilitary fighters) communicated with those *outside* of organizational boundaries (individual militants, radical publicists, members of rival groups, and so on). Here, a German term—*Spannungsfeld*—is suggestive. Usually translated as "area of conflict" or "zone of tension," but possessing electrical connotations as well (*Spannung* can mean "current" or "voltage"), the term is suggestive of the area of mutual attraction/repulsion in which militants and ideas moved in complex interplay; the area in which competing claims were weighed, assessed, and acted upon, inside or outside of the formal boundaries of discrete political parties.[23] In this study, the area "between" the "radical extremes" is to be understood to mean precisely this *zone of conflict,* the second of our spatial metaphors.

The interaction between militants belonging to political movements and those in the zone of conflict is important for two reasons. First, as observed earlier, the discourse out of which the two movements constituted themselves was in part a creation of those outside the movements, and indeed, it was precisely these militants to whom the extremist movements often tried to appeal. More fundamentally, however, it helps us avoid reifying these movements into monolithic blocks, a danger that Klaus-Michael Mallmann has warned against with respect to the KPD.[24] This study rejects easy assumptions about the ideological and organizational coherence of radical mass movements, which seek by their very nature to mythologize themselves as expressions of popular will.[25] Instead, it emphasizes the constructedness of these movements, in particular the constructedness of their "popular" element. Communism and Nazism sat nestled among a multitude of groups, sects, and tendencies, each promoting their own vision of some of the very same ideas animating the two "successful" mass movements.[26] We might do well to ask what accounted for the profusion of purposefully *small* radical sects—numbering many hundreds in the Weimar Republic—in an "age of the masses." What were their members looking for that could not be found in the larger movements to which they could easily have belonged, and which stood a better chance of seizing power? And what of the many revolts and rebellions within the Nazi movement itself, ranging from incidents of insubordination to full-scale rebellion threatening (temporarily) Hitler's authority and the continued cohesion of the movement? How were they consistent with the "total" claims of a movement united by the will of one dictator? What, for that matter, is the historian to make of the dizzying array of "nonparty" formations—purposefully positioned at the fault line between left and right—hatched by a Communist movement seeking to extend its historic right to speak for the working classes into the right to speak for the nationalist masses as well?

Attempts to answer these questions have found only a marginal place in the historiography.[27] The overriding tendency has been, with National Socialism, to focus above all on explaining its catastrophic rise to power in hopes of preventing a recurrence, and with German Communism, to understand how it fought—or, more often, failed adequately to fight (or even inadvertently aided)—the rise of the Nazis.[28] The resulting historical narratives tended, quite understandably, to focus on the rise and fall of the two mass movements in the context of the structural weaknesses and inadequacies of Weimar democracy. This "great party" approach to history has problems, however, not least the risk of inadvertently re-peating the stories of monolithic will and historical inevitability that the extremist movements told about themselves.[29] It is necessary, moreover, to recognize that political parties or "movements" are only imperfect institutional approximations of social forces and pressures; and more, that they do not just mirror but seek to shape and direct, both organizationally and (as we will discuss in a moment) discursively. If we are thus to consider radical movements in interwar Germany in their proper, dual sense—as expressions of a revolt against the conditions of modernity that are simultaneously linked with an attempt to channel and capital-ize on that revolt—then we need to focus not only on those doing the channeling (leaders, propagandists, party organizations) or on those being channeled (activ-ists, voters—the "rank and file") but on *what* was being channeled and *how*.

But where are we to look for this essence? And with what tools? The histo-riography on radical mass movements (and on fascism especially) has, from the beginning, faced the problem of how much weight should be given to the *actual* bases of a movement's social support as opposed to what the movement had to *say* about itself.[30] The problem was especially acute with fascism, since so much of what fascists had to say about themselves seemed at variance with the facts as understood by liberal democrats or scientific socialists. Most heavily disputed of all was the fascist claim to be "revolutionary," a subject of fierce dispute with representatives of the left-wing movements who called attention to fascism's ties with conservative social strata and business interests and pointed out with appar-ent justification that a revolutionary could not "serve both God and Mammon." The more radical the talk—as in the case of Nazism, which loudly and often pressed its claim to be a revolutionary movement on par with Bolshevism (even while positioning itself as a bulwark against Bolshevism)—the more fierce the reaction of the left and the more desperate the countermeasures. Early interpreta-tions of fascism, almost exclusively the work of Marxists, focused heavily on the contradiction between fascism's revolutionary talk and its reactionary aims (as far as the former could be concretely deduced from the relatively impoverished fund of fascist writings). These interpretations ranged from the vulgar Marxism of the

1935 Comintern definition—fascism as the "open terrorist dictatorship of the most reactionary, most chauvinist and most imperialist elements of finance capital"—to the sophisticated insight of Walter Benjamin, who recognized in fascism an "aesthetization of politics" that served to resolve the contradiction between fascism's "revolutionary" appearance and its careful avoidance of any threat to existing economic power structures.[31]

With respect to the Nazis in particular, scholarship for years focused heavily on the realm of the social, not only in response to Marxism's early interpretive monopoly (as a response to the various Marxist arguments that fascism was but a creation of finance capitalism that drew on the lower middle classes for its shock troops)—but as a means of combating the demagogic claims of the Nazis themselves.[32] Some of the most heavily disputed issues related to National Socialism had to do with the bases of its social support, an early emphasis on the middle-class nature of Nazi support gradually giving way to a recognition that National Socialism was indeed—as the Nazis themselves claimed—a popular mass movement that cut across class lines and achieved substantial support among the working classes.[33] But it is quite clear that, the importance of adjusting the earlier "middle-class thesis" of Nazi support aside, the focus on social class has obscured as much as it has revealed, especially where Nazism's relationship with its left-wing competitors is concerned.[34] It has been important—to cite a topic that was not so long ago the subject of heated scholarly debate—to determine the percentage of Nazi paramilitary fighters who were industrial workers.[35] But it is at least equally important to recognize that both Nazis and Communists, for differing reasons, frequently talked and acted as if the Nazi paramilitary wing was a "proletarian" formation with all the cultural and ideological baggage that entailed. And further, to recognize that one effect of the unmooring between social and affective reality that accompanied the rise of modernity was to give social class a largely *symbolic* character, a maneuver that—pushed to its *locus extremis*—was one of the hallmarks not only of fascism but of Bolshevism as well.[36]

More than any movement before it (except perhaps for Bolshevism), fascism was a movement based on the reconfiguration of symbols. This was true not least because of its "latecomer" status on the political scene, a point that could be made about Bolshevism as well.[37] Fascism sought not just to change the meaning of left-wing symbols but to create articulations between traditionally left-wing concepts such as class struggle and others, such as "nation," that by the time of fascism's birth had become the province of the right.[38] For this reason alone, any treatment of Nazism and Bolshevism must, on some level, treat the radical extremes as what William Sewell calls a "semiotic community" operating on multiple levels.[39] But we can go further if we think of political parties and movements, as Sewell has proposed we do, as "cultural authorities" whose key activity is to "order" the sources of radicalism giving rise to them, and of the adherents of these movements as actors who may, under certain conditions, dispute this ordering.[40] The Communist and National Socialist parties in the Weimar Republic attempted, at an organizational level, to gain numbers, to become "mass movements," and to do so, especially, by channeling "popular violence" into political organization, binding young men into what Michael Mann has termed the "social cage" of paramilitary organization.[41] This was true not only on the right (for which Mann uses the term) but equally on the left, as will be seen. The necessary prerequisite to such organization, however, was the construction of narratives that could make sense of the impulses fueling radical activism. An edifice of meaning had to be constructed before Mann's "cage" could have the power to contain the impulses it was designed to hold. But if politics is a "struggle over meaning," it is also, as Ronald Grigor Suny points out, a struggle "for the right to be authorized to speak."[42] And indeed, the narratives created by the extremist mass movements were heavily disputed—often both from below (by those whom Mann's "cage" was designed to hold) and from without (by political opponents offering supposedly better alternatives).[43]

To focus on the creation of meaning as a prerequisite to political organization does not represent an abandonment of the terrain of the social—far from it; the present study utilizes, indeed, the classic source materials of social history, capturing the voices of the rank and file through their fragmentary writings, police reports, the work of political spies, and so on. In this sense, the work represents "history from below," although not of a very inspiring type. Absolutely characteristic of the type of politics involved, however—and here we touch on one of the book's main arguments—is that it is a "from below" so heavily mediated (and in some instances, indeed, "faked") that we catch only glimpses of the mind of what Mann calls the "fascist subaltern" (or, for that matter, the Communist subaltern).[44] What the sources really give us is a view of the way in which Sewell's "authoritative cultural actors"—in the guise, largely but not exclusively, of the Communist and Nazi parties—speak not just *for* the masses but literally *in the voice* of the masses, playing a heavily mediated version of grassroots populism back to the grass roots in an attempt not only to gain political influence and win adherents but also to bring together seemingly irreconcilable opposites: the spirit of revolt against the increasing bureaucratization and regimentation of daily life (i.e., against aspects of modernity) with the widespread longing for mass, collectivist solutions to these problems. The question here is thus not one of "antimodernism" in the sense usually employed in debates on fascism—that is, not one of the extent to which National Socialism (as opposed to Communism) did or did not represent a rejection of Enlightenment ideas of progress—but rather one of the particular ways in which radical mass movements of the interwar period drew on and sought to direct a rebellion against barriers to popular participation.[45]

Thomas Meyer posits two types of "symbolic politics": "symbolic politics from above" and "symbolic politics from below." The former is a semiotic practice of pure appearance in which symbols emptied of real meaning are used by the powers that be for purely manipulative purposes; the latter calls attention to its own semiotic practice—as, for example, in the street theater and happenings of the 1960s—using actions *as symbols* in order to subvert official narratives.[46] Fascism and Communism, too, used actions as symbols, the most striking and effective of these being the appearance of marching masses and, with fascism in particular, violence itself. But what is remarkable about the symbolic practice of the radical movements in the Weimar Republic is precisely the way that they blurred "from below" and "from above." This phenomenon reaches its *reductio ad absurdum* in *Zersetzungsschriften* such as *Der Freiheitskämpfer*, designed to look like the work of oppositional Nazis and playing back Nazi grievances with a "Communist" inflection.[47] But it informs the entire dynamic of the relations between and within the Communist and National Socialist movements in the Weimar Republic; for in offering competing Marxist and anti-Marxist versions of populism, these two "totalitarian" movements attempted to portray a revolt that protected the fundamental integrity of the hierarchical relations desired (in different ways) by both the leaders and the led.[48]

If this seems paradoxical, it is also supremely logical, for the interwar period was an "age of the masses" in two senses: an age, first of all, in which large events and processes—the total mobilization and industrialized slaughter of the Great War; revolutions and the fall of empires; the uncertainty of national borders and the disjuncture between "states" and "nations"; large-scale economic and social breakdown calling for large-scale interventions—reinforced the need for collectivist solutions to society's problems; an age in which collectivist impulses were fueled in part by the *threats* posed to collectivities of various kinds. But it was also an age in which solutions were being sought to the question (perhaps *the* question of modernity) of how the masses were to be integrated into the life of nations. And here lay another paradox, for within the push toward collectivist solutions lay a deep and abiding unhappiness with "mass-ness," a rejection of the increasing bureaucratization and atomization of modern life—of what, in the postwar period, has been called the "managed society"—which also resonated strongly *within* the very mass organizations aimed at the overthrow of this type of society.

Walter Benjamin correctly divined that what fascism offered the masses was not subjugation but rather "a chance to express themselves"; and this self-expression was elaborated in terms of a *revolt* that operated across and within institutions.[49] The widespread currency of the term *Bonzen* ("bosses" or "big shots")—aimed by the Social Democratic rank and file at their leaders, and a term of abuse par excellence for Nazis and Communists contemptuous of Social Democracy's allegedly bourgeois character (and, as we will see, for Nazis and sometimes also Communists unhappy with their own leaders)—was no accident; it expressed perfectly the idea that impersonal forces were controlling the destiny of the "little man" and that these forces had human representatives who could be fought and perhaps defeated. Here lies also the secret of one of the main features linking radicals of left and right: their shared contempt for the bourgeoisie. Here, again, social class was largely symbolic (and, we should add, heavily gendered): "bourgeois" (confined to the private sphere, petty, concerned only with money, sedentary and cowardly: "female") was constructed as the spiritual opposite of "proletarian" (public-minded, self-sacrificing, capable, warriorlike: "male"). The important point here is that the bourgeoisie was hated by both Fascists and Communists, not as a class per se but, in the words of François Furet, as "a synonym for modern society."⁵⁰ Contempt for "bourgeois individualism"—defined by the Nazis as the failure to put "the common interest before self-interest"—was, simultaneously, contempt for the impersonal social forces symbolized by the bourgeoisie.⁵¹ The assault of the extremist movements on parliamentary democracy was thus only in part a matter of the "hatred of democracy [becoming] democratic," as Furet puts it. It was a matter of competing visions of popular representation—competing ideas about what form of society would arise from the "unprecedented integration of the popular masses into the politics of modern states."⁵² The liberal democratic version—democracy as voting in periodic elections—was found wanting on both ends of the political spectrum, precisely because it precluded new, more authentic forms of collectivity, whether based on race or class.⁵³

One source of conflict within mass movements, then, was that the spirit of revolt they channeled against society operated within the movements themselves. But there was another more specific and tangible cause of conflict—one that goes to the heart of what this study intends to reveal—that was rooted in the very nature of the politics practiced by extremist movements. These movements attempted to shape the radicalism of their followers by playing with symbols, arranging these in certain ways in order to channel that radicalism in particular directions; in doing so, they took an active role in shaping culture, a phenomenon that has been the subject in recent years of a turn toward "performative" notions of culture.⁵⁴ The concept of *performance* in this study functions in several ways. First, it pertains to this active element in the creation and employment of culture; that is, it refers to the way in which cultural authorities tried to control meaning in order to control people. This active element has been understood in terms of the creation of *cultural productions*—newspapers, speeches, parades, rituals—offering "interpretations [of reality aimed at] stimulating political action."⁵⁵ In this study the term "performance" will function, in its first sense, as a synonym for the creation of cultural productions.

In particular, "performance" will denote several unique characteristics of this active element of culture as they apply to the radical politics of the Weimar Republic. First, it will suggest the physical dynamism associated with extremist movements, which posed the bodies of their followers in serried ranks, choreographed them in living expressions of ideology, and employed them in violent domination of public space. Second, it will suggest the active element of speech, capturing the way in which the extremist movements spoke in the voice of their followers, as if placing words in the mouths of actors. Third, the term will be used here to capture the essential inauthenticity, the "fakeness" of the cultural productions produced by extremist movements, a fakeness represented in their most pronounced form by cultural productions such as *Der Freiheitskämpfer.* "Performance" will refer here, in its second sense, to the mimetic element in the cultural productions created by two opposing but mutually constitutive radicalisms. Finally, "performance" will refer to the overall aim—present in all political movements but particularly in the totalizing extremist movements of Weimar—of the staging of the forms of radicalism associated with a movement for purposes of constructing the appearance of monolithic unity and focused mass will. In this sense, "performance" is related to the third spatial metaphor employed in this study, the vertical distinction, within political movements, between "top down" and "bottom up." That is, "performance," in the broadest sense used here, refers to the process by which the "from above" stages the radicalism of the "from below."

A central contention of this study, however, is that the "from below"—that is, the people on whom the productions designed by cultural authorities were meant to act—was not passive. It participated in the performances staged by the "from above," but it also—crucially—resisted them. To understand why, it is necessary to examine what the mass movements performed. At a basic level, they performed versions of mass solidarity based on their respective foundational precepts (for the Nazis, the solidarity of race and nation; for the Communists, the solidarity of class). But they also performed a set of cultural values that supplied the basis of what will be referred to in this study as "revolutionary legitimacy." These values had the potential to cut across ideological and organizational boundaries, were compatible with both class- and race-based collectivities, and—as we will see presently—supplied the standards by which movements were judged by their followers. They stemmed primarily from four sources: the ideal of youth and youth revolt; militarism and the ideal of warriorhood; an idealized version of social class (that is, of "working class–ness"); and notions of manliness and male honor. From these four sources stemmed the qualities of the ideal revolutionary: heroism, sincerity, honesty, youthfulness, freshness, guilelessness, determination, solidarity, self-sacrifice, hardness, and strength, among others. To perform deeply-held cultural values for instrumental purposes was to play with fire, however, for as this study will demonstrate, radicals evaluated the movements to which they belonged primarily in terms of whether these movements lived up to the values they performed. This was true not only because the values in question were central to various types of identity—central, above all, to the self-image of the revolutionary—but also because ideology itself was frequently constructed in relationship to them. Indeed, in the debates about revolutionary legitimacy in and around the mass movements—how it was to be defined, who had it, who did not—ideological and cultural concerns were intimately bound together.

The active relationship of the "from below" to the performances staged by the "from above"—the resistance to being staged—will be understood in this study through the concept of "authenticity."[56] The theme of authenticity runs like a red line through the sources used in this study. Standing out in the voices of Nazi and Communist activists captured in the reports of police agents and spies, in the printed output of rebel groups big and small, Marxist or anti-Marxist, it appears as a central motif in the conflicts in and around the mass movements during the Weimar Republic. The youth radicalism of that Weimar Republic, like that of the 1960s, was characterized by a "cult of authenticity and realness."[57] This cult of authenticity helped lend the Youth Movement its uncompromising edge and filtered out to influence the radicalism of the era more generally. But "authenticity" in this study refers not only to the concept as understood in the Youth Movement (e.g., escaping the corruption of bourgeois life, eschewing the compromises and dishonesty of "politics"), but also to the broader insistence, on the part of Weimar radicals, on being able to independently evaluate and, if necessary, resist the performances staged by cultural authorities. That is, it has to do with the desire to retain agency within the confines of a mass movement. Authenticity, as this study will demonstrate, occupied a central position in the debates around revolutionary legitimacy that characterized the conflicts within the two mass movements and the smaller groups in the conflict zone between them. The desire for authenticity, in terms of our three spatial metaphors, may be seen to represent a countervailing force to the attractive power of the magnetic poles represented by the two parties; a central determinant in the debates over revolutionary legitimacy in the conflict zone between them; and the resistance of the "bottom up" against the shaping and ordering of the "top down." "Authenticity" functions here, in other words, as a synonym for resistance to "performance."

This book will discuss the conflict between authenticity and performance—understood as a conflict between radicalism as staged and radicalism as felt and experienced—as it relates to the struggle between the NSDAP, KPD, and their smaller competitors to gain the upper hand of meaning in the long Weimar Republic. The following chapter lays out the terms in which this struggle was carried out using the example of a well-known political trial of the late Weimar Republic. The trial and its aftermath brought the propaganda struggle between the NSDAP and KPD to a fever pitch, laying out in striking fashion the cultural parameters of this struggle between them. Chapter 3 examines the Nazi version of this radicalism, exploring the history of conflict within the Nazi movement as a means of teasing out the various strands of its radicalism. Chapter 4 explores the Communist version, focusing in particular on Communist attempts to turn Nazi radicalism in an explicitly left-wing, anticapitalist direction of the sort represented by *Der Freiheitskämpfer*. Chapter 5 examines how the Nazis win the battle over meaning, gaining, after Hitler's accession to power in January 1933, the opportunity to suppress alternative visions of radicalism. Throughout, the struggle between the mass movements is placed in the perspective of the Youth Movement, the National Bolshevik groups, and the various splinter groups. In looking at how the conflict functioned within movements, how it conditioned relations between them, and how it fueled the activities of noninstitutional actors in the zone of conflict who tried to intervene in it, this study will attempt to uncover and understand the distinctive radical conjuncture of the Weimar era.

Chapter 2

FACES OF SOCIAL MILITARISM
IN THE WEIMAR REPUBLIC

※

*O*n 27 February 1931, a celebrated Hitler supporter, serving a prison sentence delivered in one of the biggest political trials of the Weimar Republic, announced, to the shock and surprise of everyone, that he had decided to join the Communists. This political bombshell—a supporter of Adolf Hitler defecting to the party of Moscow and Stalin—exploded at a time of growing crisis in Germany. The Great Depression was in full swing, producing mass unemployment and social unrest. Government was breaking down, with rule by emergency decree and back-door machinations by a small cabal of schemers around the aging president, Paul von Hindenburg, replacing functioning democratic politics. Endemic street violence between left and right contributed to an atmosphere of civil war. The growing electoral success of the NSDAP signaled the growing appeal of extremist politics. It also exposed latent tensions within the National Socialist movement. Nazi radicals charged that participation in "the system" was destroying the meaning of National Socialism as a revolutionary movement. The Communists, in hopes of winning over disaffected Nazis and hastening Hitler's demise, did everything they could to support such charges and to win over those making them. The public defection of 27 February—by a young army lieutenant named Richard Scheringer—was seen as this strategy's first notable success.[58]

Scheringer, the twenty-six-year-old son of an officer killed in the Great War, had been a defendant in the celebrated Ulm Reichswehr trial held in Leipzig in the autumn of 1930. The trial revolved around three young army officers—Richard Scheringer, Hans Wendt, and Hanns Ludin—who in violation of regulations restricting army officers from political activity had agitated on behalf of the Nazi movement, traveling to surrounding garrisons to proselytize their fellow officers and even meeting with Nazi officials. Scheringer had begun his career as an officer at a time when the political neutrality (*Überparteilichkeit*) of the Reichswehr was being eroded under the impact of multiple crises, including the growing parliamentary impasse, the world depression of 1929, and the rising influence of mass antidemocratic parties.[59] Not only did the army leadership—with ultimately disastrous results—take an increasingly active hand in trying to steer Germany out of crisis, but portions of the officer corps fell increasingly under the influence of the radical right.[60] From the end of the 1920s, the Nazis' intention of winning the support of the army for their campaign against the Republic was openly announced in organs such as the *Völkischer Beobachter* and the *Deutscher Wehrgeist* (German Military Spirit).[61] The former published, in a special army issue, a speech by Hitler mocking the army leaders for their "wonderful un-political attitude" and challenging them to take up their rightful place as defenders of the nation against Bolshevism.[62] As the trial of Scheringer would illustrate, such arguments came to find an increasing audience among the younger officers.[63] The Reichswehr at the end of the 1920s exhibited something of a generational split, with older officers who still remembered the days of the *Kaiserreich* largely opposed to the Nazis and younger officers heavily—though by no means unanimously—in favor.[64] In his opposition to the conservative *Burogenerale* (desk generals), Scheringer was part of a larger trend in the officer corps to favor radical solutions to Germany's problems.[65] The strong reaction—widely regarded as excessive—to the young officers' breech of discipline by the head of the army, General Groener, was a product of the fear that such views threatened the discipline and cohesion of the army.[66]

When Scheringer stepped across the line into illegal activity—accompanied by two colleagues of the Ulm garrison, Hans Friedrich Wendt and Hanns Ludin—it was in the hopes of preparing the army to become the kernel of a "people's army of national liberation."[67] His choice of the Nazis as a "political partner" was conditioned precisely by what he saw as the needs of this "people's army." The national uprising must not be a simple *Putsch* but an uprising of the entire people. Because it must necessarily include the proletariat, this uprising must be based on a politics with a social, anticapitalist component. To Scheringer and his friends, it was the NSDAP that most closely embodied their ideal of a truly *social* nationalism that would bring the workers in on the side of the army.[68] The "socialist" planks of the NSDAP's political program played a role in these calculations.[69] But far more important for Scheringer and his friends was the Nazi paramilitary wing, the SA. Not only did the stormtroopers offer the Nazis a real chance at seizing power in the streets, but they also seemed to represent precisely the intersection of working-class radicalism and nationalist militarism that would be necessary for the coming "peoples' war."[70]

Scheringer, Wendt, and Ludin were arrested on 10 March 1930, and charged with making preparations to commit high treason.[71] Their trial took place before the Federal Court in Leipzig from 23 September to 4 October 1930. The so-called Ulm Reichswehr trial was a key event in the National Socialist march toward power in Germany. Coming immediately on the heels of the Nazis' startling gains in the Reichstag elections of 14 September, which made the NSDAP the second-largest party in Germany, and following in the wake of a dramatic increase in the national profile of the NSDAP resulting from the campaign against the Young Plan,[72] the trial marked a further increase in Hitler's political visibility and a dramatic increase in his credibility with conservative elites.[73] The trial gave Hitler, in the words of his foremost biographer, "the chance, now with the eyes of the world's press upon him, of underlining his party's commitment to legality."[74] In his testimony Hitler distanced himself from those Nazis who toyed with the idea of "revolution," citing the case of the recently excluded Otto Strasser, who had fallen out with Hitler and left the party over the question of "socialism" in July 1930.[75] Threatening, to a courtroom ovation, that heads would "roll" after the NSDAP came to power, Hitler swore that the NSDAP would achieve this power only through legal means.[76] Hitler took special pains to assuage the fears of the army leadership—raised in part by Hitler's own previous attacks on the political neutrality of the army—about the consequences of a National Socialist accession to power. Hitler's overtures to the army played no little role in creating the atmosphere for subsequent negotiations that paved the way for the army's assent to his eventual assumption of power.[77]

The Ulm trial extended the arrival of the Nazis on the national stage begun in 1929 and allowed Hitler to express his ideas before a sympathetic audience and gain a great deal of free publicity.[78] But the long-term benefit of the trial for Hitler's position *vis à vis* Germany's conservative elites was partially offset in the short term by the trouble it caused him with his own followers. Already during the campaign for the Reichstag elections of September 1930, the Berlin SA under the leadership of Walther Stennes had gone "on strike" against the party, angered by a perceived lack of respect on the part of the "civilian" party *Bonzen* ("big shots") for the "sacrifices" of the SA.[79] Issues of pay and outfitting were in the forefront, but simmering discontent over the NSDAP's participation in electoral politics also played a major role. Hitler's "oath of legality" (*Legalitätseid*) at the Ulm trial contributed to an exacerbation of these tensions that found expression in a second revolt of the Berlin SA, the so-called Stennes Revolt of April 1931. Ironically, however, the negative consequences of Hitler's testimony at the Ulm trial came out most forcefully in the subsequent actions of defendant Scheringer. With his co-defendants, Hans Wendt and Hanns Ludin, Scheringer had engaged in extensive discussions about Hitler's performance at the trial, about the nature of revolution, and about the meaning of National Socialism.[80] Sentenced on 4 October 1930 to eighteen months of custodial imprisonment, Scheringer continued his political deliberations as an inmate at fortress Gollnow in Mecklenburg-Pomerania. Here, in daily contact with Communist fellow prisoners, Scheringer began to question his commitment to National Socialism.[81] Disturbed by Hitler's statements at the trial, Scheringer sought assurance that the NSDAP really was serious about its professed commitment to social revolution. He took the opportunity of a prison furlough to visit Joseph Goebbels in Berlin (further evidence, if any more were needed, of the leniency with which right-wing extremists were treated by the judicial system of the Weimar Republic), traveling from there in the company of Goebbels to see Hitler in Munich.[82] Scheringer was far from reassured by his visit with Hitler, who, unaware or heedless of the extent to which such opulence bothered many of his followers, spent most of the audience extolling the virtues of the recently completed Nazi headquarters—the palatial "Brown House"—on the Brienner Strasse. Goebbels assured Scheringer that Hitler's oath of legality at the Ulm trial had been nothing but a ploy to disguise his true intentions. He admitted, however, that the Nazis had no intention of nationalizing industry, nor did he attempt to disguise his contempt for what passed as anticapitalist theory in the NSDAP. Regarding Gottfried Feder's writings on the "breaking of interest-slavery," Goebbels sarcastically observed: "The only thing that will be broken is anyone who tries to read Feder's nonsense."[83] Scheringer returned to his prison cell disillusioned. Less than a month later, on 19 March 1931, a letter announcing his conversion to Communism was read out in the Reichstag by the Communist deputy, Hans Kippenberger.[84]

Hans Wendt and Hanns Ludin—although sharing Scheringer's views in essential respects—declined to join him in the ranks of the Red Front. Equally disgusted with "Hitler the legalist," Wendt declared his solidarity not with the KPD but with the Nazi rebels around Stennes and Otto Strasser. Ludin, not without misgivings, chose to remain loyal to the NSDAP, arguing that the fighting spirit of the SA outweighed any shortcomings Hitler might have as a revolutionary leader.[85] Significantly, Scheringer agreed about the significance of the SA—indeed, he spent almost his entire effort in the remaining years of the Weimar Republic, as we will see, trying to convince Hitler's stormtroopers to follow him to Communism. As they set off on their independent trajectories—Scheringer into an uncertain life as a Communist; Wendt into an even more precarious future as a renegade Nazi; Ludin into a high leadership post in the SA—the three continued to share a common desire to pursue a revolution that was both social and national. The fact that these three friends, sharing very similar goals, could go in three divergent directions says much about the lability of extremist political affiliation in the Weimar Republic. More importantly, as we will see, it illustrated the key importance of cultural factors in the construction of political ideology.

That it was largely Scheringer rather than Wendt and Ludin who captured the imagination of contemporaries is indicative. In stepping from one side of the barricades to the other, he bridged irreconcilable opposites, in the process confirming preexisting ideas about the fundamental similarities between Nazism and Communism. Scheringer's defection caused a sensation that was reported on extensively in both the domestic and foreign press.[86] An array of fears and hopes were projected onto the twenty-six-year-old lieutenant. The liberal *Vossische Zeitung* interpreted his act as a characteristic sign of the ease with which young activists were able to cross the political barricades.[87] For a conservative writer,

Figure 2.1 "Why I was a National Socialist and how I became a Communist." Richard Scheringer in the *AIZ* Nr. 40, 1932. Bundesarchiv.

who took the case as a clear example of the dangerous forces at work in the supposedly "national" NSDAP, the case proved "better than a thousand arguments that a straight road leads from National Socialism to Communism."[88] Leaders of the Nazi paramilitary wing worried about Scheringer's possible influence on working-class stormtroopers disappointed by the NSDAP's "bourgeois" course.

The Communist Party trumpeted Scheringer's "brave deed" on the front page of its newspaper, the *Rote Fahne,* citing his defection as a welcome sign that the magic spell of Hitler's demagogy was beginning to lose its hold.[89] Joseph Goebbels lamented his missed propaganda opportunity, confiding to his diary: "Too bad about the kid! I would have made something out of that one." Goebbels attempted to soften the embarrassment by speculating that Scheringer must be suffering from some kind of "prison psychosis."[90] But Scheringer was not suffering from a psychological disorder, nor did his behavior admit of any of the simple explanations put forward by those hoping to confirm prejudices or capitalize politically. On the contrary, Scheringer was acting with a deep internal logic, and his road-to-Damascus performance highlights, in a striking way, key aspects of the relationship between the radical extremes in the Weimar Republic.

Scheringer's defection was rooted, first of all, in a specific aspect of Communist policy in the Weimar Republic, the nationalist turn taken by the KPD in the second half of 1930. The party had been rather slow to recognize the danger posed by the NSDAP, and indeed, the ultra-left strategy adopted in 1928 treated the "social fascist" Social Democratic Party (SPD) as an even bigger threat than the "national fascist" Nazis. But the growing electoral success of the NSDAP from the end of the 1920s, and the national visibility achieved by the Nazis through the campaign against the Young Plan in 1929, forced the KPD to begin taking the danger posed by the Nazis more seriously. Aware of the NSDAP's success in mobilizing cross-class support by exploiting opposition to the Treaty of Versailles, the KPD tried to stake out nationalist territory for itself, a maneuver it had attempted once before in 1923.[91] The centerpiece of this second wave of KPD nationalism was the "Program for the National and Social Liberation of the German People," unveiled during the campaign for the Reichstag elections of September 1930.[92] Promising to annul the Treaty of Versailles and destroy all other obstacles to Germany's national self-determination,[93] the program forcefully argued that the KPD, not the NSDAP, was the true representative of Germany's national interests.[94] This strategic amendment to the idea of proletarian internationalism—representing nothing less than the adoption of all the main demands of the radical right by the KPD—was followed by the policy of *Volksrevolution* (People's Revolution), a line for which Ernst Thälmann successfully argued at the Eleventh Plenum of the Executive Committee of the Communist International in Moscow in March 1931.[95] The concept of *Volksrevolution* was an attempt to extend Communist influence to those groups with which the Nazis were enjoying the greatest electoral success and the Communists the least: rural voters, white-collar employees, and civil servants.[96] It had the twofold aim of winning the middle class for Communism while preventing further Nazi inroads into the working class, a concern of the KPD from the early 1920s.[97] This attempt to show that the KPD was more national socialist than the National Socialists was neither convincing to most nationalists nor acceptable to many Communists. It was criticized, for example, by Hermann Remmele, who argued that the party's position on the national question was shallow and unconvincing both within and without the party.[98] The nationalist turn did, however, provide an ideological justification for Scheringer to jump from one side of the barricades to the other, even if his conversion was devalued (at least as an expression of the superiority of the idea of proletarian internationalism) by the fact that it was facilitated by what amounted to the KPD's capitulation to nationalist chauvinism.[99]

Yet there is more to Scheringer's switch than the artificial nationalism of Communist propaganda. His underlying motivation—so much a part of common wisdom in the Germany of 1931 that it scarcely elicited comment—was the desire to align himself with the party that he held to be most authentically warlike. The figure who managed Scheringer's conversion to, and subsequent activity for, the KPD was a peer of sorts. Head of the KPD's secret Military Department, Hans Kippenberger was himself a decorated combat veteran, commander of a machine-gun regiment on the Western Front during the Great War and one of the military leaders of the Communist uprising in Hamburg in 1923.[100] When Kippenberger visited Scheringer in prison, it was to emphasize not the KPD's opposition to war but its *fitness* for war.[101] It was the KPD that would carry out the anti-Versailles war of *national* liberation desired by Scheringer, as *one* front in an internal, anticapitalist war, a *civil* war of class against class. The letter written by Scheringer and read out by Kippenberger in the Reichstag praised the KPD's support "for the militarization of the entire working people, for a prepared and militant German Red Army," and quoted Lenin on the necessity of revolutionary war: "We are going to become 'defenders of the Fatherland' … we are going to become the most 'warlike' of the parties." The wording of Scheringer's conversion left no doubt as to what he considered important about the KPD: "I reject … pacifism and take my place as a soldier in the ranks of the fighting proletariat."[102]

Scheringer's conversion was thus less a shift from right to left than a displacement of hope for a people's war against the Versailles powers from one army (the Reichswehr) onto another (a German Red Army backed by the power of the USSR). The provisional nature of his conversion comes out clearly in the correspondence reprinted in a Communist-financed pamphlet. To a Generalleutnant a.D. Dietrich, Scheringer wrote of his desire for a "war of liberation against the West" to be carried out "over the rubble of the Weimar Republic." In another letter he wrote that because "more and more of the proletariat and the middle classes are collecting themselves in the KPD to fight for the revolutionizing and arming of the working classes to fight against capitalism and for a war against the Western powers, I have decided to put all doubts behind me and extend a hand to the 'reds.'"[103] Left-wing critics of the KPD's nationalist turn were quick to note the apparent shallowness of this conversion. For Leon Trotsky, Scheringer was someone who looked "favorably upon the cause of the Communist Party as the direct continuation of [the Great War]," who saw the dead of that war as "heroes who have fallen for the freedom of the German people." Scheringer and his ilk agreed to accept the "people's revolution," Trotsky continued, but only as a means "of mobilizing the workers for their 'revolutionary war.' Their whole program lies in the idea of *revanche* (revenge)."[104] The radical journalist Carl von Ossietzky—a rather more convincing antimilitarist than Trotsky—mocked the sudden awakening to the military virtues of a party that had only recently heartily criticized the "sort of people" who went into the Reichswehr.[105] This skepticism was shared by many in the KPD, few of whom would go as far as one exasperated (ex)-Communist functionary who proclaimed the Scheringer line "fascism" pure and simple, but many of whom recognized that as a nationalist and a militarist with "social" aspirations, Scheringer still had more in common with the Nazis than with the Communists, his new vocabulary of "proletariat" and "Soviet Union" notwithstanding.[106]

Yet key aspects of the KPD's radicalism—the privileging of will, struggle, and ruthlessness; the eliding of the distinction between "militant" and "soldier"; the conflation of "internal" with "external" war, "social" with "national" struggle— were familiar to National Socialists. Both movements were expressions of a rampant militarism in Weimar society, a *social militarism* that went beyond a mere "historically inappropriate glorification of the military"—associated traditionally with the political right—to posit war as a vehicle for societal transformation and a source of spiritual values.[107] This involved not merely the adoption of values and vocabulary drawn from the war experience but, as we will see, an essentializing approach to social reality that created collective categories for a demonized other. The infusion of war and its "virtues" into civilian politics is, of course, a hallmark of fascism. But in Weimar Germany, social militarism, in various shades and with differing degrees of radicalism, spanned the political spectrum, providing a common language and sensibility not only for radicals on the right but also for their counterparts on the extreme left. This social militarism developed in tandem with a new type for which both left and right supplied the source material: the "revolutionary soldier." This type arose out of a transformation of the idea of soldierhood and a new model of the revolutionary, both developed in the context of the changing nature of militarism in post–World War I Germany. The radical right after the war attempted to keep alive, organizationally and culturally, the classical militarism of the *Kaiserreich,* simultaneously updating it with the new "spiritual" content provided by the Great War. The "spirit of 1914" (the myth of national transcendence associated with the enthusiasm of the first days of the war) and the "community of the trenches" (involving the alleged erasure of class divisions in the service of the nation) became central components of what George Mosse has called the "Myth of the War Experience."[108]

During the war, notions of comradeship and self-sacrifice, combined with estrangement from civilian life and suspicion toward the home front, found expression at the rank-and-file level in an outpouring of trench newspapers.[109] Letters, journals, and personal accounts of the war were filtered by publishers and government authorities both during and after the war in a way that reinforced the "soldierly virtues" and "front spirit" (*Frontgeist*) of the troops. This soldierly nationalism was carried forward in the postwar period by the *Wehrverbände* or "military associations." The most important of these, the *Stahlhelm* (Steel Helmet), the *Jungdeutscher Orden* (Young-German Order—commonly known as the

Jungdo), and the *Wehrwolf,* saw themselves not only as vehicles for the political mobilization of veterans, aimed at combating the revolutionary left, but also as articulators of "soldierly" solutions to the problems of government and society.[110] The *Stahlhelm,* founded in December 1918 by Franz Seldte, played a particularly major role in the mythologization of the war experience, propagating the concept of "Front Socialism" (*Frontsozialismus*) and providing—sometimes not completely willingly—a space for the development of more radical themes.[111] The *Wehrwolf,* founded in January 1923 by Fritz Kloppe, enjoyed a close association with the *Stahlhelm* and acted initially as a sort of unofficial youth wing.[112] The *Jungdo,* founded in January 1919 by Arthur Mahraun, sought to recast Prussian authoritarianism in the spirit of the German Youth Movement, helping create a link between militarism and youth revolt that would unfold more fully at the end of the next decade.[113] These groups sometimes differed from each other in important ways—the *Jungdo,* for example, nominally accepted the democratic Weimar system—but all shared in the spirit expressed in the founding proclamation of the *Jungdo,* which invoked "the moral virtues which must not remain the exclusive privilege of the military order."[114]

The new, radicalized postwar militarism was borne in its most extreme form, organizationally and culturally, by the *Freikorps.* Demobilized soldiers, embittered and shocked by the suddenness of defeat, psychologically unprepared for peace, flocked to join volunteer formations created by officers to maintain the organizational and spiritual continuity of the army. Although hardly representative—the majority of ex-soldiers, as Richard Bessel has demonstrated, successfully reestablished themselves in civilian work—the fighters of the *Freikorps* helped set the tone for successive postwar iterations of soldierly identity.[115] As volunteers—in many cases volunteers twice over who had answered the call in 1914—and as, in many cases, officers with a greater vested interest in the military life, the soldiers of the *Freikorps* embodied a positive evaluation of the war experience. These fighters—formally unpolitical, heralds of restless action, embodying a brutal nihilism that had much in common with fascism—earned their notoriety in the postwar ethnic warfare on Germany's eastern frontiers and in the crushing of far-left risings in Berlin, Bavaria, and the Ruhr. Their *raison d'être* was a politicized continuation of the war experience—fueled by resentment against civilians, Marxists, and Jews—that became an end in itself. The fledgling Nazi movement profited heavily from the infusion of these types, who came to occupy many of the movement's leadership positions. More important, thanks to the efforts of talented literary apologists such as Ernst Jünger and Ernst von Salomon, the *Freikorps* came to occupy a key place in the mythologization of the war experience later in the Weimar Republic. The ideal of the political soldier was first hinted at in the nihilistic activity of the *Freikorps,* which, although formally "unpolitical," linked moral qualities with action (hardness, decisiveness, will to combat, and self-sacrifice).[116]

The focus on the moral makeup of the warrior articulated easily with conceptions of moral virtue involving honesty, sincerity, and willingness to sacrifice.

Encoded within this warrior ethos was a potential for political transformation. If the bases of action were primarily moral, and if the purpose of politics was to create room for right action in the world (defined in warrior terms), then the potential for crossing the political barricades was automatically created. Right action, defined morally, was fundamentally nonparty, both in the sense that it was inconsistent with politics as practiced in a liberal democracy, and in the sense that it could find more than one political expression. The very revealing self-image of *Freikorps* fighters as "Bolshevists of the right," and the well-known potentiality of these (normally fiercely anti-Communist) *Freikorps* fighters to actually join the Communists, must be seen *not* merely as an a-ideological commitment to action for its own sake but as an expression of a deeper, more profound set of motivations in which politics is only an epiphenomenal expression of ethical behavior. This idea of political soldierhood was key to Nazism and was taken wholesale into the SA, becoming a central component of the ideology of the Nazi paramilitary wing.[117] The SA took pains to distinguish itself, for example, from the *Stahlhelm,* according to the proposition that "the SA man was a political soldier and not— like a *Stahlhelmer*—a solder who also made politics." This distinction—between "political soldiers" and "soldiers who play politics"—was based entirely in the realm of motivation, that is, on the moral core behind the activism.[118]

The radical left supplied its own version of the ideal of political soldierhood. Here, the important source was Russian Bolshevism, particularly the experience of the Russian revolution and civil war. The military organization of a political party was of course, as Stanley Payne has pointed out, an innovation not of fascism but of Leninism.[119] Lenin was explicit in his admiration for the modern army as an organizational form, and he conceived of the Bolshevik Party "as the military staff of the proletariat."[120] This theoretical/practical conception received confirmation in the course of the revolution, which relied heavily on military formations such as the Red Sailors of the Baltic Sea naval fortress Kronstadt, and the civil war, which required full-scale military mobilization and the use of ex-Tsarist military officers. The Red Army under Trotsky's leadership developed a reputation for hardness and ruthlessness against opponents of both right and left. The distinction between "soldier" and "revolutionary" was essentially erased, as suggested by Lenin's repeated use of the phrase "soldiers of the revolution." This military orientation was transplanted more or less whole into Germany after the revolution of 1918. The early history of the KPD was marked by repeated attempts at armed insurrection (in 1919, 1920, 1921, and 1923), creating a "militaristic legacy" that heavily influenced its subsequent history.[121] The paramilitary *Rotfrontkämpferbund* (Red Front Fighter's League or RFB) possessed "an indigenous military ethos" that made it something more than simply a counterweight to the rightist combat leagues.[122] One of the chief tasks of this organization—founded in 1924, banned by the government in 1929, and continued illegally thereafter— was to keep alive both the "memory" and the "technical knowledge" of the Great War as a means of "defending against nationalist-military propaganda in favor of a new imperialist war."[123] The youth wing of the *Rotfrontkämpferbund,* the *Rote*

Jungsturm, was founded to carry out the "spiritual militarization of proletarian youth" and, along with its parent organization, uphold the memory of "the glorious days of the Red soldiers in Russia and the whole world."[124]

Alongside this emphasis on the "moral" elements of proletarian warfare, the KPD emphasized technical know-how, publishing a number of military-political texts that were circulated within the party's secret *M-Apparat* or "military" bureau.[125] Among this department's several tasks were preparations for a military uprising (for which it gathered arms and published the technical journal *Oktober*), the internal policing of the party and defense against espionage (the *M-Apparat* was sometimes known as the "German GPU"),[126] and the subversion of both the armed forces of the state (police, army, navy) and "enemy" paramilitary formations, including the Social Democratic *Reichsbanner,* the Nationalist *Stahlhelm,* and the SA. The goal of subversion was suggested in the occasional use of the designation "*AM-Apparat*" ("antimilitary department"), which also reflected, simultaneously, an attempt to disguise the department's own insurrectionary designs.[127] To be sure, *opposition* to war—especially "imperialist war" (i.e., a war of the West against the USSR)—was a key aspect of Communist rhetoric; but the goal of civil war inherited from the Bolshevik revolution in Russia and reinforced by the KPD's early insurrectionary experiences produced a sense—parallel to that on the radical right—that being a warrior was an intrinsic good.[128]

These two competing but complementary versions of political soldierhood had, as their common basis, one key idea: that the virtues required to be an effective revolutionary were the same as those required to be a good soldier. The moral values out of which the "revolutionary warrior" could be constructed—the basis of revolutionary legitimacy—were thus ones that the radical extremes could and did share. The political conversion of Richard Scheringer is significant not simply because Scheringer was the most prominent of the militants who followed the narrow path provided by the KPD's nationalist program from one side of the barricades to the other; nor because his deliberations with his codefendants illustrate the sorts of debates that went on about the opposing programs of National Socialism and Communism; it is rather because he illustrates the key importance of a moral understanding of politics to the political radicalism of the Weimar Republic, a moral understanding whose terms were drawn from war, and through which—crucially—ideological programs were interpreted and debated. Scheringer's prominence derived, indeed, from precisely the fact that he represented an articulation between "warrior" and "revolutionary" at a time when the two concepts had become fused together and linked to one of the most powerful forces in the Weimar Republic: the rebellion of youth.

The Revolution of German Youth

In a famous study published in 1957, the West German sociologist Helmut Schelsky wrote of the distancing of early postwar youth from involvement in politics.[129] Schelsky positioned this "skeptical generation" in sharp contrast to the youth of the Weimar era, who were marked by their extreme idealism. The contemporary social philosopher Helmuth Plessner, a keen observer of the radicalism of the Weimar era, wrote of a "new youth" filled with a "heroic conception of life" and marked by a sharp break with the values of the parent generation.[130] Youth were, for Plessner, the primary locus of a "social radicalism" that, by placing community—whether understood in terms of a *Volksgemeinschaft* or of a brotherhood of all workers—above all else, threatened to destroy the social distancing between individuals that made civilized life possible. This radicalism, according to Plessner, entailed "the conviction that genuine greatness and goodness arises only from a conscious return to the roots of existence; the belief in the healing power of the extreme; and the method of opposing all traditional values and compromises."[131] It motivated not only the Youth Movement, argued Plessner, but also the extremist movements of left and right, which offered up for the consumption of restless youth both "blood" and "ideal" based versions of community.[132]

The new youth sensibility of which Plessner wrote developed in Germany around the turn of the century, above all among middle-class youth who began to question the staid bourgeois world of their families. The *Wandervögel* founded in Berlin in 1901 gave expression to the desire to escape the strictures of this world, escaping into nature in the search for authenticity, comradeship, and adventure. The spirit of the *Wandervögel* was simultaneously elitist and egalitarian—although not yet militaristic—antimaterialist and idealistic, rejecting adult society and its compromises, above all those represented by the word "politics." Thousands of young volunteers of the *Wandervögel* fell in the Great War, above all in the Battle of Langemarck in November 1914, which subsequently became a key myth in the linkage of youth and nation by the radical right.[133] The carnage of the trenches rendered the romantic escapism of the *Wandervögel* quaint, and the postwar atmosphere of social dislocation and political polarization had a corrosive effect on the independence of the youth, which was increasingly targeted by political parties seeking mass support among the young. The Youth Movement had two key aspects in common with the radical extremes: the rejection of bourgeoisie (in this case largely by members of the bourgeoisie) and the rejection of "politics" in favor of something deeper, spiritual, more "representative."[134]

The myth of the Front Generation grew up in a society obsessed with the idea of youth revolt, a theme explored in countless books, articles, plays, and films.[135] The messianic mission of youth was celebrated by authors such as Friedrich Nietzsche, Julius Langbehn, Paul de Lagarde, and Stefan George, whose works found a corresponding resonance in the publications of the interwar youth movement.[136] Social scientists and youth pedagogues wrote of the revolution represented by the changing social and sexual mores of the young generation. More important than the ever-changing landscape of youth organizations was the dissemination of the ideas and spirit of the Youth Movement, which crystallized in a wide variety of groups across the political spectrum, developing within these groups "youth factions" pressing the revolutionary claims of the new generation.[137]

All political parties and tendencies in the Weimar Republic tried to instrumentalize this impulse, with varying degrees of conviction and success. On the left there were the Socialist Worker Youth (SAJ) and the Young Socialists, both associated with the SPD; the Socialist Youth Association of Germany (SJVD), affiliated with the SPD-offshoot Socialist Workers Party (SAPD); and the Communist Youth Association of Germany (KJVD), controlled by the KPD.[138] Cutting across and acting within these groups were elements of nonparty youth associations such as the International Youth Alliance and the Free Proletarian Youth. On the right were the youth groups of the nationalist *Wehrverbände* and patriotic associations, various militarist youth associations, and the mass organizations of the Nazis. These groups, stretching right across the political spectrum, advocated many of the same ideas, often using "almost identical language."[139] The mainstream parties, with few exceptions, failed to effectively appeal to youth—association with parliamentary democracy was a death sentence as far as youth support was concerned.[140] The well-known declaration by a leading member of the Free German Youth that the "young generation would dispense with political parties" is indicative of the general attitude.[141] Parties were ambivalent about youth anyway. Unsure about youth's revolutionary potential from the beginning, the *Stahlhelm* founded its own youth organization only in late 1923.[142] The *Stahlhelm*'s journal, *Die Standarte,* was employed as a "safety valve" in which the young could let off steam, but in the end it only accentuated cleavages between leaders seeking political respectability and young radicals demanding action. The writings of these young radicals—among them the novelist Ernst Jünger—proved sufficiently embarrassing to the *Stahlhelm* leadership that it took away the official status of *Die Standarte* (while continuing to fund it) in March 1926.[143] Similar problems with youth were experienced by organizations of the left. The Social Democratic Party enjoyed some success in mobilizing young people, and indeed, the pro-Republican *Reichsbanner,* the largest paramilitary group in the Weimar Republic, organized more young men, even on the eve of the Third Reich, than the SA and *Stahlhelm* put together.[144] But as a governing parliamentary party, long since disassociated from any sort of social-transformative aspirations, the SPD found it difficult to appeal to the romantic utopianism of Weimar youth.[145]

The more radical ethos of the younger generation was far more effectively embodied by the Nazis. National Socialism was a strikingly young movement; 80 percent of the membership of the NSDAP in 1931 was under the age of thirty-five.[146] The party's emotional appeal to youth was captured in Gregor Strasser's phrase of 1927: "Make way, you old ones!"[147] The youth radicalism that the Nazis successfully tapped was based on a fundamental rejection of "politics," a word synonymous with what was widely held to be an illegitimate and unrepresentative parliamentary democracy. This was expressed well by an article titled "The Young Revolutionary," published in the journal of the National Socialist Student League in 1927: "We National Socialists believe that the unrefined [*unverbildet*] youth who hurl themselves with ardent hearts into political activity … will accomplish greater historical deeds than all the 'politicians' of today."[148] A young contemporary, the journalist Ernst Erich Noth—who, after fleeing Nazi Germany in 1934, published a remarkable book on the (dashed) hopes of the young generation—wrote of the way that Adolf Hitler understood best how to exploit the fighting spirit of youth.[149] A key to this ability was the paramilitary SA, which treated young stormtroopers as full-fledged "adult" members of the movement.[150] During the years 1929 to 1933, 60 percent of SA men were under twenty-five years old.[151] Already a mass movement by 1930, the SA had a membership equivalent in age to that of the *Stahlhelm*'s youth organization, and it embodied the Nazi success in crystallizing its claim to lead "young Germany."[152] This success is instructive, for it was the way in which the SA embodied the ideal of the young, manly revolutionary warrior that made it the most radical and dynamic of paramilitary formations.

If the Nazis were successful in part because of their ability to appeal to youth's "sense of mission" (*Sendungsbewusstsein*), National Socialism's relationship with youth was also a construction set up in characteristically military terms. The linkage between youth and war was made explicit in a number of forums, in none more strikingly than Otto Strasser's program of 1930, which directly linked the "German Revolution" with

> the Great War ... that mighty revolution of the twentieth century, of which the "World War" was only the first act, of which all "putsches," "rebellions," "battles" are only parts. ... Thus we youths feel the heartbeat of the German Revolution pounding, thus we front soldiers see the face of the near future before us and experience, humble-proud, the role of the chosen ones, to fight, to win the battle of the twentieth century, satisfied to see the meaning of the war, the Third Reich.[153]

The biggest part of the myth the Nazis set about constructing after the "seizure of power"—that it represented a spontaneous uprising of German youth—was, similarly, cast in military terms. When Joseph Goebbels wrote in April 1933 that the predecessor of the Hitler Youth had been not the young romantic of the youth movement but the private soldier of World War I, it was a characteristic example of the Nazi attempt to control the meaning and legacy of the Youth Movement.[154]

This attempt was an extension of the link between youth and warriorhood begun during the Great War. If the Nazi vision of a specifically National Socialist youth revolution was overstated, the rising success of the Nazis from the end of the 1920s did proceed apace with an overall "militarization" of the Youth Movement and of the idea of youth itself, which was in many ways consonant with the precepts and worldview of National Socialism. The war had affected the self-image of youth as well as the view of youth's role in society, delegitimizing the old generation while transforming youth into "hope-bearers" of the nation.[155] The "positive" content of the war—above all, the idea of the "community of the trenches" in which everyone had allegedly shared and shared alike regardless of social class—was seen to prefigure a future "socialist" organization of society. The idea of the *Frontgemeinschaft* concealed class differences in a way that paralleled that in the right-wing version of socialism. In romanticizing the brutal reality of military power relationships—officers and ranks as "one big happy family," with no callous expenditure of human life or draconian punishments to be seen—the myth of the *Frontgemeinschaft* elided class distinctions between officers and men, while simultaneously allowing the officer of upper-class background to don the mantle of the "simple soldier." In this way, the "militarization" of the idea of socialism both mirrored fascism's eliding of class differences and provided the basis for a bourgeois identification with the working classes.

The dream of authentic community derived from the prewar Youth Movement, displaced onto the trenches of the Great War, became connected with the idea of the Front Generation, the cohort of youth that supposedly embodied the new form of the *Volksgemeinschaft* created in the trenches.[156] Ironically, however, it was not that generation itself but the following one that actually came to embody the social myth of the Front Generation. The identification between youth and war more fully achieved with this "postwar generation" was a product, on the one hand, of the relentless hammering on nationalistic and militarist themes by patriotic extremists and, on the other, of the tireless efforts of members of the actual Front Generation to instill the "military virtues" into the consciousness of the younger generation. The latter goal was achieved, in particular, by the formation of youth groups led by former frontline and *Freikorps* officers, which sought to eliminate the civilian elements surviving from the prewar Youth Movement.[157] The combined effect was to bring about a "hardening" of the Youth Movement, a process complete, in the judgment of one scholar, by about 1927.[158]

The militarization of youth was accompanied by the construction of a "pop culture" version of the war that obscured its horror while making combat appear highly attractive to young men and boys. War, as it existed in the consciousness of youth, had little to do with "the dreadful reality of the trenches" but was drawn instead, as Richard Bessel writes, "from films, cheap children's novels, and playing soldier with … school comrades."[159] Popular literature, in particular, underwent a pronounced militarization from the end of the 1920s. A "war literature wave"—accompanying a general shift of writers from left to right in the late Weimar Republic—reached a first highpoint in 1929–30. The "*Volksgemeinschaft* of the trenches" was pushed in countless books and articles. The idea of youth became increasingly bound up with the idea of the warrior. The explosion of war literature was explicitly linked with "the young generation's claim to rule" and thereby to calls for political action. Young militants of the late Weimar Republic were advised in a popular pamphlet to take the struggle from "from the trenches to the streets."[160] This impulse was supported and fostered above all by the Nazis, who protested vociferously against any manifestation of "pacifism," leading demonstrations, for example, against the 1930 German opening of the film version of Remarque's *All Quiet on the Western Front* (the film was subsequently banned by the Republican authorities).[161] Hitler's attempt to commission a novel from

Figure 2.2 The dead of the Great War haunt Erich Maria Remarque. *Die Brennessel,* January 1931. Bundesarchiv.

Fritz Ewers, a writer criticized by the press magnate Alfred Hugenberg—as an ally of Hitler, far from squeamish about his associates—as the author of "patriotic revolver-pornography," was characteristic of the importance placed by National Socialism on the militarization of youth.[162]

The ten-year time lag between the end of the war and the "war wave" in German culture was no doubt, as George Mosse suggests, a product of the time necessary to achieve psychological distance from the war.[163] It is surely also no accident that it coincided with the overall radicalization of the political climate accompanying the Great Depression and reflected the drift toward authoritarian government from the late 1920s.[164] But the delay also related to a characteristic of youth culture detected by historians of the postwar period but seldom commented upon in histories of the Weimar Republic: the way in which ideas appealing to the members of youth subcultures are bastardized and radicalized through their successive reproduction in various media and through their adoption by successive waves of young adherents.[165] The Youth Movement of the Weimar Republic was, to be sure, much more firmly integrated into the adult world than the youth "scenes" of the post-1945 period; the "teenager" as a consumption-based youth type did not yet exist, and the Weimar youth organizations were strongly stamped by the shaping influence of adults in general, and ex-military men in particular. Yet there is evidence that the process of exaggeration and caricaturization that characterized the post-1945 period was prefigured in the youth scene of the Weimar Republic. The primary site of this process was the set of groups known collectively as the *Bündische Jugend* (*Bündisch* youth). The *Bündische Jugend* were the product of a sort of identity crisis in the Youth Movement. Facing increasing pressure from the adult world, in particular from political parties and groups hoping to instrumentalize the spirit of youth revolt, the *Bündisch* groups attempted to forge an autonomous sphere of youth activity. The strength of the *Bündisch* scene, as Otto Ernst Schüddekopf has observed, was precisely a product of a great "refusal" against what was perceived as "the lack of ideas and directionlessness of [both] the ruling regimes and the *Bonzakratie* of the radical extremist parties."[166]

* * *

Yet while based on a rejection of official politics and mass parties, the *Bündisch* concept proved adaptable for a variety of political orientations. Indeed, with a membership numbering in the tens of thousands, the *Bündisch* groups reflected a bewildering array of orientations and emphases.[167] The "idealist" or "independent" wing—represented above all by the *Deutsche Freischar,* with some twelve thousand members—came closest in spirit and goals to the old Youth Movement, having inherited some of the pro-Republican and liberal ideas associated with the prewar *Freideutsche Jugend.*[168] The "völkisch-nationalist" wing encompassed a number of groups—*Adler und Falken,* the *Artamanen,* the *Geussen,* and the *Schilljugend*—operating in the orbit of the NSDAP and cooperating with the Nazis on a level up to and including (in some cases eventual) organizational fusion. The "national revolutionary" wing, while sharing a commitment to the idea of "National Socialism," pursued a policy of strict independence from the Nazi movement and (in some cases) resisted the consolidation of the regime after 1933.[169] This wing provided a field for the activity of the "National Bolshevik" element and invited the attention of the KPD during those periods (1923, 1930) when the party sought cooperation with the radical right. The chief spokesman of this wing was the *Bündisch* publicist Karl Otto Paetel, whose groups—the Arbeitsring Junge Front at first, and later the Group of Social Revolutionary Nationalists (GSRN)—sought to bring together radicals of left and right in pursuit of a "Third Way" between the Nazis and the KPD.[170] This goal was elaborated in a number of influential newspapers, including *Die Tat* (The Deed), edited from 1929 by Hans Zehrer, which struggled to establish a "Third Front" between the NSDAP and the KPD to "mobilize for a true German socialism."[171] Especially associated with the *Bündisch* scene and expressing its heterogeneity was *Die Kommenden* (The Coming), a supra-*Bündisch* weekly that acted as a sort of clearinghouse for radicals of varying stripes. Representatives of the Hitler Youth were allowed space, for example, in which to rebut *Bündisch* criticism of, among other things, the NSDAP's participation in Weimar electoral politics.[172]

The *Bündische Jugend* had a very pronounced "countercultural" aspect. The most influential figure in the development of a youth countercultural identity in the Weimar Republic was Eberhard Koebel (aka "Tusk"), a leader in the *Deutsche Freischar*, who formed his own youth group in late 1929.[173] The *Deutsche Jungenschaft vom 1. 11. 1929* (shortened to "d.j.1.11") effected a highly influential updating of the content and style of the Youth Movement. Unlike the *Wandervögel*, it adopted an open attitude toward science and technology, modern art, design, and philosophy. The *Jungenschaft*'s sources of inspiration were eclectic and crosscultural, embracing Russian and Scandinavian literature, folklore and mythology, and the heroic ideal of the Japanese samurai warrior.[174] Members adopted various indicators of folk authenticity—Russian peasant blouses, the playing of the balalaika—sat "Indian Style," and explored the classics of Eastern philosophy.[175] Koebel himself composed songs and designed clothing for the movement. These expressions of eccentricity were not meant to privilege individuality over youth's great emancipatory mission; on the contrary, the task, as Koebel saw it, was to "fight the *Zeitgeist* of selfishness, of the loner."[176] Lifestyle and politics were intimately linked, with "culture clubs" formed to discuss and teach issues of "Revolution and Socialism" and communes established to allow students and workers to live and work together.[177] The name given by Koebel to these communes—"Red-Gray Garrisons"—is instructive, for the social-emancipatory longings of youth were by this time increasingly linked with the idea of soldierhood.[178]

The *Bündisch* scene was one of the key sites in the elaboration of a "protofascist" milieu in Weimar Germany. The term is used here in the sense suggested by Roger Griffin—as signifying the working out of fascist ideas prior to their incorporation into a mass movement.[179] The key aspect of this milieu was an interplay between left- and right-wing ideas, on socialism and revolution, and on the idea of the *Volksgemeinschaft*.[180] "Only the youth," wrote Helmuth Plessner,

> achieved what theoretically could never have been achieved, nor what permitted an intelligible defense without contradiction. They fused the teaching of Nietzsche and Marx into an enthusiastic and heroic affirmation of community. ... From the former came the antidemocratic spirit, the obligation to create form, exclusiveness, the longing for greatness, self-sacrifice and irrationality; from the latter came an opposition to society and civilization ... and a love of the army" [!].[181]

Ernst Erich Noth made a similar observation, writing of the "[fine line] between socialism and fascism" in this scene, whose members were united in the dream of a (more or less anticapitalist) *Volksgemeinschaft* to be achieved through the vision, self-sacrifice, and heroism of the young.[182] A glance at the debates splashed across the pages of *Die Kommenden* and other papers—about the correct attitude toward the Soviet Union, the meaning of the term "socialism," whether or not the *Völkisch* conception of the state admitted the concept of class warfare (the same sorts of debates engaged in by Scheringer and his codefendants in the Ulm trial)—reinforces the impression of extreme ideological flexibility connected with the "youth revolution" in Weimar Germany. The vagueness of the ideas involved only added to the revolutionary mystique. As Birgit Rätsch-Langejürgen puts it, simply combining the words "socialism" and "nationalism" "worked a magic so strong that no further explanation was necessary."[183]

The broad-based fascination with the idea of the *Volksgemeinschaft* supplied the mythic source material for German fascism. It was at once broader and deeper than the membership of its ultimate beneficiary, the Hitler movement, a fact that goes a long way toward explaining why the NSDAP was embraced by these circles only with difficulty, and even then, in many cases, incompletely.[184] The militarization of the *Bündische Jugend* was accompanied by both a masculinization and a politicization. "Under the direct influence of 'front-soldierly' elements," writes Karl Rohe,

> the *Bündische Jugend* moved further and further away from their original inspiration. In place of the "friends of the forests" now came the "problems of state and nation"; the "discussion of Eros" was replaced by the "forum on the social order"; in place of loose groups were formed "cohorts and marching columns"; in place of "mixed groups with girls allowed" came "boys' groups" and "young men's groups"; a change, that is, in outward style as well as in inner attitude: compared with the *Wandervögel* of the prewar period, the *Bündische Jugend* had become more taut, more political, more soldierly.[185]

These changes affected youth on the left as well. The "hypermasculinity" connected with the warrior virtues was shared not only by the NSDAP but by the KPD and occasionally by Social Democrats.[186] In the KPD, what Irmtraud Götz von Olenhusen calls "soft" youth—that is, those remaining under the influence of the less militarized, individualistic values of the old Youth Movement—were mostly driven away during the period of "Bolshevization" in the mid-1920s. In their place remained young people willing to march in uniform, train with weapons, and follow orders.[187] The KJVD placed great emphasis on military values, and on the connection between military and revolutionary values. *Die Junge Garde,* the primary organ of the KJVD, became a key site in the elaboration of a youthful militarism that paralleled very strongly that of the youth groups of the radical right, even if the specific ideological content was different.

The SPD was also affected by the militarization of youth in the Weimar Republic. Under the pressure of attacks from the right and criticism from the left, the SPD felt constrained to "learn from the enemy" and adopt a more warrior-like pose. This attempt was hindered, however, both by the SPD's ambivalent attitude toward violence and by the political inability of the SPD to make use of it as a weapon against the right.[188] An elite troop within the *Reichsbanner,* the *Schutzformationen* (Schufo), did achieve some success in drawing and organizing more combative members.[189] There were pressures within the SPD to adopt more militaristic means. As the Social Democrat Theodor Haubach argued in 1931, "Our movement must learn … that ceremony, order, and firm discipline are by no means antidemocratic, and most definitely not unsocialist."[190] The political ineffectiveness of the SPD and its paramilitary aside, working-class youth organized by the SPD and the KPD took part in the overall militarization of the working-class youth organizations. Militarism was encoded in the very language of militancy, even for the SPD. Thus an SPD flier inveighed against militarism in the same breath that it called upon "young comrades [to] march together in the freedom battalions of youth. … Youth to the front!"[191] Militarism was encoded in clothing style as well. "Despite their ideological differences," writes Frank Bajohr, "the [Socialist youth, the Communist youth, and the Hitler Youth] were almost indistinguishable in their outer appearance."[192] The existence of surface similarities, as Bajohr points out, did not necessarily imply a similarity in ideological content; but this development of style did signal an increasing acceptance of a certain conception of young-manliness that provided a common visual (and in some ways conceptual) language for militants across the political spectrum.[193]

* * *

Debates about the relationship between socialism and the nation, the meaning of revolution, the importance of the Soviet model, and so on were thus carried out according to certain basic assumptions. But alongside ideological debates was another, more fundamental debate having to do with the relationship between the individual and the mass. In contrast to the mass youth organizations of the left, the Youth Movement had traditionally been organized around the principle of the "elite," a character reinforced by the tutelage of militarist adults. The *Schilljugend,* founded by the ex-*Freikorps* leader Gerhard Rossbach in 1927, is a case in point. An important precursor to the *Bündisch* groups, the *Schilljugend* represented a fusion of the *Freikorps* tradition with the traditions of the Youth Movement. Combining a "bündisch spirit of voluntary subordination to a compelling leader-personality" with an "emphasis on cultural renewal through folk music and dance," the *Schilljugend* took as its chief goal the spiritual militarization of youth.[194] The *Schilljugend* explicitly positioned itself as an elite antidote to the mass radical parties: "[The *Schilljugend*] is no party youth. It is no social club. We are unpolitical and do not tolerate the influence of parliament-*Bonzen* in our ranks."[195] Although it embraced the ideas of Adolf Hitler—indeed, embraced the idea *of* Hitler as a mythological focal point—the *Schilljugend* was "critical of the mass character and low quality of many of the [NSDAP's] members and leaders."[196]

Increasingly by the end of the 1920s, the *Bündisch* groups faced hard political choices. The intensification of social warfare between the KPD and the NSDAP—and the challenge, especially, posed by the rising popularity of the latter from 1930—forced them to grapple with the inexorable logic of mass politics.[197] In some cases, the *Bündisch* groups tried to stem the threat posed to their identity by National Socialism. The *Freischar Junger Nation* organized a summit in May 1930 aimed at combating the "strong sympathy [recently being exhibited by members] toward the NSDAP. The rally will attempt to counter this trend and to put the ideas of the *Bund* in the foreground."[198] Other groups saw no problem in the decision to join the mass organizations of National Socialism, arguing, in Mathias von Hellfeld's words, that the NSDAP was simply "the current manifestation of a perpetually building national socialism."[199] *Die Kommenden* proclaimed in July 1932 that it was permissible for *Bündisch* youth to join the Hitler Youth "as a means for accomplishing our *Bündisch* tasks."[200]

The *Bündisch* exclusivity and "sense of youth mission" was, in part, a construct. It was, to be sure, the expression of a widespread sense of generational mission; but the specific political content of this mission was a matter of great dispute. The idea of a "young generation" was a type of "social myth," the content of which was open to interpretation. The relative resistance of youth to incorporation into mass groups comes out clearly in the comments of those who attacked this reluctance. "We are ready," wrote Franz Matzke in a high-profile book of 1930, "to form great bands and associations, to strive forcefully for a goal. We are ready to place ourselves under leaders. And we look with contempt upon those—typical of yesterday or the day before yesterday—who [fear for] the many superficial vanities of the ego if just once they had to obey an order from someone else."[201] Eberhard Koebel exemplified the dichotomy between elite and mass, hoping for his *Jugendschaft* to operate as elite within the larger Youth Movement and calling simultaneously on youth to resist selfishness and avoid the path of individualism. It is not mere adolescent male fantasy that made Eberhard Koebel seize on the image of the samurai warrior of medieval Japan as the leitmotif for his "d.j.1.11" group, but rather the way in which the samurai blended military values of honor and bravery with individuality and agency.[202] And here we come to a key dichotomy: The *Bündisch* movement resonated with fascism in its celebration of the elite; yet it also came into conflict with fascism as a mass movement because the mass nature of fascism drew in people who were not elite and therefore, by extension, not revolutionary.

This dichotomy reproduced that at the heart of fascism itself, for it stemmed from the very nature of fascism's project as it was rooted in the experience of the Great War. One of the most salient effects of World War I was to destroy or seriously weaken the idea of the warrior elite. Ideas of cavalry charges and chivalry soon gave way to the depersonalizing stalemate of trench warfare, where the warrior was reduced to a dehumanized cog in a machine. The war thus destroyed military agency in favor of a "massification" that made man a servant to machines. Tactically, military agency was retrieved by the creation of "shock troops"—elite commandos, sheltered behind the lines until the moment of attack, who developed the methods of infiltration with small arms, grenades, and flamethrowers that prefigured the small-unit tactics of World War II. These formations—a privileged military elite held aloof from the mass of the army until the moment of attack: the "special forces" of their day—were personified after the war by their best-known representative, the writer Ernst Jünger.[203] It is thus no surprise that shock troops became key bearers of fascism. Spiritually, warrior agency was regained through the postwar celebration of the wartime shock troops and their spiritual successors in the *Freikorps* (as in the work of Jünger) and, more generally, through fascism's celebration of the warrior elite and the values with which it was connected. Fascism was an attempt to retrieve agency lost in the Great War, but it held a similar tension within itself, between elite and mass. The "elite" became equivalent to those who were charged with the spiritual mission of combat; the mass, those who came aboard when it was "safe," when the hard work of the elite was done. This dichotomy between elite and mass passed into the paramilitary organizations of the Weimar Republic, above all the SA, and was reflected not only in conflicts between the SA and the party but also in relations between the small splinter groups and the mass movement. The "small band of picked fighters"—an analogue to the shock troops of the Great War—became the resistance metaphor par excellence on the radical right (on the left, as will be seen, a far more positive evaluation of the mass was operative). The idea of political soldierhood elaborated in the SA can thus be seen as a means of resolving the conflict between elite and mass stemming from the Great War and passed into the mass politics of Weimar. It also held, as we will see, the seeds of conflict within the Nazi movement and supplied the terms in which that conflict was fought out.

"Virile hate has been replaced by feminine lamentation"

The warrior identity reclaimed and expanded after the war was above all a male identity. Fascism's attempt to reclaim agency for the warrior was simultaneously an attempt to reclaim a masculinity asserted in that war and challenged in the return to peacetime, both by pacifism and by the women's movement. The "revolutionary soldier" through which this reclamation was accomplished was a heavily gendered type. Part of the "war mood" of 1914, which was a response to the perceived boringness and meaningless of civilian life, was the search for a new manliness. Steps in the creation of a new masculine identity had already been taken in the late nineteenth century, and the new masculinity seems to have developed in tandem with the consolidation of the nation-state.[204] A German fascination with the ideal of manliness—the *Mannesideal*—is discernable from the time of the Wars of Liberation.[205] But the Great War brought about a strengthening of male gender stereotypes, creating, in the words of the novelist Arnold Zweig, "an upsurge of public and private male-manliness."[206] The war further solidified the link between this new masculinity and the type of the warrior-revolutionary. "The feeling that the war had created a new masculine type existed all over Europe," writes George Mosse; "this man would be free of the dead-weight of a middle-class past just as the front-line soldier ... had left that past behind him."[207] The idea of the "new man" born in the war and carried forward into the birth of fascism was bound up with the articulation of a "militant masculinity."[208] The heroism celebrated by fascism was a male heroism, the deeds it demanded manly deeds. Thus the very idea of radical activism, the call for a politics of "deeds," was, as Wolfgang Lindner has pointed out, inherently male—there were no such thing as "womanly deeds."[209] The "contempt for women" celebrated by F. T. Marinetti in the "Futurist Manifesto" was at once contempt for peacetime civilization and for the feminized bourgeoisie with which it was connected. Fascism's celebration of physical activity and action for its own sake was explicitly understood as celebration of a masculine ideal of physical prowess. The "decadence" against which fascism ranged itself was understood as a synonym for "effeminacy."[210]

The new manliness had specific links with the concept of youth revolt elaborated during and after the Great War. The Battle of Langemarck, especially, became connected with the myth "of war as an education in manliness." This manliness, in turn, "meant the idealization of youth's vigor and energy."[211] Wartime propaganda—including the trench newspapers of the frontline rank and file—feminized and racialized Germany's adversaries. "Shirkers" on the home front, as well as "racial enemies" such as the Slavs, were consistently portrayed in feminine terms contrasting them to the manliness of the frontline fighter.[212] The exaggerated idea of manliness was carried forward into the postwar period by the *Freikorps,* which fetishized the ideal of masculine togetherness and hatred of the feminine derived from the war experience. "A powerful myth grew up around the members of the Free Corps," writes George Mosse, "as real men who in their camaraderie exemplified the best of the nation."[213] *Freikorps* leaders such as Herman Ehrhardt and Gerhard Rossbach were looked up to as role models by young people precisely because they were seen to represent the apex of manliness and warriorhood.[214] These manly ideals played an important role in the *Bündisch* groups. The latter repackaged old *Freikorps* songs, whose lyrics spelled out a domain absent of women.[215] Increasingly, women were excluded in a movement that fetishized male-togetherness and an adolescent fantasy world of campouts and "adventures."[216] The moral values associated with the youth revolution and connected with the new revolutionary warrior type were also heavily gendered. The version of manliness that arose in the trenches privileged the ideal of comradeship—connected with the ideal of the *Männerbund*—as intimately related to the notion of self-sacrifice. "The ideal of comradeship," writes George Mosse, "had provided many soldiers with the noblest expression of their manliness. It seemed to approximate that *fin-de-siècle* longing for a community of affinity which had been so strongly opposed to the artificiality of bourgeois life." This ideal of comradeship—which, in the form of the "community of the trenches," was bound up with the idea of classlessness, and thereby with the idea of socialism—came to be regarded as "the noblest expression of . . . manliness." Decisiveness was another key virtue, lauded not only in the speech and action of fascist militants but also in memorial depictions of the fallen.[217]

The ideal of the young, manly revolutionary soldier was epitomized by the stormtroopers of the SA, who represented, in Richard Bessel's phrase, "machismo in uniform."[218] Likewise, the brand of socialism upheld on the radical right in general, and in the SA in particular, was a highly gendered concept—a socialism of manly fighters. The head of the SA, Ernst Röhm, in his widely read autobiography, drew a clear connection between soldierly manliness and virility.[219] Characteristically, he posited "hate" as an essential quality of antibourgeois radicalism opposed to what he dismissed as "feminine lamentation."[220] When it became necessary to tame the SA's activism after the Nazi consolidation of power, it was not just done by the blood purge of 30 June 1934; it was done, as George Mosse has shown, by reinforcing aspects of the bourgeois family that placed limitations on the "lone wolf" character of young male activists."[221] By "feminizing" the movement's paramilitary fighters in this way, the party attempted to blunt their revolutionary urgency, to rob them of agency. One of the more obvious gender elements associated with the paramilitary activism of the SA has been the role played by unemployment and loss of status within the family. A number of scholars have noted the importance of paramilitary activism as a means of reasserting a threatened masculinity.[222]

Like the militarism with which it was connected, the new ideal of manliness was not confined to the political right.[223] The celebration of "masculine strength and bravery" was a key component of the Communist self-image as well, as studies by Eric Weitz and Pamela Swett have shown.[224] But more generally, all the various uniformed formations of the Weimar Republic, to the extent that they shared in the overall militarization of youth culture, shared in its masculinization. Militant masculinity, as a key component of radical identity in the Weimar Republic, provided one important axis of communication between left and right. Richard Scheringer, for example, was attracted to Hitler's SA not on ideological grounds but, as he later put it, because of his deep attachment to the *Männerbund-romantik* of the interwar years.[225] Similarly, Scheringer himself was attractive to both left and right because he embodied the militant ideal. As a political "martyr" exemplifying the virtue of comradely self-sacrifice, he was seen to represent moral qualities important to both sides. Ideas of heroic young manhood derived from the trench experience of the Great War provided the filter through which Scheringer's conversion to Communism was interpreted, making it intelligible to militants of all stripes (even Communists otherwise disgusted by the KPD's dalliance with nationalist chauvinism). Most young nationalist militants, to be sure, rejected Scheringer's contention that the KPD offered a convincing vehicle for the particular type of violent revolution they sought; but all understood the language of militancy, heroism, and sacrifice—the hallmarks of authenticity—in which his decision was presented.

Conclusion

By the end of the Weimar Republic, more than a quarter of the four million young men between the ages of eighteen and twenty-five belonged to paramilitary organizations, with an additional significant number belonging to nonparamilitary youth groups.[226] This mass paramilitarization arose with the generational wave and developed in parallel with a simplification and amplification of ideas connected with the preceding, so-called Front Generation. If Richard Scheringer's conversion to Communism and his subsequent celebrity as a crossover figure of the radical scene in the Weimar Republic illustrates the cultural commonalities that allowed dialogue and understanding across the political barricades, the divergent paths taken by him and his two codefendants in the Ulm Reichswehr trial illustrate the way that this cultural content was expressed in the context of conflict over a series of antinomies. The first of these, the dual question of national and social revolution, represented in many ways the characteristic dilemma of political militancy in the Weimar Republic. "Everybody was indeed a socialist … in the Germany of 1930," observed Walter Laqueur in his classic study of the German Youth Movement, "just as everybody was against the Versailles treaty. But what did this all mean?"[227] A veritable obsession, in the Weimar Republic, with the idea of socialism—deeply connected to a spirit of generational mission and the spiritual values of the war experience—existing outside of and parallel to the mass parties, supplied the centerpiece of a multifaceted discourse that provided the motive force for extremism of both left and right.

The question of the extent to which this socialism would be national—or more properly, on the right and among the *Bündisch* youth, of the extent to which nationalism would be social—was a subject of fierce debate.[228] For militants, whether caught in the magnetic pull of one of the two great mass movements, like Scheringer and Ludin, or eking out a politically marginal existence in the zone of conflict between them, like Wendt—who last appears in the sources in October 1931, a fugitive terrorist on the search for explosives—the issue was one of how much weight was to be laid on each of these principles, the national and the social.[229] These were, to be sure, elastic conceptions; the content of "socialism" in particular, as we will see, occupied a key position in dialogue between the radical extremes, and much of the struggle over meaning we will examine in the following chapters had to do with how it was to be defined. Linked to the question of ideological ratio was a question of means: was the struggle to be pursued within one of the two great mass movements, National Socialism or Communism, accepting the tortured claims of the former to be "social" (Ludin) or of the latter to be "national" (Scheringer), or was it better to remain independent and therefore pure (Wendt)?

This question of means—which was, simultaneously, a question of the relationship between the individual and the mass—was ideological inasmuch as it had to do with questions of nationalism, socialism, and revolution, but on a more fundamental level it was the expression of a *moral* conception of politics. The divergent paths taken by the Ulm defendants—three young friends from the same garrison pledging their allegiance to, respectively, Adolf Hitler, Otto Strasser, and Joseph Stalin—is unintelligible without reference to the role played by shared cultural assumptions about the value of social warfare generally, and warrior virtues in particular; but they are also unintelligible without reference to the ideas of moral legitimacy with which the concept of being a revolutionary soldier was connected. Scheringer chose the KPD not only because it seemed to offer a better answer to the question of ideological ratio posed above, nor because it was radical and militant and thus shared his values, but because it seemed to be the party that was most *sincere:* the party that meant what it said when it said it was going to make a revolution.[230] Scheringer chose the KPD because he became convinced that it represented in fact what the NSDAP said but did not really believe—that the solution to Germany's problems demanded *both* a social and a national revolution. He chose the KPD, in short, because it had, in his eyes, a greater revolutionary legitimacy. Scheringer himself became important for the same reason—in facing prison for his beliefs, he became a symbol of authenticity.

Similar considerations guided Wendt and Ludin in their choices.[231] Wendt could not embrace Communism, in part, because he could not take seriously its claims to be national. Ludin chose to remain with the NSDAP because he saw it as having the best chance to actually put a "national socialism" into practice.[232] In highlighting the centrality of this moral understanding of politics, the Ulm defendants illustrate a key determinant in relations within and between the radical extremes in the Weimar Republic. Alongside shared cultural preconceptions about what it meant to be a soldier, a revolutionary, and a man, this moral understanding of politics allowed radical extremists to talk to each other, to participate in the discourse of social radicalism. But these same concepts provided the language through which battles over content were fought out, both within and between movements. Conflicts over ideological ratio (a necessary component, in particular, of a syncretic movement such as National Socialism); of elite versus mass; of moral purity fought out around cultural symbols characterized conflict within National Socialism and conditioned its relations with both Communism and the myriad radical groups of the *Völkisch* scene. The ideological warfare between the KPD, NSDAP, the *Bündisch* groups and others, and also within these organizations, arose out of attempts to define these issues, to assign a particular inflection to the radicalism of followers or opponents. It is to these conflicts that we now turn.

An uns allein wird der Bolschewismus zerschellen

Figure 3.1 "On us alone will Bolshevism be shattered." *Der SA-Mann. Organ der Obersten SA-Führung der NSDAP,* Munich, Saturday, 26 November 1932, Jg. 1. Bundesarchiv.

Chapter 3

NATIONAL SOCIALISM AND
ITS DISCONTENTS

*T*wo weeks before the Reichstag elections of 14 September 1930—elections that would bring the NSDAP 107 parliamentary delegates and make Nazism a major player on the German political stage—a series of anonymous fliers began appearing on the streets of Berlin, Leipzig, and other German cities. "We are nationalists and socialists," the authors of the first flier proclaimed, "but we are above all revolutionaries. For that reason, the plan to take place in the government after the elections is treasonous." Any kind of alliance with the bourgeois "parties of the goldsacks," any kind of participation in the system, they continued, was a "betrayal of socialism," a betrayal of the slogan—"the common good over the individual good!"—enshrined in the NSDAP's own program.[233] The liberal *Frankfurter Zeitung* observed, not without sarcasm, that although "the matter has a distinctly Communist flavor, the directness of the language and the undisguised hate that rings out of every line speaks for its authenticity."[234] Others were not so sure. Police authorities in Pomerania, where the fliers were also in circulation, attributed them to the rebel group around Walther Stennes and Otto Strasser.[235] The Nazi Party, in contrast, charged the fliers to the account of the KPD. A memorandum from the party in Berlin reproduced parts of the flier in order to illustrate what it called "typical phrases" used by Communist propagandists, such as "the only thing that will help now is ruthless openness"; "is there a point to fighting the Marxist and bourgeois parties when in our own party ..."; and so on.[236] The disagreement about the provenance of the fliers represented, in the first instance, a general recognition that a variety of groups were making similar claims, if only for purposes of subversion. But it also suggests the extent to which the NSDAP had been successful, by the end of the 1920s, not only in capturing the support of workers but also of blurring the boundaries between its anticapitalist claims and those of the KPD.[237]

The question of Nazism's borrowing from the left is intertwined with the question of its own revolutionary claims. Like fascism generally, but to a more pronounced degree, Nazism drew on the symbolic repertoire of the working-class movement. This borrowing was linked in part with what the sociologist Juan Linz has called fascism's "latecomer" status. Attempting to win space for itself in the established party-political spectrum by elaborating various "anti-" positions (anti-Marxism, antiliberalism, anticonservatism), fascism also attempted, with varying success, to, as Linz puts it, "incorporat[e] elements of what [it] rejected."[238] More importantly, fascism's borrowings were shaped by the character of its struggle with the revolutionary left as a struggle between revolutionary competitors. Acting to rally the threatened middle classes against the specter of Communist revolution while simultaneously putting forward its own vision of revolution—a new, radical, organic, spiritual national community—fascism had necessarily to grapple with the left's monopoly of mass-mobilizing symbolism. To accomplish its foundational maneuver—the binding of the working masses to the flag of the nation—fascism had to break, through violence where necessary, the left's hold over the masses. At the same time, in order to seal its own claim to rule and to cement the affinity between the working masses and the national community, fascism had to adopt and reconfigure the left's symbolic repertoire. Nazism, while lacking the left-wing pedigree of fascist movements in France and Italy analyzed by Zeev Sternhell and others, developed an *affective* leftism of great potency, a fact noted by contemporaries.[239] Unorthodox Marxists such as Walter Benjamin and Ernst Bloch identified National Socialism's key maneuver in its privileging of appearance over reality, its substitution of revolutionary *affect* for revolutionary *effect*. Writing in 1933, Bloch called attention to Nazism's "propaganda ... [of] sheer revolutionary appearance," noting especially what he called its "thefts from the commune."[240] A number of historians since have noted the highly effective way in which the NSDAP employed "leftist" rhetoric to its advantage.[241] Gerhard Paul has demonstrated very convincingly how Hitler repackaged the symbols of the working-class movement to accomplish this end. Iconic images of the Marxist working-class movement, such as the closed fist or the tool employed as a weapon, were used by the NSDAP, writes Paul, as a "visual representation of its readiness to overthrow the 'system' and its decisive will to power." Appealing directly to the emotions, these symbols were meant to bypass the intellect. "Flags and standards, insignia and colors," writes Paul, "were for [Hitler] magical forces and a means for control over the masses." Here was the root of Hitler's socialism—it was precisely these symbols that were to serve a "socializing function," binding the masses together in a community of sentiment linked to race and nation.[242]

The Nazi version of socialism was, of course, indelibly linked to racist and ethnic nationalist conceptions. In this, it distinguished itself not only from the Marxist left but from other fascisms for which, in most cases, race played a secondary role.[243] The primacy of race in the construction of National Socialism has led many scholars to try to exclude it from more generic conceptions of fascism, although the trend in the historiography of recent years has been to include it, while recognizing its unique characteristics.[244] Nazism was an outgrowth of the *Völkisch* scene in Germany, ultimately gaining primacy over—and incorporating aspects of—a plethora of groups sharing a combination of ethnic-romantic, racial-environmental, anti-Semitic mythologies. Nazism's ability to "nationalize the masses" stemmed, in part, from its ability to racialize them.[245] Yet Hitler's theft of the left's symbolic repertoire can be seen as part of a larger fascist project that had its roots, as Zeev Sternhell has shown, in the synthesis of national and socialist ideas among French and Italian thinkers from the end of the nineteenth century.[246] This project received a decisive impetus from the Great War, which demonstrated, first of all, the severe limitations of social class as a constitutive element of political action. The myth of the nation in arms, free of crippling class divisions (as in the *Burgfrieden* of Germany or *L'union sacreé* in France) was proven considerably more powerful than the myth of international proletarian solidarity dashed by the rush to the colors in 1914. Second, the war demonstrated once and for all the bankruptcy of old-style conservatism with its disdain for the masses, demanding a "modernization" that would link the productive and combative capabilities of the lower classes with the creation of a new national community. These ideas were carried forward during and after the war by men such as the Marxist renegade Benito Mussolini, for whom the war seemed to open the way forward into a new era of radicalism freed of humanitarian or ideological constraints. This was fascism—or "proto-fascism," if we wish to follow the distinction proposed by Roger Griffin—that sought only the creation of institutional vehicles for its practical realization.[247]

The linkage between the masses and the nation demanded by fascism required a reconfiguration of the idea of social class. This involved, first, the positioning of the state as the new revolutionary subject, captured most famously in the idea of the "proletarian nation" elaborated by Enrico Corradini in 1910. This concept played a key role in fascism's redrawing of the lines of conflict between left and right, allowing the war-prepared nation in arms to occupy the conceptual space previously occupied by the proletariat. This transformed the struggle, as Michael Mann has written, from one between "bourgeois" and "proletarian" to one "between 'workers of all classes,' 'the productive classes,' ranged against 'unproductive' enemies, usually identified as finance or foreign Jewish capitalists." In this way, "nations [replaced] classes [as] the true masses of modernity."[248] In Germany this fusion of nation and class was elaborated in racial terms. The concept of "German Socialism" laid out in the writings of Oswald Spengler and elaborated by later writers such as Moeller van den Bruck as "Prussian Socialism" held a dual thrust, suggesting potentially both a "national" socialism (i.e., a socialism bound to the nation) and a "racial-ethnic" socialism (i.e., a socialism constructed in opposition to a racialized other). The latter could and did easily articulate with anti-Semitism, which provided a vehicle for linking nationalist chauvinism with anticapitalism. The inherent ambiguity of this formulation played a key role in enabling National Socialism to draw disparate interests together in a common goal, but as will be argued below, it also created the potential for severe conflict over the meaning of National Socialism.

The radical right's attempt to destabilize class as a category received unexpected support from the Communist left. Communism manipulated Marxist categories to include elements of the middle classes among the "oppressed," and by placing the nation—sometimes explicitly—at the forefront of the class struggle.[249] At its Second Congress in 1920, for example, the Comintern drew a "distinction between two types of states, 'exploiters' and 'exploited nations,'" echoing the distinction made a decade earlier by Corradini.[250] During the first of the KPD's overtures to the radical right in 1923, the Comintern's representative in Germany, Karl Radek, argued that the working class must "put itself at the head of the nation, to accept the burden and honor of leading the German people and fuse the class struggle with the quest for national emancipation."[251] The fusion between class and national aims implicit in the shift toward "socialism in one country" in the mid-1920s, and made explicit in Stalin's elaboration of an indigenous "National Bolshevism" from the early 1930s,[252] paralleled some of the thought of the German "national revolutionaries" and accounts in part for their fascination with the Soviet Union.[253] Ernst Niekisch saw in the combination of "Russian strength and Prussian spirit," in Birgit Rätsch-Langejürgen's words, "the synthesis of the future."[254] In creating "a Russian socialism organized like a military camp," Stalin supplied an image with great appeal for *Bündisch* youngsters and political theorists trying to eke out a Third Way between left and right.[255]

Right-wing admiration for Communism could only go so far, however, for the primary goal of right-wing extremism in Germany was not the elevation of class to an organizing principle but the erasure of class as a threat to the unity of the nation. What was retained by the right—the most important thing it borrowed from the left—was the *emotional charge* of class. The bourgeoisie was, for both left and right, a symbol of corruption, weakness, and effeminacy; the proletariat, a symbol of deep productive forces, masculine combativeness, strength, and energy. Even as it sought to eliminate the class struggle to the benefit of the nation, breaking the hold of Marxism on the working classes, fascism sought to incorporate this energy. The elevation of the nation as revolutionary subject—and the destabilization of the concept of class with which it was connected—was accompanied by the transformation of class from a socioeconomic to a *moral* category. The cultural meaning of the class struggle—its religious sense of inevitability, its righteous indignation and moral authority—were retained; its underpinnings in the reality of class exploitation were jettisoned. The moral qualities supposedly associated with the proletariat and the class struggle (simplicity, determination, will, hardness—the latter fetishized by Bolshevism to an almost unbelievable degree) were turned into positive goods, revolutionary virtues that articulated, as we have seen, with soldierly virtues.[256] The symbolic attributes of social class—referred to hereafter in this work as "symbolic social class"—were developed on both right and left and became available for use in the construction of radical identity by fascism.[257] National Socialism's theft from the left attained not just to symbols but also to a "revolutionary essence" expressed in an affective "working-class" identity that Nazis played with in big cities such as Berlin. This was, of course, only one Nazi identity—as William Sheridan Allen showed long ago, and as a number of scholars have confirmed since, National Socialist propaganda was fundamentally instrumental in the way in which it bent itself to the requirements of locale and clientele.[258] Yet even where it shied away from "leftist" associations—in favor, say, of the pet resentments of shopkeepers and armchair militarists—National Socialism profited from what it stole from the left, which was not merely a fund of symbolic imagery but the idea of *revolt* itself.

This theft was perpetrated in the context of a violent reaction against the threat of Communist revolution in the wake of World War I. A series of revolutionary misadventures in 1919 in Germany or along its eastern borders—the Spartacist Uprising in Berlin in January; the Bavarian Soviet Republic in Munich in the spring; the Red Terror in Hungary under the dictatorship of Bela Kun in the summer—compounded the shock of the lost war and galvanized a middle-class reaction against the threat of social revolution. This reaction was centered initially in the citizens' defense militias (the so-called *Einwohnerwehren*), in the *Freikorps* volunteer formations of ex-soldiers, and in paramilitary *Wehrverbände* such as the *Stahlhelm* and the *Wehrwolf*.[259] Although initially by no means the most important of these groups—the NSDAP was merely one of many on the *Völkisch* right for most of its first decade—National Socialism was the ultimate inheritor of the force of this backlash. Much of its initial dynamism derived from its incorporation of the anti-Communist paramilitarism of the *Freikorps,* and its self-image as the defender of Germany (and later Europe) against Bolshevism was central to National Socialist identity.[260] It is true, as Walter Laqueur has pointed out, that in the early days of the party, anti-Semitism and opposition to the Treaty of Versailles trumped anti-Marxism as concerns, and that "Marxism" in the parlance of the NSDAP almost always referred to the SPD rather than the Communists.[261] Nevertheless, anti-Communist atrocity tales and the scare image of a coming "Red Germany" played a key role in Nazi propaganda both before and after 1933 (see Figure 3.1).[262]

The anti-Communism of the Nazis—simultaneously visceral and instrumental—was heavily alloyed with respect and admiration. As early as 1919, leading Nazis were involved in efforts to recruit among Communists in southern Germany.[263] Dietrich Eckart, an early and important influence on Hitler, came out in favor of a "German [as opposed to Jewish] Bolshevism," and Adolf Hitler himself made similarly provocative utterances.[264] Hitler's prediction to Hermann Rauschning, that it was not Germany that would go Bolshevist but rather Russia that would go National Socialist, is well known. Joseph Goebbels's early characterization of Stalin as a "National Socialist" was later picked up by Otto Strasser, and Goebbels himself remained subject to periodic "National Bolshevist relapses" that signaled an ongoing fascination with Soviet Communism.[265] What the Nazis most admired about Bolshevism was its fanaticism and uncompromising ruthlessness, and indeed, these qualities were often what seemed to link them together. What was "left" about Nazism, in the eyes of conservatives, was not its economic program—the left-wing aspects of which were underplayed and not infrequently contradicted by Hitler and other leading Nazis—but its "gutter" quality, a quality it was seen to have in common with Bolshevism.[266] When the theorist of totalitarianism Waldemar Gurian termed Nazism a "Brown Bolshevism," he was commenting not on its program but on the "spiritual qualities" of plebian ruthlessness it allegedly shared with Russian Communism. The Nazis themselves noticed the link, and some of them—one thinks here above all of Goebbels—in this sense at least, seem to have considered the comparison a compliment.[267]

The janus face of National Socialism's attitude toward Bolshevism came to especially pronounced expression in the SA. As the spearhead of National Socialism's anti-Communist offensive, the physical embodiment of the National

Figure 3.2 "This is how it's done." *Der Angriff* 39, 16 October 1930. Bundesarchiv.

Figure 3.3 "Brother Worker! People's Comrade!" *Der Angriff* 39, 30 September 1929. Bundesarchiv.

Socialist "idea," instrument of propaganda both physical and ideological, the SA played a key role in mediating Nazism's relationship with Communism.[268] The entire mythology of the SA was constructed out of its battle in the streets with Communist opponents. Especially in "Red Berlin," where Goebbels took over as *Gauleiter* in 1926, the struggle of the SA against the Red Front became a key component of Nazi propaganda and self-understanding, although, as Gerhard Paul has pointed out, it was not until after 1933, when the Nazis had all the repressive power of the state at their disposal, that the "storming of the Red bastions" became a reality.[269] Arguably more destructive for the working-class movement in Germany than the SA's physical assault was its ability to penetrate the working classes, to take advantage of breakdown of class allegiances and problems within the SPD and KPD to win over workers. From a social perspective, the SA represented National Socialism's bridge to the working masses and, in particular, to Communism's target constituency, the industrial proletariat.[270]

Der Tag des Erkennens — der Anbruch des Dritten Reiches

Brüder eines Volkes —

Figure 3.4 "The Day of Recognition." *Der Angriff* 32, 4 July 1932. Bundesarchiv.

Just as important was the SA's symbolic function. It was the SA that was the vehicle for Hitler's attempt to steal weapons of propaganda from the left and to take back the street physically and aesthetically as a site for propaganda. Here, it was the SA man himself who was the "decisive propaganda medium."[271] As the formation in which the proletariat became integrated with the lower middle classes proletarianized by economic crisis, as well as with higher-class officers, the SA represented the coming together of militarized youth and the nation, becoming, in effect, the embodiment of the Nazi version of a "classless society." Joseph Goebbels, in particular, was fond of portraying the SA as the collective embodiment of "young Germany." He emphasized the proletarian makeup of the SA (particularly in Berlin) in order to draw the connection between class and the nation, using the SA as a living, breathing symbol of the proletarian nation. The SA represented an "embodied National Socialism" (Ernst Röhm) that reproduced, in physical reality, concepts (in Gerhard Paul's words) such as "the *Volksgemein-schaft*, values like selflessness, readiness for action and sacrifice, and [a] nationalist and socialist will."[272] These values were widely understood and overwhelmingly approved of by radicals in the Weimar Republic. In showing "socialist" (i.e., ple-bian) masses, young, manly masses, marching for the cause of the nation, the SA represented what everybody—the youngsters of the *Bündisch* groups, the Na-tional Revolutionaries, and, on some level, the Communists—thought *should* be happening. For the KPD, obviously, the SA was a threat that had to be combated, but even here, there were strong differences of opinion about whether this would be better accomplished with carrot or stick, and about whether SA men were better seen as murdering thugs for finance capital or as admirably radical but "misled" proletarians hoodwinked into following the demagogue Hitler.[273]

Tactical considerations aside, the key importance of the SA was recognized by all the revolutionary contenders of the Weimar Republic, which accounts for the heavy emphasis placed on the SA in attempts to blunt, subvert, or redirect Nazi radicalism. The SA was the site of National Socialism's most important "theft" from the revolutionary left. The National Socialists "stole the street," wrote Ernst Bloch, "the pressure it exerts. The procession, the dangerous songs that had been sung." The SA was central to Nazism's ability to, in Bloch's words, "[pretend] to be merely workers and nothing else."[274] The French anarchist Daniel Guérin, traveling in Germany in the early 1930s, made a similar observation. Of an old socialist song appropriated by the Nazis, he wrote:

> The Nazis have appropriated this song, just as they have done with the red flag, May Day, dramatic recitations, the five-year plans, and a thousand other things. The *blood red* flag has simply become the *swastika* flag, and the workers' *world*, considered too internationalist, has become the workers' *state*. No need to exercise your brain. What's essential is that the masses maintain the illusion of singing a revolutionary song.[275]

The SA was, in effect, the site at which was stored the "revolutionary charge" stolen from the left by National Socialism.

Yet it was precisely this role of the SA that was potentially problematic for the Nazis. As a vehicle for recruitment of militant opponents, including Com-munists, the SA was expected to provide its recruits with sufficient preparation to win people over. The NSDAP made much of the presence of ex-Communists in the ranks of the SA and attempted, in much the same way as the KPD, to prosely-tize in the enemy's ranks.[276] Yet implicit in the SA's role as a bridge to the working masses was the dangerous potential that any tendency of Communists to switch sides might be matched by an opposite tendency on the part of SA men, and that proletarians (especially ex-Marxists) in Nazi ranks were prone to be susceptible to Marxism and therefore fundamentally suspect (the flip side of an essentialist view of the SA's social makeup that fueled Communist efforts to subvert the SA). This fear would come strongly to the fore after the seizure of power, as will be seen in chapter 5. The SA was thus a source not only of pride but also of worry for Nazi leaders. At times of particular stress in the movement, SA and party leaders were prone to warn of the danger that their charges might defect to the KPD. This was sometimes done for effect, as when Hitler tried to shock Bavarian authorities into supporting him by warning of potential defections from the SA to the Red

Front.[277] Sometimes it really happened, especially in the crisis year of 1932; but the idea that the SA represented a sort of "Brown Bolshevism" with the potential to play into the hands of Moscow was more important as a potential—as a representation of hopes and fears—than an actual occurrence.[278] It was, nevertheless, both a cause and a consequence of the SA's being signed as "left."

The Nazi Left(s)

The idea of Nazi leftism has typically been treated in a very reductionist manner, either located solely in the "National Socialist left" around the Strasser brothers (powerless after being outmaneuvered by Hitler in 1926, their impotence proven by Otto Strasser's failure to drag substantial numbers along with him when he quit the NSDAP in the summer of 1930); seen to be purely affective, a central component of Marxist interpretations; or read backward from the Third Reich, with the regime's actions after 1933 overwriting the beliefs and expectations of its followers before 1933.[279] Yet the NSDAP's leftist aspect was more diffuse and harder to pin down than these approaches suggest. Gottfried Feder's distinction between *raffende Kapital* (exploitative capital) and *schaffende Kapital* (productive capital)—which was also, or primarily, a distinction between "Jewish" and "Aryan" capital—played an important role in the movement, as did his concept of the "breaking of interest slavery" (*Brechung der Zinsknechtschaft*), Joseph Goebbels' cynical remarks to Richard Scheringer notwithstanding.[280] Hitler wrote at length in *Mein Kampf* about the importance to him of Feder's ideas.[281] The 25-point party program composed by Feder and released in 1920 contained a number of left-wing or anticapitalist points.[282] These were constructed entirely in anti-Semitic terms and were implicitly understood as such by many in the movement, but in practice they informed the populist radicalism and submerged class resentments that motivated much of the day-to-day agitation of Nazi activists.[283] Feder's ideas predated those of the Strasser brothers and in many ways were more important. On the other hand, as Barbara Miller Lane has pointed out, the Strassers were themselves "widely influential publicists" whose ideas were by no means out of step with the broader movement.[284] The ideological centerpiece of Otto Strasser's activity after leaving the NSDAP—the "Fourteen Theses of the German Revolution"—was the object of public congratulations from Joseph Goebbels upon its publication in July 1929.[285]

It is certainly true that attempts to theorize and codify Nazi anticapitalism were bound to fail where they came against the charismatic leadership of Hitler, who refused to be bound by any program that would limit his freedom of action. Feder, for example, in no way held the place normally occupied by a theorist in a political movement, and the "unalterable" party program was never in any way regarded as binding by Hitler. As to Strasser, although his propagation of a racialized anticapitalism resonated strongly in the NSDAP, his ideas were gospel only to a small coterie of followers, and their particular prescriptions were seen by very few in the party as grounds for a break with Hitler. When Strasser announced "the socialists are leaving the NSDAP" in July 1930, very few "socialists" came with him.[286] This fact has often been used to argue that his ideas were not influential or widely shared in the movement, but it is probably more accurate to say that many Nazis who shared his anticapitalist views, despite concerns over the NSDAP's increasing respectability, continued to feel that they could pursue their socialism *within* the movement. The nature of the NSDAP's anticapitalism—the primary "ideological" subject of dispute in the Nazi movement—was, moreover, essentially irrational and emotional. The "anticapitalist longing" referenced by Otto's brother Gregor in his famous Reichstag speech of 1932 required little in the way of theory—it was, like everything else in the Nazi world of ideas, subject to a whole host of different inflections, to the extent of being all but immune to rational discussion. It thus means very little that few Nazis followed Strasser out of the party, or that Hitler was never serious about anticapitalism, for there is evidence that anticapitalism was taken very seriously indeed in the National Socialist movement. Christian Striefler, and more recently Pamela Swett, have, for example, called attention to the many similarities in National Socialist and Communist rhetoric.[287] In Nazi newspapers such as the *Völkischer Beobachter* and *Der Angriff*, points out Striefler, "the rejection of capitalism was so understood that one could point out examples [of anticapitalist rhetoric] in almost any issue."[288] That these anticapitalist flourishes were, like all aspects of Nazi propaganda, fundamentally instrumental simply proves the point—they were used because they had wide appeal, a fact confirmed by many observers across the political spectrum.[289] These ideas were *not* mere window dressing; on the contrary, they appear frequently in the sources, not only in discussions of people for whom programs, to a greater or lesser degree, mattered—political seekers such as Richard Scheringer or the militants of the *Bündisch* groups[290]—but from the mouths of Nazi radicals, such as the stormtroopers involved in the Stennes Revolt, who saw them as critical totems of the NSDAP's anticapitalist commitment.[291]

It is thus somewhat misleading to speak of a "Nazi left" that was defeated by Hitler in 1926–30, for in the mythic-emotional register in which fascism operated, Nazism was always (and never) "left." This leftism had several levels; alongside the anticapitalist theory of people such as Feder and Strasser was a heartfelt rank-and-file anticapitalism fused in many cases with a thinly veiled class resentment, an emotive soldierly idea of socialism as a community of shared sacrifice, and a vague but powerful myth of the *Volksgemeinschaft*.[292] But the sources of Nazi radicalism did not lay in ideology as such but instead worked in an emotional register linked to a broad "refusal" expressed in cultural terms. This resistance was shot through with contradictions and ambiguities, but was characterized by several interrelated elements, all having to do with a morally construed politics constructed around issues of agency and authenticity: (1) an "elite" identity connected with a deep and abiding ambivalence about the nature and meaning of

Nazism's attempt to be a mass movement; (2) a (more or less pronounced) "military/militant" identity, linked with a rejection of "civilian" values understood in gendered and racialized terms, and linked to the attempt to recover military agency as a synonym for male agency; (3) a "spiritual" as opposed to "materialist" worldview, linked with a suspicion of "self-interest," itself linked in turn to "politics" seen as the ultimate expression of "self-interest;" (4) barely disguised class resentments—sometimes the expression of real grievances on the part of proletarian or lower-middle-class members—"deproletarianized" and linked with ideas of the ultimate good of the national and racial community, but capable of expression in terms not that different from those of the radical left; and (5) hatred of bureaucracy and other depersonalizing forces of modernity, expressed in the creation of essentializing categories through which these forces were personified and rendered fightable.

The latter—expressed above all in the figure of the *Bonze*—is in many ways the key to the rest. The language of National Socialism is replete with conglomerating terminology linked to the demonization of enemies—Jews as *"Juda"* (the Jew), Communism as *Die Kommune* (the Commune)—which reduced human beings to the status of clichés easily demonized.[293] The idea of the *Bonze* was by no means an invention of the Nazis but was, on the contrary, a term of long usage in the SPD. In its use by the Nazis, as Gerhard Paul points out, the concept was depoliticized and turned into a purely emotional critique.[294] But it still suggested the party boss who ignores the real needs of the workers, and in this way it was another of Nazism's thefts from the left. The idea of *Verbonzung* captured a process of ossification suggesting lack of responsiveness or lack of real connection between the leaders and the led; it thereby became intimately associated with the idea of politicians, of the "system" for which they were responsible. Opposition to the "system" was a key element of Nazi identity, one that tapped a deep vein of outrage running through Weimar society, one capable of being attached to varied targets, one allowing Nazism to play the victim, to wear the garments of the martyr on the altar of moral corruption, and to dip deep into the pool of affective radicalism of the left (see Figure 3.5).[295] Here again we encounter symbolic social class, for to be a member, or beneficiary of, the "system" was to be "bourgeois," whereas to be opposed to it was to be, if not a "proletarian," at least a "producer"—and/or "soldier"—constructed as underdog and victim. The figure of the *Bonze* carried all the negative connotations of the bourgeois stereotype (see Figure 3.6). Aloof rather than responsive, sedentary rather than active, effeminate rather than manly, corrupt rather than honest, the *Bonze* was the spiritual opposite of the soldier/militant. *"Bonze"* was, as Susanne Meinl puts it, nothing less than a synonym for "not revolutionary" and, as such, functioned as the term of abuse par excellence for representatives of the "system" in general and of the SPD in particular.[296]

The idea of the *Bonze*—lifted from the vocabulary of the Marxist working class as a code word for unresponsive leadership–was intimately connected, furthermore, with the idea of "treason." In its Marxist iteration, the *Bonze* stood for

Figure 3.5 National Socialism destroys the "System." *Der Sonntags-Beobachter. Zentralwochenblatt der NSDAP* Nr. 8, 5 June 1932. Bundesarchiv.

betrayal of the led by their leaders. In its adoption by the radical right, this meaning was retained, but a secondary meaning, derived from the experience of the war and its aftermath, was layered onto it. The treason of the *Bonze* as social type was an analog to the larger betrayal of the SPD leadership, marked, in the right's terms, as a *national* betrayal linked to the overthrow of the old regime and the signing of the Treaty of Versailles—Hitler's "November Criminals"—and, in the Communist left's terms, as a *social* betrayal arising from the SPD's efforts to crush working-class insurrection from 1919 on.[297] The connection of the *Bonze* with *treason* could, in both cases, be used to position the SPD and the system against ideas of military honor, and in opposition to the virtues of the "revolutionary soldier." In this "treason" iteration the idea of the *Bonze* could and did, for Nazis, stand in for a civilian society lacking in the moral authority to be gained only through the experience of manly struggle in the trenches.

Figure 3.6 "Our Ruin. The Big Shot." *Der Angriff* 77, 19 April 1932. Bundesarchiv.

The virtuous warrior ideal connected with the struggle against the system and its representative the *Bonze* was understood and portrayed in explicitly racialized terms. In Figure 3.7, an SA man prepares for action under a flapping swastika flag. In the background, a collection of enemies, ranging from stereotypical Jews in the clothing of cabinet ministers to a "society lady" and a gun-wielding Bolshevik, dance together in an orgy of heedless disregard. The implication—that a "housecleaning" is necessary—could not be clearer. The racial element in society's

Figure 3.7 A storm trooper prepares for battle. *Der SA-Mann. Organ der Obersten SA-Führung der NSDAP,* Munich, Saturday, 12 November 1932, Jg. 1. Bundesarchiv.

degeneration, and the necessity of military virtue in combating it, comes out with special clarity in Figure 3.8, in which an SA man gives the Hitler salute while various monstrosities—the hats of the Jew, the Catholic clergyman, and the bourgeois gentleman readily discernable atop their heads—swarm at his feet. Images like these, reproduced in various Nazi media—rather more revealing, or revealing in a different way, than the images drawn from electoral propaganda analyzed by Gerhard Paul—were an attempt to appeal to racist sentiment in the

Figure 3.8 The SA man as soldierly bulwark against social-biological menace. *Der SA-Mann* Nr. 29, 7 September 1929. Bundesarchiv.

Nazi movement, but they were also an attempt to racialize the more generalized spirit of revolt in the movement against the system and the *Bonze*. Ideological training in the SA also emphasized this racialization. One of the aims of the Reich Leadership School (*Reichsführerschule* or RFS) founded in the summer of 1931 was to link the radicalism of the SA more closely with the biological-racist goals of the Nazi leadership.[298] Alongside lectures on practical (i.e., military) matters and attempts to inculcate military values of duty, comradeship, and honor were lectures on topics such as "*Volk* and Race" and "German history from a racial-biological standpoint."[299] This particular linkage took on a greater force after 1933, as we will see later. The important point here is that National Socialism drew its strength from a revolt, a refusal, and that this revolt was associated very strongly with the stormtroopers of the SA, in part because of essentializing ideas about the proletarians in their ranks. This revolt had strong "socialist" elements, but the meaning of this socialism was a subject of dispute both within and out-side the movement.

"You rebelled for socialism"

The NSDAP was a fractious movement within a fractious scene. The *Völkisch* movement of which it was a part comprised more than a hundred similar groups and was subject to constant splits and realignments.[300] The groups had in com-mon, in varying degrees, a *Völkisch* (i.e., ethnic/racial) nationalism, a fierce anti-Marxism, contempt for what they saw as an ineffectual and foreign parliamentary democracy, and a desire to restore national honor and to deal with traitors against it (above all the signers of the Treaty of Versailles), and to replace the Weimar Republic with something more "authentic," whether some form of monarchy or some sort of new dispensation along the lines of a "national socialism." It was only with great difficulty that Adolf Hitler was able to rise to primacy in this scene, and only then because of a unique charisma and a gambler's instinct, com-bined with an ability to resist compromise in such a way as to present would-be allies and followers alike with unavoidable either/or choices.[301] Hitler portrayed himself as a man of unalterable will, and the story of his rise to power has often, not without reason, been presented as one of how Hitler outwitted his opponents and profited from the mistakes of feckless conservatives or sheer dumb luck. But it is worth digging a little into the history of revolt within the Nazi movement for what it tells us about what Nazis thought was important, and about what other people (especially other radicals) saw was important about the Nazi movement. A focus on revolt—and the symbolic terms in which it was fought—allows us to step outside of the "National Socialism's march to power" rubric to capture something of the spirit of radical politics in the Weimar Republic.

The early history of Hitler's rise to mastery, first over the German Workers' Party he joined in 1919, and later of the *Völkisch* movement in southern Germany, has been recounted many times, as has his defeat of the northern German faction of the NSDAP at the Bamberg party congress in 1926.[302] The history of conflict between the NSDAP and its paramilitary wing is equally well known, although its significance has often been underplayed or misunderstood. The most salient crisis in the SA's relationship with the party, the so-called Stennes Revolt of 1931, has appeared in the literature largely as a bump in the road on Hitler's way to power. This judgment makes sense from a certain perspective, for although the revolt accelerated a partial reorganization and realignment of forces within the Nazi movement, it had little lasting impact on its overall fortunes.[303] Yet a close examination of the revolt has much to offer the historian of radical extremism in the Weimar Republic, for the terms in which the crisis was fought out—and how it was understood by those outside the movement—are deeply revealing of larger issues. Walther Stennes held the post of OSAF-Ost (SA Deputy Leader–East).[304] From Berlin, he commanded the SA in Berlin-Brandenburg, East Prussia, and Mecklenburg-Pomerania. This amounted to forces totaling about a third of the entire SA. His revolt had specific causes connected to the history of relations between the SA and the Nazi Party. Founded in August 1921, the SA was meant to serve as a protection squad for Nazi meetings and leaders. Its effective commander, the ex-Reichswehr officer Ernst Röhm, had larger ambitions, hoping to mold the SA into the core of a revolutionary army aimed at overthrowing the Weimar Republic. The failed *Putsch* attempt of November 1923 reinforced Hitler's doubts about the military character of the SA, and after the refounding of the party in February 1925, Hitler resolved to mold the SA into a propaganda and protection squad tied closely to the party. When Röhm resigned in disagreement, Hitler appointed as OSAF Franz Pfeffer von Salomon. In a letter to the new SA leader, Hitler emphasized that the SA was not to be a military organization but a propaganda and marching unit aimed at "the conquest of the streets" from the party's Marxist opponents. The activism of the SA was to be channeled in directions "expedient to the party."[305] The competencies thus spelled out proved to be a source of latent conflict within the movement, which, however, lay largely dormant until the end of the decade. Disagreements over the role of the SA were exacerbated by conflicts over funding and outfitting. In the conditions of economic crisis from the beginning of the 1930s, the SA's financial dependence on local party administrations was a constant source of tension, one that was increasingly interpreted in terms of a lack of respect on the part of the "civilian" party *Bonzen* for the "sacrifices" of the SA.[306]

A number of issues more general to the movement were also at work. Tension between the SA and the party was, first of all, a product of the SA's claim to meaningful participation in the affairs of the larger movement and, in this sense, must be seen as symptomatic of a broader push for participation that, it has been argued here, was characteristic of political radicalism in Weimar as a whole.[307] There was, moreover, widespread unease in both the party organization and the Hitler Youth about the "embourgeoisement" of the Nazi movement, a process symbolized above all by the NSDAP's participation in electoral politics. The

NSDAP had always been oriented strongly against electoral politics, which were understood to be the most corrupt in a system of corrupt practices. The formative experience of the movement—the failed Munich *Putsch*—symbolized this orientation, and there continued to be many in the party, especially among the SA leadership, who preferred, on both practical and moral grounds, to seize power by force.[308] The intensification of Nazi electoral activity from 1929—crowned by growing success but nothing approaching total power—intensified the disagreement. The needs of successful participation in the "system"—reputation, connections, aid from wealthy backers—conflicted with the Nazi self-image. It was often felt that the allies necessary for such success were not worth the price in lost credibility. Participation in the campaign against the Young Plan at the side of the nationalist press magnate Alfred Hugenberg—a critical step, as events would prove, in Hitler's rise to power—was bitterly resented, as was the party's entry into governing state coalitions.[309] The necessary concomitant of such success—the dilution of the NSDAP by bourgeois opportunists (the term "bourgeois" understood implicitly to refer not to actual class background but to lack of revolutionary sincerity) threatened to bring with it a catastrophic loss of identity. As a Hitler Youth leader who quit the party in July 1930 in connection with the Strasser crisis put it, "The entry into the party of countless reactionary and capitalistic personalities, the alliance with Hugenberg, ... the coalitions in Thuringia and Saxony, show the openly antisocialist and unrevolutionary character of the NSDAP."[310]

Such complaints represented a crisis of authenticity—that is, a crisis over revolutionary self-image—against which the conflict between the party and the SA must be read. The first open outbreak of tension came during the campaign for the Reichstag elections of September 1930. Matters came to a head in late August, when a delegation of the Berlin SA under Stennes traveled to Munich but was denied permission to see Hitler. Upon his return to Berlin, Stennes launched a series of extraordinary meetings, circulating an announcement that the SA would refuse all further duty (including campaign work for the coming Reichstag election) until its demands were met.[311] Joseph Goebbels was given to understand that if Stennes's demands were not met, his appearance before a mass meeting scheduled in Berlin's Sportspalast would have to proceed without the protection of the SA. Goebbels made assurances to Stennes and the two patched up their differences. Stennes, in turn, cabled Hitler in Munich with a declaration of the SA's loyalty.[312] This might have marked the end of the matter, had not Stennes and his lieutenants discovered, during a meeting on the very same day, a spy from the SS eavesdropping on their proceedings. The buildup of the SS as a counterorganization to the SA (to which it was technically subordinate) was a major source of tension, and the spying incident was seen as an intolerable provocation. The SA stormed the *Gau* business offices, assaulting the SS guards with fists and broken-off chair legs and seizing the party's election materials and files. Siege was also laid to Goebbels's apartment, and order was restored only by resort to the police.[313] A panicked Hitler rushed up from Munich to control the crisis. A first meeting with local SA leaders—held only after Hitler himself had made the rounds of the local SA pubs to gauge the mood of the rank and file—produced mixed results. The next evening, at a meeting at the *Kriegervereinhaus,* Hitler pulled off a masterful propaganda performance, tearfully recognizing the sacrifices of the stormtroopers and promising to redress the grievances of the SA. To an enthusiastic reception, Hitler announced that he himself was assuming the post of OSAF.[314]

Hitler's personal intervention put an end to the crisis, but not for long. The NSDAP's success in the parliamentary elections of 14 September (the NSDAP elected 107 deputies) did little to mitigate tensions between the SA and the party. One of Hitler's measures in the wake of the fall crisis was the appointment of Ernst Röhm to take over effective administration of the SA. As chief of staff, Röhm reorganized the SA with the aim of limiting the autonomy of regional SA leaders such as Stennes.[315] Continued tensions between the SA and the party were stoked by Hitler's prohibitions on SA street fighting and public speaking in February of the following year, the continued growth and increasing independence of the SS, and Hitler's oath of legality at the trial of Richard Scheringer. The situation was brought to a head by Chancellor Brüning's emergency decree of 28 March, which gave the government the authority to ban meetings and dissolve political groups. Stennes intensified his criticism of the party, calling for Röhm's dismissal and sharply attacking Hitler's decision to abide by Brüning's decree.[316] Hitler seized the opportunity presented by Stennes's open insubordination to preemptively dismiss him from the party, pushing Stennes, unprepared, into revolt.[317] Stennes occupied the premises of Goebbels's newspaper *Der Angriff* and "deposed" Goebbels as *Gauleiter.*[318] Despite his lack of preparation, Stennes found himself with considerable support.[319] Some 30 percent of the Berlin SA went over to him immediately, as well as 20 percent of the Hitler Youth.[320] Where the crisis of the autumn had been confined to Berlin, the revolt of the spring extended into the several regions of Stennes's command. Stennes received declarations of support from the leaders of the SA in Silesia (Kremser) and Pomerania (Lustig), and by May he had strong followings in those two regions as well as in Brandenburg and Mecklenburg.[321] Of the twenty-five thousand SA men in eastern Germany, Stennes had at least the provisional support of some eight to ten thousand.[322] Stennes founded his own group, the *Nationalsozialistische Kampfbewegung Deutschlands* (NSKD); a youth wing, the *Revolutionäre Arbeiter und Bauern Jugend,* and a newspaper, *Arbeiter, Bauern, Soldaten* (Workers, Peasants, Soldiers).[323]

Two features of the revolt stand out. First, it saw the spirit of revolt central to Nazism turned back against the NSDAP itself. All the animosities central to National Socialism—above all, resentment against *Bonzen* as compensation for the lack of true representation, corruption, materialism, and self-seeking behavior—were directed against the party leadership. Second, resistance against these negative features of modernity—against which were opposed the virtues of the soldier-revolutionary—were placed onto the person of Stennes. This personalization of the revolt—"in the person of Captain Stennes the whole SA is being attacked"—made the name "Stennes" synonymous with "revolutionary SA," a linkage that, as we will see below, was rather misleading.[324] The *Niedersächsische Zeitung* urged its readers to avoid any premature *Schadenfreude* at the expense of the Nazis, warning that the radical elements detached by the revolt were likely to find their way to an organization with even more dangerously radical credentials, the KPD.[325] The *Kölnische Zeitung* similarly worried that by expelling the most radical elements in the SA, Hitler was rewarding the Communists with a large cadre of "largely untapped activist forces."[326] Stennes and his supporters worried openly about the possibility of losing rank-and-file SA men to the KPD, and in particular about the danger posed by the example of Richard Scheringer. "It is not an exaggeration," complained one of Stennes's lieutenants, "when people say that either something will be done, or our people will abandon us [and] go over to the enemy." He went on to add that activists who might be expected to join the SA were joining the local Antifa instead: "The bearing of Lieutenant Scheringer … has made a powerful impact. Are these warning signs not enough for Munich?"[327]

Grandiose expectations greeted the Stennes Revolt in the Communist camp, with the Russian newspaper *Pravda* expressing the hope that the "proletarian elements" in the SA would now turn their backs on the Nazis and "march to the left."[328] The KPD hailed the revolt as evidence that the long-predicted split in the Nazi movement was finally at hand.[329] Hans Kippenberger, the head of the Communist department charged with instigating unrest in the NSDAP, saw the revolt as evidence that the Nazi movement was finally coming apart under the strain of reconciling its contradictory elements.[330] The divide was understood, first and foremost, as a class divide between a bourgeois-reactionary party organization and a proletarian-revolutionary paramilitary wing. This was, simultaneously, a divide between officers and ranks, a view that had a certain grounding in reality.[331] Kippenberger's interpretation of the revolt as an "officer's mutiny" with only tenuous support among the rank and file was confirmed by police authorities in Berlin, who noted, for example, that "with the exception of its leaders," the "most heavily proletarian *Sturm*" in Berlin had refused to join the revolt.[332] Kippenberger's view was contradictory, however, for he simultaneously located the motive force of the revolt in the increasing unwillingness of proletarian stormtroopers to be "misused" in the NSDAP's campaign for the defense of finance capital. Hitler was trying to rid his movement of these social-revolutionary elements, argued Kippenberger, in order to ingratiate himself with the bourgeois elites whose help he sought in the parliamentary struggle. Stennes's "objective role" in this context was thus to prevent the rebellious proletarians in the SA from following the example of Richard Scheringer, a deterministic interpretation no doubt reinforced by the way in which Stennes played up his socialism to the plebian SA rank and file.[333]

Richard Scheringer was the figurehead for the KPD's efforts to profit from the revolt. "The case of Scheringer," argued a Communist speaker at a meeting of the KPD's propaganda apparatus in March 1931, "shows what success is possible [with] intensified ideological education."[334] Scheringer's "conversion" of 27 February 1931, was still fresh in the minds of everyone upon the outbreak of the Stennes Revolt a little over a month later. The revolt seemed to confirm the hopes Scheringer placed in the stormtroopers' revolutionary capabilities. Scheringer made a number of appeals to the SA, emphasizing their common interest in overthrowing the system. The influence of Hans Kippenberger came out clearly in these appeals, which highlighted issues of class and ideology. In a flier distributed on 3 April and printed in the *Rote Fahne* on 5 April, Scheringer criticized Stennes's failure to "break ideologically ... with Hitler and Goebbels and the counterrevolutionary NSDAP."[335] Rather than trying to attain "a rebirth of national socialism," Scheringer argued, the rebels should place "themselves decisively on the side of the revolutionary war for the social and national liberation of the working people."[336] Follow-up appeals by the KPD similarly emphasized the iron logic of Communist ideology: "SA proletarians and workers of the NSDAP! Even if you honestly try to disagree with the ideology and goals of Marxism, you, like Scheringer, will be unable to find a counterargument."[337]

But despite the lip service paid to the need for the rebels, in Scheringer's words, to go beyond "the pseudosocialist phrases" of the Nazis, ideology played a secondary role.[338] Scheringer's appeals were cast fundamentally in cultural terms, drawing on the vocabulary of revolutionary soldierhood ("Draw the consequences from the decline of the NSDAP, from the fraud and betrayal of your leaders!"), and in terms of individual versus mass ("Don't let yourselves be captured by political sectarians. Don't despair of liberation; rather, throw everything behind you and come here to us! We will form the German Red Army of workers, farmers, and soldiers!"). The real problem was one of choosing the correct army for which to fight, the army that was most serious about combining a class war with a war against the Western powers.[339] And in this sense, activism was, for Scheringer as it had been for Stennes, an end in its own right. Scheringer had come to understand that only the KPD was in a position to "turn Nazi phrases into deeds."[340] A KPD flier advised SA men: "Not Hitler, nor Stennes, Scheringer shows you the way!" It praised the stormtroopers for their resistance to the reactionary Nazi leaders ("SA proletarians! Berlin's revolutionary working class has followed with great interest your fight against the bossified and legalistic party leadership") and reminded them of Hitler's "treachery" at Scheringer's trial in terms of revolutionary pathos:

> As Hitler stood before the court and—in high tones and with pathetic gestures—swore the legality of his party to the judges of the present system ... many of you believed that it was just a ploy, occasioned by tactical considerations. [But soon even] in the circles of your leading activists people began to stop short; the gesture with which Hitler denied the German revolution were too real, [his promises] to uphold the laws of the current social order too forceful.

It was now becoming clear, the authors went on, that Hitler's oath had been no "ploy"—he really meant it. This was proven by the fact that his party had no answers for those—such as Scheringer—who had questions about the party's commitment to the social revolution: "Men from your ranks," the flier continued, "who have given their confession of faith, before all of Germany, for the revolutionary freedom-fight of an oppressed people, have expressed what many of you today also think and feel." In an attempt to place the stamp of meaning over the revolt, the flier concluded: "You rebelled for socialism."[341]

This was true in a certain sense: the rebels were motivated by a desire to retain or achieve something they called "socialism," connected in the minds of many with a more or less pronounced aversion to capitalism, connected in many cases with bitter experience of poverty and class injustice, in which hatred of Marxist internationalism obscured the extent to which the ideal of the *Volksgemeinschaft* served merely as an alternate, ethnic-nationalist version of the classless society desired by Communism; but the KPD misunderstood—or rather, denied to itself on ideological grounds—the nature of this socialism and the way it was understood by its protagonists. The tendency to see in the SA revolt a critical impulse of the German revolution was not just an anomaly of Communist policy. Oppositional Nazis such as Otto Strasser felt the same way. After departing the NSDAP in the summer of 1930, Strasser had formed his own organization, the *Kampfgemeinschaft Revolutionäre Nationalsozialisten* (KGRNS), which he tried to position as a revolutionary alternative to the NSDAP.[342] Strasser's response toward the outbreak of the Stennes Revolt was initially guarded, but he quickly came to invest high hopes in it.[343] Like Scheringer and Kippenberger, he saw in the revolt the opportunity for a realignment in which the "socialist" and/or "proletarian" wing of the Nazi movement would become available for a revolutionary project free of the "deformed" aspects of Nazism. In the 5 April edition of his paper, *Die Deutsche Revolution,* he located the source of the conflict in the Nazi movement in the opposition between "the revolutionary sensibility of the SA" and the "reactionary tone of the bourgeois leadership of the Hitler party."[344] This line of analysis was similar to the Communist one, inasmuch as it divided the Nazi movement into reactionary and revolutionary wings, and inasmuch as it saw revolutionary energies in the Nazi movement—above all in the SA—that could only be effective if harnessed to the right type of political content. And much like the Communists, Strasser understood "revolution" in terms of "anticapitalism." "For a long time," he wrote, "strained relations have existed in the Hitler party between the revolutionary-socialistic elements and the bourgeois-nationalistic. If one were to grossly simplify the problem, one would find as the decisive question: 'How do you stand on the sanctity of private property?'"[345]

This was of course not at all the source of the conflict between Hitler and Stennes, a fact that Strasser acknowledged.[346] The "opposition between the 'revolutionaries' and the 'legalists'"—that is, between those who supported Hitler's strategy of gaining power legally and those who wanted to seize it by force—appeared as the main issue, argued Strasser, only because the deeper issue, the issue of socialism, was never mentioned by either side. Neither the SA leadership nor the party leadership, according to Strasser, had any interest in addressing the issue of anticapitalism. Yet Strasser asserted that this anti-capitalism did exist in the NSDAP and had to be located in the SA and party rank and file: "The feeling of the overwhelming majority of SA people, but also numerous political functionaries of the lower ranks, answers distinctly: 'Because we want the overthrow of capitalism, there can be for us no sanctity of private property.'"[347] Much in the same way as the Communists, Strasser saw the lower ranks as the chief repository of socialist, anticapitalist sentiment in the NSDAP. To be sure, the "anticapitalist longing" in the SA identified by Otto's brother Gregor was real enough, but conflict between the SA and the party was being fought, as Strasser would find out, not in ideological but in cultural terms.[348]

Indeed, the conflict was fought out on both sides according to a series of antinomies derived from the war experience: steadfastness versus dereliction, honor versus betrayal, comradeship versus treason. Hitler compared the rebellion to the "stab in the back" of 1918.[349] The rebels denounced the party's failure to recognize the SA's sacrifice of "blood and lives" on behalf of the movement as a "betrayal" intimately linked to the "civilian" party leadership's failure to observe the laws of comradeship that were commonsense aspects of the soldier's creed.[350] "Selfish" (*eigennutzige*) party leaders—a term lifted deliberately from point 24 of the party program, "The common interest before individual interest" (*Gemeinnutz vor Eigennutz*)—were accused of introducing "fratricidal warfare into the ranks of the party," leaving the SA no choice but to continue the fight on its own. The rebellion was explicitly linked with key tenets of Nazism—the SA represented a "cumbersome conscience reminding people of the betrayed party program and demanding the fight for the old ideals of National Socialism"—but the "betrayed" party program really served a symbolic function: failure to honor its "socialist" provisions provided an opportunity to level charges of betrayal that carried a greater emotional charge than the provisions themselves.[351]

Yet socialism and soldierly virtue were, in the event, synonymous. A self-justificatory essay published by Stennes shortly after the revolt reprinted an open letter to Hitler from an "anonymous SA man"—probably Stennes himself—which sought to link the fight against the party with National Socialism's fight against bourgeois corruption (the use of the "anonymous SA man" simultaneously attempting to achieve "rank-and-file" credibility while calling up associations of "unknown soldierhood"). Formerly a revolutionary movement, the letter argued, the NSDAP now served, "like all the other parties[,] only as a crib for *Bonzen.*" The hallmark of the *Bonze* was, again, his inability to respect the laws of comradeship: "Every big shot," the letter continued, "cares only for himself, and asks only: 'How can I suppress all the sincere fighters so that my position won't be endangered when the posts are distributed in the Third Reich?'" The ascendancy of *Bonzentum* in the party proceeded in parallel with the NSDAP's transformation from a *movement* to a bourgeois *association,* a change over which Hitler presided as "president of the NSDA club" (belonging to a bourgeois leisure club being the ultimate insult for a revolutionary in the Weimar Republic).[352] Stennes's supporters in the Pomeranian SA took up a similar theme, accusing the NSDAP of leaving "the revolutionary course of true National Socialism" and becoming a reactionary "coalition party."[353] In portraying the revolt as a struggle against "the system," the rebellion transformed bureaucratizing tendencies in the NSDAP into a synonym for the system against which National Socialism struggled.

If there was little in all this of the socialism that the KPD and Otto Strasser (or, for that matter, worried conservative commentators) saw in the revolt, socialism was nevertheless key; it simply held a meaning that, as will be seen, rendered it impervious to meddling by outside, "unsoldierly" elements. Socialism in the language of the SA was both a radical egalitarianism and a revolutionary intransigence that rejected compromise with the system; it was a synonym for soldierhood and self-sacrifice, where socialism equaled "comradeship"—a connection straight out of the postwar radical right's fantasy of a "trench community" or "socialism of the trenches." *Bonzentum,* which represented both a rejection of egalitarianism and a betrayal of the party into alliances with reactionaries, the primacy of "civilian" over "military," of "female comfort" over "manly struggle," was the opposite of socialism.

These ideas were concretized in one of the biggest issues, and one in which Nazi socialism was most seen to be at stake, the so-called Brown House in Munich. The new party headquarters, located in the former Barlow Palace at 45 Brienner Strasse, were calculated to impress, with a "grand staircase [leading] up to a conference chamber, furnished in red leather, and a large corner room in which Hitler received his visitors beneath a portrait of Frederick the Great."[354] The refurnishing of this Brown House came at a time when "Strasserism" was being purged from the party, when Hitler was enjoying increasing success in gaining funding from conservative backers interested in supporting an anti-Communist movement, and the NSDAP was actively pursuing an alliance with the *Stahlhelm.* It was also a time, however, when the party was making a push to capture industrial workers—in part through the founding of the NSBO (Nazi Factory Cell Organization), a project viewed with unease in some parts of the party leadership but taken very seriously in others, especially in Berlin—and during which there was growing disenchantment with the party's strategy of winning power through elections.[355] The Brown House thus became a sort of lightning rod for the anger of the revolutionaries in the Nazi movement.[356] Both Richard Scheringer (during his trip to see Hitler with Joseph Goebbels in February 1931) and Walther Stennes (during his visit to see Hitler in August of the previous year) saw the Brown House, and neither came away with a favorable opinion of it, or of Hitler.[357] After the latter meeting, in which Hitler's authority was openly challenged, one of the SA officers present complained of Hitler's "un-German" actions, writing that "a man who busies himself with the building of palaces is no longer capable of struggle, no longer capable of a liberating deed."[358]

When the Stennes Revolt broke out a few months later, the Brown House occupied a high spot on the list of grievances. "Today they build the 'Brown House' in Munich at a cost of millions," read the flier announcing the outbreak of the revolt, "whereas the individual SA men have not a penny with which to repair their torn boots."[359] During a mass meeting of the Berlin rebels on 4 April, noted a journalist for the *Vossische Zeitung*, "especially sharp words were found against the building of the Brown House in Munich at a time when individual SA men can hardly come up with the money to eke out a living." The building of the Brown House was explicitly connected to the rise of *Bonzentum* in the party, in turn connected with its "bourgeoisification."[360] When two of the new SA leaders promoted in the wake of the revolt—Edmund Heines and Paul Schulz—made the rounds of the Berlin SA taverns in a desperate attempt to win pro-Stennes stormtroopers back to the party, they had to specifically address the issue of the Brown House. It had to be decivilianized, debourgeoisified, and gendered male.[361] At a meeting in the *Sturmlokal* "Wespenneste" in the Schöneberg district, Heines debated with Stennes's lieutenant Wetzel and assembled rebel junior officers in an unsuccessful attempt to bring them back to the fold.[362] In meetings of his own command, Heines tried to recast the symbol of the SA's greatest anger—the Brown House—in positive terms. The party headquarters, he assured his men, was a "noble monument" to the sacrifices of the SA, where the names of SA dead would be inscribed in marble and flanked by banners.[363]

The conflict had to be fought out in cultural terms in part because there was no real ideological difference between the rebels and the party; but at a deeper level, the conflict was fought out in these terms because they expressed what was really important to the participants. Unlike those who grounded their decision to leave the Nazi movement in more or less ideological terms—Otto Strasser and, to a lesser extent, Richard Scheringer—Stennes understood National Socialism in terms of pure activism. His chief criticism of Adolf Hitler was that he had allowed himself to become linked to a "National Socialism of words," against which Stennes proposed a "National Socialism of deeds."[364] For Stennes, authenticity depended—that is, his self-image as a revolutionary depended—on the promise of being able at some favorable moment to seize power by force. What Stennes really wanted was to turn back the clock to the early days of National Socialism, retrieve the "old National Socialism" of the *Putsch* in place of the "new National Socialism" of alliances and elections. Hitler's crime in Stennes's eyes was less a failure to honor the "socialist" planks in the party platform than his abandonment of the real and essential socialism represented by the movement's antibourgeois fighting spirit. Paradoxically, as a consequence, Stennes found it difficult to make a final break with Hitler because, for the majority of militants in the movement, it was Hitler himself who embodied this "socialist" essence. A reporter for the *Vossische Zeitung* present at the mass meeting of 4 April was struck, indeed, by the extent to which Hitler escaped direct censure; the stormtroopers' ire was directed rather against those around Hitler who needed to be "cleaned up."[365] Because there was no programmatic difference between the rebels and the party—complaints about funding and administrative competencies aside, the real conflict took place in the cultural aether of affective social identity ("soldier" vs. "bourgeois")—there was no basis on which to mount a thoroughgoing critique of Hitler per se. The second of the broadsheets released by the rebels made the point explicitly: "Stennes and the independent SA stand in unchangeable loyalty to National Socialism, and continue toward the goal for which they have long been fighting at the side of the old [!] Adolf Hitler."[366]

Yet it was also, paradoxically, impossible for Stennes to pursue a revolt against the party without attempting to establish an ideological-programmatic position for himself. For just as revolutionary politics in the Weimar Republic could only be pursued under the rubric of "revolutionary soldierhood," so too was it necessary that these politics be elaborated in terms of a "national socialism" expressed in a political program. Nothing less than this could be expected to appeal to militants looking for a place for themselves in the radical scene. In the wake of the revolt, Stennes moved quickly to attempt to establish programmatic legitimacy for his movement. Characteristically, this involved an attempt to appear "left wing" ("left" here being a category meaning "not conservative")—elaborated in terms designed to reinforce the legitimacy of the connection between leaders and ranks and expressed, in part, in the "voice" of the latter. That is, Stennes, like the Nazi movement to which he had belonged, had to perform the radicalism of the rank and file. One of Stennes's chief aims—aside from differentiating himself ideologically from the NSDAP—was to prevent rank-and-file stormtroopers from drifting off to the KPD. His fear of this possibility had a number of bases: essentializing assumptions about the political behavior of SA men from Berlin's working-class neighborhoods; knowledge of the way that Nazism's assault on the idea of the class struggle itself drew on barely sublimated class resentments; firsthand experience of the low level of ideological training and commitment in the ranks; and awareness of the KPD's ongoing efforts to infiltrate and subvert the SA. Stennes appears to have had difficulty in attracting and holding the allegiance of the SA rank and file, and there is evidence that his motives and leadership were not immune from criticism. The anonymous fliers that appeared in Berlin and Leipzig in late 1930 and early 1931 warned of the Nazi leadership's "fight over the gravy train," noting that both "Party and SA leadership … pursue self-serving interests and hide from us their true goals." Stennes was mentioned specifically: "Behind the demands for the participation of the SA in the spoils [of the Reichstag elections of September 1930] lie the self-seeking wishes of our Osaf-Ost. Does this correspond to our program?"[367]

This no doubt reflected both the popularity of Hitler and the failure of the rebels to show what made them different or better; but class resentments between the largely proletarian rank and file and the upper-class leadership may also have played a role. A former *Freikorps* leader and police captain of independent means, Stennes possessed contacts at the highest levels of government and society.[368] Socially, he and his fellow higher SA leaders were a world apart from rank-and-file stormtroopers, many of whom were workers living in the same neighborhoods and in the same conditions as their Communist opponents.[369] Stennes appears to have tried to bridge this gap, casting the revolt as one of the "soldierly and proletarian elements of the party" and playing up his socialism for the rank and file. In language that could have come directly out of the KPD's "Program for the National and Social Liberation of the German people," Stennes gave as the goal of the NSKD the fight for a "real social and therefore also national liberation of the productive people" (*schaffendes Volkes*). Employing the language of symbolic social class, Stennes drew a distinction between the "proletarian and rural [*bäuerlichen*] SA men" as the "valuable forces" of the movement on the one hand, and the increasingly bourgeois party on the other, placing his movement squarely on the side of socialism and against "private property."[370] Stennes's newspaper, *Arbeiter, Bauern, Soldaten* (Workers, Peasants, Soldiers), echoed in its title the social makeup of the "Red Army" dreamed of by Scheringer and preached loudly by the KPD via every available medium to the SA rank and file.[371] Like the KPD, and like Otto Strasser, Stennes too felt compelled to overlay "socialist" aspirations on the rebellion, to *perform* socialism.

These attempts to ideologize the revolt—to place a stamp on the rebellious activity of the SA as the most radical expression of revolutionary national socialism—took place in an atmosphere of social crisis in which Nazism in its various official and rebel iterations came to be seen by many as increasingly indistinguishable from Communism. When Stennes instituted political training for his stormtroopers, a key item in the curriculum was a section on "What distinguishes us from the KPD?" It focused on eliminating any possible doubts about where lines were drawn between "Revolutionary National Socialism" and Marxism (the former avoided the "three mistakes" of the latter: "Internationalism," "Class War," and "Materialism"). The question of how the NSKD distinguished itself from the Nazi movement was rather more difficult. In the absence of any salient programmatic difference, the focus fell on the revolutionary attitude that the rebels maintained and the NSDAP had supposedly lost. Stennes expressed this idea neatly in the following formula: the NSKD was to the NSDAP as the KPD was to the SPD. In Stennes's algebra of revolutionary credibility, the question was one not of ideology but of *seriousness* about revolution—that is, one of authenticity. Characteristically, the difference was expressed in terms of symbolic social class: the *Spiesser* (bourgeois philistines), according to Stennes, were to be found in the NSDAP, not the NSKD.[372]

Stennes's "leftist" talk aside, his real aims were fairly routine versions of the ideas current within the radical right at this time. A list of Stennes's "demands" published in July called for a set of fairly routine (for the interwar German radical right) measures centered on the establishment of a dictatorship that would abrogate the Young Plan and carry out a series of economic measures leading in the direction of autarchy, including an increase in production, work creation schemes, and the resettlement of workers in the countryside.[373] Stennes's supporters among the eastern German SA leadership were by no means "social revolutionaries," and indeed, although they shared Stennes's anger at Hitler's electoral strategy, they were more concerned with resisting the influence of "Rome"—that is, the Catholic, South German, Munich wing of the party—than anything else.[374] One of them, Kurt Kremser, rejected Stennes's alliance with Otto Strasser on the grounds that the latter was too "socialist," later going over to the *Stahlhelm*.[375]

Where for someone like Richard Scheringer, attention to the social question was a primary mark of authenticity, for people like Kremser, too much attention to the social question led precisely to the loss of authenticity by verging too far in the direction of a Bolshevism that must be fought at all costs. The same was really true of Stennes as well, despite his attempt to perform socialism for the benefit of his ally Strasser and in order to capture the imagination of the SA rank and file. Stennes's real focus, and his ultimate project, comes out clearly in the pages of *Arbeiter, Bauern, Soldaten,* which were filled with articles analyzing military strategy and tactics, both of the Great War and of current struggles such as the war in China. Stennes rejected the compromises entailed in the development of fascism into a mass movement. He continued to crave the "old days" of National Socialism—political activism as a surrogate for combat service. This was, simultaneously, a focus on the issue of the elite versus the mass; that is, it involved the recovery of military agency by a military elite.

* * *

This dynamic came out clearly in Stennes' alliance with Otto Strasser. The revolt started out strong. Some 30 percent of the Berlin SA and 20 percent of the Berlin Hitler Youth switched over to Stennes immediately.[376] With the support of Kremser in Silesia and Lustig in Pomerania, Stennes held the nominal allegiance of some eight to ten thousand of the twenty-five thousand SA men in eastern Germany.[377] This strong initial response dissipated rather quickly, however. A combination of Stennes's tactical errors, the unwillingness of many of his sympathizers to convert words into deeds, and a vigorous response by the party leadership prevented the revolt from taking hold and spreading. Almost a thousand stormtroopers and party members were expelled within a few days of the revolt,[378] and almost half the SA leadership of *Gau* Brandenburg had been relieved by mid-April.[379] Enough mid-level SA leaders were lost to the revolt that many posts had to go unfilled for lack of qualified replacements, but key higher posts were quickly filled with Hitler loyalists.[380] The alliance between Stennes and Strasser, concluded in early June, was very much one of convenience; each saw in the other an opportunity to expand his influence in ways otherwise closed to him.[381] Strasser saw the alliance as a way to extend his influence to the activist forces freed up by the Stennes revolt.[382] Stennes appears to have grudgingly accepted that his newly independent SA formation required some sort of political organization, and Strasser was a logical choice. The alliance was arranged by Herman Ehrhardt, notorious *Freikorps* leader, participant in the right-wing Kapp *Putsch* of 1920, one-time supporter and now opponent of Adolf Hitler. An inveterate political schemer, Ehrhardt appears to have been attempting to use Stennes and Strasser to fulfill conspiratorial designs of his own.[383] It was he who convinced Stennes of the necessity of the arrangement, and his offer of financial support was of decisive importance in getting Stennes to accept.[384]

The new organization, the NSKD, was fairly successful for a time.[385] By August, it had attained a membership of some ten thousand.[386] More importantly, it had won a location for itself on the mental map of the militant scene in Weimar. The KPD, for example, considered Strasser's new movement even more danger- ous than the NSDAP, a fact that, if it supplies further evidence of the KPD's well-known inability to realistically assess threats, also suggests a more profound truth: revolutionary rhetoric—in particular, a sharpening of rhetoric that declared oneself to be more revolutionary than someone else—was seen to be, simulta- neously, something that had to be taken seriously and something that was po- tentially dangerous. Yet the problems inevitable in an arrangement such as that between Stennes and Strasser were not long in appearing. Indeed, Stennes's alli- ance with Strasser is remarkable for the way in which it reproduced the problems that had led to Stennes to break with Hitler in the first place. The gulf between the paramilitary and political wings, always latent and not infrequently open in the NSDAP, continued to persist in the rebel organization. This became evi- dent in an otherwise very successful meeting in Brandenburg on 14 June, during which the rebel stormtroopers kept an aloof distance from the "civilian" members of the NSKD.[387] Disinterest in questions of theory and political training was an- other problem.[388] Stennes's stormtroopers were expected to learn and understand Strasser's "Fourteen Theses of the German Revolution," but this is something in which they exhibited little interest.[389] Stennes echoed their mood in an article in *Arbeiter, Bauern, Soldaten:* "One can't bring up fighters with discussion evenings, popular meetings and … more or less unintelligible speeches. The fighter wants to act!"[390]

The importance of symbols and revolutionary legitimacy came out forcefully in the way in which Stennes and Strasser struggled to gain the support—or to appear to have the support—of Scheringer's codefendant in the Ulm trial, Hans Wendt. Much in the same way that the KPD tried to use Scheringer's credibil- ity—as a soldier, as a martyr—to make inroads into the Nazi's "socialist" base, the Stennes rebels and the Strasser circle competed to associate themselves with Scheringer's comrade. Wendt shared Scheringer's disappointment with the NS- DAP but was unwilling to make the jump with Scheringer all the way to the KPD. He was enthusiastic, however, when he heard the news in prison that a re- volt had broken out in the SA. Like Scheringer and the KPD, and like Otto Stras- ser, Wendt located Nazism's revolutionary potential in the stormtroopers, where he thought he imagined the coming together of the working class and the nation. In a declaration from prison published in Strasser's *Die Deutsche Revolution* on 2 April, Wendt called for ruthless struggle behind the "socialist slogans of revo- lutionary National Socialism."[391] In a subsequent appeal, parallel to Scheringer's appeal from his prison cell to the Berlin SA on behalf of the Communist Party, Wendt greeted the Stennes Revolt as the true "revolution of the German working people."[392] Accusing the NSDAP of pursuing a "bourgeois reactionary" course, Wendt wrote, "The traitors sit in Munich. They accuse us of intending to carry out a *Putsch* [simply] because we have retained our revolutionary momentum. … We belong where the revolution of the German working people is being pushed forward. I therefore renounce, like my comrade Scheringer, Hitler and his fascism [*sic*]."[393] After his release from prison—upon which, arriving at the Friedrichstrasse station in Berlin, he was allegedly paraded through the streets in triumph by a mixed crowd of some sixty Communists and National Socialists—Wendt made a tour in the company of the Pomeranian SA leader Hans Lustig to win stormtroopers over to Stennes's cause.[394] The symbolic importance of Wendt as "young rebel" and "soldierly martyr" came out most clearly during the breakdown of the alliance between Stennes and Strasser, which featured competing declarations of support from Wendt (one obviously falsified), and an offer by Strasser (which he was in no position to make) for Wendt to take command of the rebel SA.[395]

Ironically, the movement showed the same tendency to break down into constituent parts on the basis of moral disputes as did the NSDAP. Indeed, as soon as the presence of Hermann Ehrhardt behind the scenes was discerned—on 29 June—the movement was thrown into an uproar, which led fairly quickly to its dissolution. As a former *Freikorps* leader, participant in the Kapp *Putsch,* and organizer of postwar terror cells, Ehrhardt was seen by the people around Strasser as an arch-reactionary. This fact highlights perfectly the way in which "revolutionary legitimacy" in the zone of conflict between the mass movements was a fragile and fleeting quality. The involvement of Ehrhardt shattered Stennes's carefully constructed pose as a "leftist," a pose of which many were already suspicious.[396] The revelation of Ehrhardt's role was a severe embarrassment for Strasser—he denied everything in *Die Deutsche Revolution*—and resulted in a split between Strasser and the editor of *Die Deutsche Revolution,* Ulrich Oldenburg, who seized control of the paper from Strasser. The scandal was such that by early July, in the words of Patrick Moreau, all of "politically informed Germany [was talking about] operation Ehrhardt."[397]

Two important aspects of the affair stand out. One was the continuing importance of symbolic personages (Wendt, Ehrhardt); another was the difficulty of pursuing a Third Way between Communism and National Socialism. And indeed, the crisis precipitated the departure of a number of Strasser's supporters to the KPD. The moment when German fascism became ideologized—that is, the moment when an appeal other than to spirit and the emotions was made—it became susceptible to the blandishments of Communism. Informed that the NSDAP intended to "put an end once and for all" to the NSKD, its leaders requested that Stennes send a contingent of SA men to protect the big meeting in Hamburg on 18 July. Stennes refused—much the same maneuver he had carried out against Joseph Goebbels in September of the previous year—and the result was a disaster for the NSKD.[398] In the absence of Stennes's SA men, Strasser turned to the Communist *Kampfbund gegen den Faschismus,* or KgdF (Fighting League Against Fascism), to protect the meeting. This was, in effect, the same as giving the meeting over to the KPD, and in the event, 750 of the 1000 attendees present at the meeting were associated with the Communists. The protection of the meeting was wholly in the hands of the KPD, and speakers from the party and from the Revolutionary Trade Union Opposition were given the floor. The result was a resounding propaganda success for the KPD and a deep embarrassment for Strasser. NSKD members at the meeting wondered aloud why the organization should be anti-Communist when its meeting had to be protected by the Communists.[399]

Two days later, Ulrich Oldenburg, the editor of *Die Deutsche Revolution,* was expelled from the NSKD. Branches of the NSKD in Spandau, Bernau, and Neukölln left on the same day. On 3 August, the Hamburg group of the NSKD castigated Strasser for his ties to reaction and left to go to the KPD.[400] A number of junior Hitler Youth leaders who had shifted over to Strasser's youth group, the *Revolutionäre Arbeiter- und Bauernjugend,* also joined the Communists. The further shift of these young idealists to the KPD was a serious blow to Strasser, but it was, it will be argued here, an entirely predictable step, and one based on an iron logic derived from the elite/mass dialectic in the Weimar Republic. The loss of the cadres won by Strasser from the NSDAP and the Hitler Youth highlights the difficulty both of delineating an ideological position sufficiently striking to distinguish it from the NSDAP and the KPD and of collecting activists in a group capable of resisting the pull of those groups, the two magnetic poles of Weimar mass radicalism.[401] In a statement reprinted in the Communist paper *Aufbruch,* they said:

> For years we carried out our anticapitalist struggle in the ranks of the NSDAP and the Hitler Youth. In the year 1930 it became clear to us that the Hitler party, which had begun its struggle as an opponent of the system, has become a prop for the exploitative capitalist society. … As purposeful and revolutionary nationalists, clear in our understanding that Hitler and Strasser are betraying the interests of the working German people, we mean to deploy ourselves in the fighting ranks of the Red Front.[402]

One of the activists who signed this declaration, Herbert Crüger, later recalled the thinking behind his decision. As it had for Richard Scheringer, the KPD's nationalist program played a large role in his deliberations. But the bigger issue was one of revolutionary effectiveness. "[A] revolution is no *Putsch,*" wrote Crüger. "In [a revolution] great masses go into action. But where were the masses? At all events not with us!"[403]

No-Man's-Land

Despite its failure, the Stennes Revolt signaled, like the tip of an iceberg, the presence of widespread discontent in the Nazi movement. For every SA leader or rank-and-file stormtrooper who was expelled from the party or joined the revolt, there were many others who shared the attitudes of the rebels toward the party but had been unwilling to join them. Stennes complained bitterly about likeminded SA and party leaders who failed to back him when the decisive moment came, and there is ample evidence that the discontent that had led to the revolt continued and even increased in its aftermath.[404] Police authorities in Munich,

Figure 3.9 "Hitler is our Leader." The defeat of the Stennes Revolt depicted in *Der Angriff,* 31 December 1931. Bundesarchiv.

a southern German capital far removed from Stennes's main bases of support in northeastern Germany, noted that Stennes's failure to destroy the NSDAP by no means meant that "in the circles of the Munich SA and SS peace and contentment rule." On the contrary, the report continued, "in the SA there everyone is convinced that boss-rule [*Bonzentum*] has spread through the party leadership to an almost unbearable degree."[405] Nor was the continued low-level conflict in the Nazi movement limited to the Nazi paramilitary wing. A generalized feeling of discontent with the growth of National Socialism into a mass movement was felt in the party organization as well. Albert Krebs, *Gauleiter* of Hamburg and later editor of the left–National Socialist *Hamburger Tageblatt,* expressed a common attitude—even among those who did not share his left–National Socialist orientation—when he complained, in 1932, that the "Nazi party permits no one in its ranks who thinks independently and dares to express those thoughts."[406] The last year and a half of the Weimar Republic was marked by continued unrest over the NSDAP's electoral strategy in portions of the party organization, and the persistent threat of open rebellion in the SA. In the period between the Stennes Revolt and Hitler's appointment as Reich Chancellor, revolts, disturbances, and formation of opposition groups were reported—to cite only an incomplete list— in Munich, Nuremburg, Lübeck, Kiel, Bremen, Leipzig, Hannover, Frankfurt, Hamburg, Düsseldorf, and Cologne.[407]

Another large revolt of the SA, this time in southern Germany, took place on the very eve of the Nazi seizure of power. It was led by Walter Stegmann, the head of the SA in Franconia.[408] As in the Stennes Revolt, conflict with the local party administration played a key role. In this case, the local party leader was the notorious anti-Semitic publisher Julius Streicher. Stegmann objected to the corruption of the local party leadership, exemplified, in this case, by Streicher's obsessive focus on gutter anti-Semitism to the exclusion of all other concerns. Here again, "moral issues" were at the forefront—soldierly virtues versus corruption. The impulse behind the revolt comes out clearly in the drawing adorning the cover of the newspaper affiliated with the rebels (see Figure 3.10).[409] The lone soldier, wounded, clothing torn, carries the torch lighting the way against all enemies and villains.[410] The real cause, unhappiness within the NSDAP as a "civilian" mass movement, was reflected in the rebels' slogan: "The party *Bonzen* are our misfortune."[411] Police authorities noted that although reports in the Social Democratic press of open mutiny and disintegration in the Frankish SA were overstated, both the SA and the SS in Nuremberg were affected by a strong discontent focused above all on the manner in which leadership posts were given out and in the types of persons being appointed to these posts.[412] Stegmann made much of the danger that his stormtroopers would defect to the KPD if the situation was not rectified, a warning that was partly based on real worries—stoked by the KPD's accelerated attempts to appeal to Franconian stormtroopers—and partly a scare tactic aimed at confronting Nazi leaders with something that they were always a little worried about.[413] But the real impulse behind the revolt comes out clearly in the name given by Stegmann to his post-NSDAP political formation—it was called the *Freikorps Franken,* signaling the desire to return to the independent military roots predating even the formation of the SA.[414]

These small groups that split off from the Nazi movement bled into the zone of conflict in which all kinds of minor radical groups were trying to eke out an independent existence. Whatever their specific orientation, all of these groups arranged themselves around the NSDAP, responded to it ideologically, and tried to make a place for or steal its members. A fundamental unhappiness within the or-

Figure 3.10 The Stegmann Revolt as depicted in the debut issue of Stegmann's newspaper. *Das Freikorps. Kampfblatt für Sauberkeit und Reinheit der Nationalsozialistischen Idee,* Nr. 1, 1933. NSDAP Hauptarchiv, Hoover Institution Microfilm Collection.

ganizational confines of the mass movement, as well as disputes over moral issues related to leadership, more than ideological issues, were the root cause. Problems in the Kassel SA at the end of 1932 spread to the SS, members of which—in what was almost a parody of the contradictory impulses toward aggregation and disaggregation in the zone of conflict (particularly in the orbit of the NSDAP)— formed a *Kampfgemeinschaft ausgeschlossener und ausgetretener SS-Leute* (Fighting League of Expelled or Resigned SS Members).[415] Anger over alleged financial malfeasance was at the forefront, but the root causes were deeper. They were captured in the new group's goals: "cleanliness, order, and justice."[416]

Other groups of the *Völkisch* scene, fundamentally similar in ideology, sprang up to try to capitalize on discontent in the NSDAP. The *Kampfbund Oberland* was founded in late 1932 with the goal of recruiting among SA and SS men. It took up contact with the *Kampfbund* of General Ludendorff—"the only revolutionary worth following"—in the hopes of becoming its armed wing. Members of the group—which billed itself as a "nonparty political fighting alliance"—were forbidden to have anything to do with parliamentary politics or parties. The *Kampfbund* appealed to the SA in terms very similar to those that came to the fore during the Stennes Revolt. The failure of the NSDAP to seize power after the parliamentary elections of November 1932 was a result, it was argued, not of the system's resistance (very soon to be overcome) against letting the demagogue Hitler into power but of "betrayal" pure and simple.[417] Calling for a German revolution in the "religious, spiritual, and economic domains," the *Kampfbund* criticized Hitler as a false prophet. Rather than lead the struggle, he was content to dream of his Third Reich "in a luxurious villa in the Bavarian Alps." Not a real leader but simply a bourgeois *Spiesser* (philistine), Hitler was not planning to lead a German revolution but scheming to place Germany under the leadership of the pope.[418]

Many of the *Bündisch* groups—oriented more in the direction of the KPD than in the direction of *Völkisch* splinter groups such as the *Kampfbund Oberland*—took a similar position toward the NSDAP. The Group of Social Revolutionary Nationalists (GSRN), founded in December 1930 by the *Bündisch* publicist Karl O. Paetel, was a direct response to the challenge posed by the Nazis. Initially receptive to National Socialism, Paetel became disenchanted with what he saw as its growing lack of revolutionary legitimacy. "The fight against capitalism is still only a phrase," he wrote in May 1931, and "the 'National Socialist Revolution' is only a slogan." Tellingly, Paetel conceived of the GSRN's relationship with the NSDAP in transinstitutional terms, arguing that the GSRN itself formed "the social-revolutionary left" of the Nazi Party. Calling for a "ruthless struggle" against the NSDAP, he wrote: "The increasing discontent among individual party comrades over the fact that National Socialism is going the way of party-fication [*Verparteilichung*], as well as its ... ideological poverty [*Programmlosigkeit*] makes the union of all oppositional elements in the NSDAP an urgent necessity." Like the Communists and the Strasserites, Paetel hoped to liberate the "valuable elements" in the party: "Oppositional currents active in and around the party are to be educated and supported in their struggle against the party or particular [leaders], when possible also financially."[419]

This tendency of splinter groups to think in transinstitutional terms—to conceive of themselves as collection points for those "disappointed" by Hitler, or as elite infiltrators aiming to influence the content and direction of the Nazi movement—was more than an attempt to protect a moral or ideological purity threatened by Hitler's compromises; it was an attempt to remain autonomous, to rebel against the system while simultaneously remaining aloof from the mass movements. Many may have entertained futile hopes of building a mass movement to rival the NSDAP, but many did not *want* to be mass movements; authentic political activity could be an end in its own right. At the same time, these groups recognized that members lost from the NSDAP, especially those from the SA, were sometimes prone to find a home in the KPD, and a goal of these groups was often to prevent disappointed radicals from falling into political apathy or, worse, joining the Communists. Police authorities in Hannover reported, for example, that Ludendorff's *Tannenbergbund* hoped to form a new organization with SA members split off from the NSDAP, but that the defection of SA men to the KPD was hindering such efforts.[420]

The Nazis themselves worried about the possibility of their shock troops bleeding off to the left, yet their very approach fueled it. On the one hand, the NSDAP carried out ideological combat against the KPD, emphasizing poor conditions in the USSR, and utilizing Communist turncoats much in the way the KPD utilized Richard Scheringer and other ex-Nazis.[421] The need to ideologically battle Communism sometimes led to instances of official cooperation, in the holding of joint meetings,[422] and—most famously—in open cooperation during the Berlin Transportation (BVG) strike of November 1932.[423] Although temporary Nazi-Communist cooperation in the strike worried some observers, it had little lasting impact on relations between the two parties; but it did demonstrate a striking willingness to work together on the part of the Communist and Nazi rank and file.[424]

Indeed, the picture of a rigid separation between extremist opponents, as Pamela Swett has recently demonstrated in her work on Berlin, is no longer tenable; at least where large cities such as Berlin were concerned, the radical scene was characterized by a familiarity verging on intimacy, by political discussion rather than just fighting, and by the not infrequent switching of members from one side to the other.[425] Evidence from other cities suggests a similar pattern. In Cologne, for example, police authorities noted in October 1932 that "countless members [of the Nazi movement] have gone over to the KPD."[426] National Socialist opposition groups also actively recruited from the SA. One of them, calling itself the *Revolutionäre Freheitsbewegung*, was led by the former leader of the Hitler Youth and Otto Strasser's youth wing, Wilhelm Kayser.[427] Kayser represented the "Nazi" cause at a number of meetings organized by the *Kampfbund gegen den Faschismus* in the autumn of 1931.[428] His opposite number at one of these meetings was a former SA *Sturmführer*—the very one expelled from the SA for distributing *Der Freiheitskämpfer* that summer—who had gone over to the KPD and was making the rounds of KgdF meetings aimed at winning over Nazis.[429] Bans on fraternization of the kind described by Swett in Berlin were imposed in Cologne and other Rheinland cities. Stormtroopers were warned especially against the Kayser movement, which was accused of "attempting in every way imaginable to get at the SA [and] party organization." Forbidden to take part in either meetings or "discussions" with members of the opposition, SA men were reminded that "the SA does not debate with mutineers and undisciplined elements."[430]

In this atmosphere, ideological divisions often paled before the allure of activism for its own sake, opening the way for alliances of convenience. Krause of the *Kampfbund Oberland* took advantage of a recommendation from Beppo Römer to establish ties with the KPD, offering to help in the party's *Zersetzungsarbeit* in the SA.[431] On the run in the summer of 1931, Hans Wendt told a police agent of the need for the small terror groups he hoped to organize to work closely with the KPD.[432] Walther Stennes, who spent the last year of the Weimar Republic at the center of an increasingly small and conspiratorial group of renegades in Berlin, dabbled in alliances with the local KPD. In one celebrated incident, some of his men, in cooperation with local Communists, murdered a Hitler Youth named Herbert Norkus.[433] Fittingly, the tale of Norkus's martyrdom became a major propaganda focus for the Nazi regime after 1933. Immortalized in the 1933 film *Hitler Youth Quex,* Norkus came to symbolize the sacrifice of young Aryan manhood at the hands of inhuman Bolshevism. In reality, as Jay Baird's detailed reconstruction of the events indicates, the death of Norkus took place in a milieu in which the lines between "Red murder" and "Nazi murder" were often blurred, and in which the lines separating extremists of left and right from each other were often exceedingly thin. SA men sometimes went to the KPD, especially in 1932, but when they did, it was not typically because they had accepted Marxism-Leninism but because the KPD seemed more serious about fighting the system than the NSDAP.[434]

Conclusion

We have seen in this chapter how National Socialism was constructed in relationship to the revolutionary left, borrowing its idea of revolt and playing with class categories so as to replace the proletariat with the nation, while simultaneously elaborating a symbolic class identity based on class as a moral category linked to the warrior virtues. We have seen also how National Socialism's performance of "leftism," above all through the SA, provided a powerful yet dangerous weapon for disintegrating previous class political loyalties. The idea of a "Nazi left," while a useful shorthand for speaking of the more explicitly "anticapitalist" wing of the party—typically associated with the North German "Strasser faction" of the party—is misleading in a fundamental sense; for Nazi "leftism" operated in an affective register that made it susceptible to different interpretations. In the case of the Stennes Revolt, each of these attempts at interpreting or giving meaning to the revolt was dealt in the coin of "socialism," linked variously to the "nation"; all were ideological, inasmuch as they played with those ideas that were the political "ideas of the moment" in the Weimar Republic. But characteristically, also, each idealized class in more or less essentialist terms, employing the ideas and rhetoric of symbolic social class. Each imposed a conceptual map over the revolt in an attempt to signify reality in a way fitting its ideological preconceptions and tactical needs, a map that broke things down into "bourgeois" and "proletarian." When they referred to the Nazi Party as "bourgeois," they might mean, depending on their political orientation, either socially bourgeois or affectively bourgeois (feminine, civilian).

This perspective illustrates one reason why Otto Strasser could not have won in his dispute with Hitler, even if other factors had been aligned in his favor; in all the ways that counted (i.e., in terms of decisiveness, hardness, and so on), he was more "bourgeois" than Hitler. Characteristically, Stennes tried to elide class, even as he responded to the realities of class stratification in the SA—and in this, his behavior highlights the extent to which he differed little from the NSDAP against which he was rebelling. The Communists, on the other hand, foregrounded class, but they did so in a way that revealed an underlying discomfort with the Marxist categories available to them. Finally, each tried to speak for and on behalf of the rank and file, variously defined, in a way designed to assign a particular meaning to the revolt. The SA was considered "socialist" for several reasons: first, because it represented the intrusion of the masses into politics; second, because it represented fascism's claim to be "left," therefore becoming the "point of danger and opportunity" both for the NSDAP and for Communism in its attempts to defeat fascism; and third, because they represented the idea of the young revolutionary soldier that appealed to militants on all sides.

The NSDAP's trouble with the SA came in part from the difficulty of keeping together a group of lawless toughs, and in part from competing sources of radicalism stemming from the inherently unstable nature of Nazism's ideological and social synthesis. It was a function, also, of the ambiguity of language, above all of the term "socialism" and the multiple meanings attached to it. What was mistaken for Nazi leftism was often just people's unhappiness with the system, and this very unhappiness was one thing that allowed different interpretations to be attached to Nazi radicalism. The widespread anger over *Bonzen* was a function of this opposition to bureaucracy (aka the "system"). Disputes over material interests were often precisely what they appeared to be—petty squabbles over spoils; but often, too, they depended on items of great symbolic importance. In this, it was part of a wider phenomenon of disaffection from official politics that functioned *within* movements as well as *between* movements and the state. Fundamentally ambiguous about politics, it was easy for activists to become turned off in the course of their participation in it. In this sense, events such as the Stennes Revolt were nothing more than fascism's revolt against the "system" turned inward against the *Bonzen* ruling over a "bourgeois" party organization, a struggle to be authorized to speak, a form of resistance.[435] There was serious anticapitalism in all this, which the KPD tried to exploit, even to the extent of trying to place demands in the mouths of Nazi rebels, as we will see in the next chapter. But this was, for the KPD, only part of a bigger project of performance that was both a cause and a consequence of some of the same problems on the left that trouble in the Nazi movement revealed on the right.

Figure 4.1 "Kampfbund gegen den Faschismus." Flier, KgdF Ortsgruppe Hamm (no date). Bundesarchiv.

Chapter 4

GERMAN COMMUNISM AND THE FASCIST CHALLENGE

The key to Communist politics in the Weimar Republic lies in what the Communist Party was bequeathed by the Bolsheviks: the claim to an exclusive, scientifically legitimated role of leadership over the masses. Caught between the hammer of a Soviet Union bent on aggrandizing its own security needs at the expense of indigenous Communist parties, and the anvil of a crisis-ridden German society in the grip of patriotic extremism, the KPD faced many difficulties; but its greatest difficulties were a function not of external circumstances but of the very nature of its project. The KPD's revolutionary orientation, although clearly at the heart of Communist identity, has received remarkably little scrutiny; indeed, unlike the revolutionary claims of National Socialism, which have been treated by historians with justifiable skepticism, those of Communism have largely been taken at face value. The Bolsheviks, as Francois Furet has pointed out, assumed—and were assigned—the mantle of the great French revolution of 1789, an association that once established proved remarkably durable.[436] Yet, like the "National Socialist Revolution" of 1933, the Bolshevik revolution of 1917 had to do not just with the mechanics of seizing power but with the construction of a narrative legitimatizing that power. In both cases (as we will see in regard to the Nazis in the next chapter), the revolution consisted in channeling popular energies and silencing opposing voices, both through violence and through control of the public sphere; and in both cases, this control was exercised against both enemies and allies. In countless cases in Bolshevism's early history—in Lenin's measures against freedom of speech and press (aimed not at the Whites but at fellow leftists);[437] in the dismantling of workers' control and the "militarization of labor";[438] in the dispersal of the Constituent Assembly and the takeover of the formerly nonparty councils (Soviets);[439] in the war against allied peasant anarchists in the Ukraine in 1918–19;[440] in the suppression of the Tambov province uprisings in 1919–21 (dwarfing in size the revolution to overthrow the Tsar itself);[441] in the armed assault on rank-and-file democracy in the Baltic Sea naval base of Kronstadt in 1921[442]—the party found itself opposed to the popular forces it claimed to represent.[443]

Long before the *Black Book of Communism* with its controversial ideological baggage,[444] and long before the "historians' conflict" of the 1980s unleashed by a dubious attempt to use Russian crimes to excuse German ones,[445] critics on the left identified in Bolshevism the institution of a new counterrevolution masquerading as a movement for human emancipation.[446] Bolshevism "was denounced as illusory and dangerous," as François Furet reminds us, "not only by the 'reactionaries' but also by the majority of European socialists, by authorities on Marxism, and even by revolutionary Marxists."[447] Many Western intellectuals embraced the new regime, but others were troubled, including the British philosopher Bertrand Russell, who, despite holding the Russian revolution to be "one of the great heroic events of the world's history," came away from his trip to Russia in 1919 lamenting the harshness and fanaticism of the Bolsheviks.[448] The American anarchist Emma Goldman was similarly chagrined by her experiences in Russia.[449] The German revolutionary Rosa Luxemburg's criticisms of the Bolsheviks are well known.[450] Russian Social Democrats and anarchists, especially, were well aware of the historic disaster represented by Leninism. The former were convinced that Lenin's determination to speed up the historical processes predicted by Marxism were doomed to failure,[451] the latter that authoritarian means must inevitably lead to authoritarian ends.[452] Both were subsequently proven correct. Word of these events crept into Germany, dogging the steps of the Bolsheviks' German allies. Russian émigré anarchists in Germany accused the Bolsheviks of having substituted in place of Tsarism a "red dictatorship."[453] The German "Committee for the Defense of Anarcho-Syndicalism in Russia" complained, for example, about the "red chains" the Bolsheviks had placed around the workers' movement in Russia, lamenting that "the whole of Russia has become a prison."[454] Characteristic of this attitude was the refusal in May 1923 of anarcho-syndicalists affiliated with the International Transport Workers' Federation to sign a joint resolution with the Communist Union International against "war-danger, fascism, and reaction" unless the Bolsheviks were listed among the "reaction."[455]

These complaints about Bolshevik authoritarianism, to the extent that they were heard at all, met mostly with indifference from a world with little use for fine distinctions between shades of revolutionary socialism;[456] but that they were made—and not from the right but from the left—underlines an important point: The revolutionary project embraced by German Communism enfolded within itself a highly problematic notion of the "popular," one that contained an irresolvable tension between the claim to represent the masses and the reality of mass participation. This disjuncture was only partly a consequence of the Stalinization of the party during the 1920s, with its attendant authoritarianism, factionalism, and meddling by the Comintern. As Klaus-Michael Mallmann has recently argued, the KPD's politics were characterized by conflict between an authoritarian leadership—the "avant-garde"—and an independent-minded and sometimes refractory rank and file.[457] Mallmann's work, with its emphasis on local autonomy, is a valuable corrective to the view of a monolithic KPD implied by the thesis of Stalinization—but in reality, the two positions are hardly incompatible; the underlying assumptions guiding the Comintern and German avant-gardes was the same. Implicit in the conception of the vanguard party was "the image of [the people as] a manipulable mass—a great potential source of energy which [could] be mastered by those [with] the knowledge and the will to do so."[458] A critical part of this process of mastery was the act of naming; this was encoded in the very name of Lenin's party, which styled itself the "party of the majority" against its opponents in the Russian Social Democratic Party (the Mensheviks or "party of the minority"), even though it was the latter who made up the actual majority. This *naming* extended to the very words "revolution" (which became what the Bolsheviks did) and "counterrevolution" (which became what Bolshevism's enemies did). The will to reorder reality according to ideological or tactical requirements was expressed also in the Bolshevik use of class. As an eminent scholar of the Russian revolution has recently shown, the manipulation of class categories was a central component of the Bolshevik project.[459] The destabilization of the concept of class in Russia proceeded in parallel with increasingly close identification between class and ruling party ("proletarians" as those who supported the revolution) and between the ruling party and the state (the proletariat as "virtually synonymous with the state and Communist Party").[460] The hallmark of Bolshevism was the superimposition of symbolic categories over the map of social reality, with little regard for the real shape of the latter. This is the key to understanding the politics of the KPD in general and its relationship with National Socialism in particular.

This sort of social "mapping," intimately connected to the exclusive claim to represent the masses, conditioned the KPD's relationship with the other major working-class party, the SPD. In referring to the SPD as a "bourgeois" party, despite its overwhelmingly proletarian membership, the KPD used social class as a stand-in for political function.[461] This symbolic use of social class was intimately connected, in turn, with the need to "unmask" opposing claims to leadership over the masses, which became the key determinant in the KPD's relationship with German Social Democracy. The troubled relationship between the KPD and the SPD—to which both parties contributed—had a number of causes. Faced with the task of founding and strengthening parliamentary democracy in a Germany troubled by an imbedded and refractory authoritarianism, the SPD had little use for the revolutionary fantasies of the KPD, or, for that matter, the grassroots radicalism of the nonparty council movement that played such an important part in the German revolution. The SPD's failure to purge militarists and monarchists from leading positions in German society is well known, as is its decision to employ the right-wing *Freikorps* to crush the Spartacist Uprising and subsequent risings of the Communist Party.[462] The actions of the SPD contributed to a state of enmity between the two parties that was sealed by the events of 1 May 1929, when Social Democratic–controlled police fired on and killed marchers in a Communist-led demonstration, the so-called *Blutmai* (bloody May).[463] For its part, the SPD objected to a Communist Party that, in addition to trying on several occasions to seize state power by force, used the luxury of being in permanent opposition to direct an unending stream of criticism and abuse on the SPD leadership, issuing repeated calls for a united front as cover for attempts to steal the SPD's membership (the so-called United Front from Below, to which we will return) and appearing on many occasions to prefer the company of the radical right to that of the Social Democratic left.

The ultimate expression of this latter tendency was the "ultra-left" strategy begun in 1928–29, which placed the Social Democrats in the ranks of fascism as "social fascists." Characteristically, "social fascism" was a Soviet import designed to fulfill Soviet requirements; elaborated by Stalin and Zinoviev in the mid-1920s, the concept became official Comintern doctrine in 1928–29.[464] Adopted by the KPD at its Wedding Party Congress in June 1929, the policy of "social fascism" played a poisoning role in relations between the KPD and the SPD for the rest of the Weimar Republic (and indeed, was not abandoned until 1935). "In taunting the movement which, all over Europe, commanded the allegiance of an overwhelming majority of proletarians with being a fascist movement," wrote the Austro-Hungarian–born Communist Franz Borkenau, "the communists cut their class ties with it. From now onwards communism was no longer part of the labour movement."[465] Yet the KPD had to get at the workers controlled by the SPD if it were to make good its claim to represent the working masses. This was the genesis of the strategy of the United Front from Below, in which the term "united front" meant exactly the opposite of what the term would usually suggest. "To carry out a 'revolutionary United Front policy,'" proclaimed Ernst Thälmann, the leader of the KPD, "means to pursue a relentless struggle against social fascists of all shadings."[466] If it were to represent the masses, the KPD had to gain control over the masses, and the masses belonged to the SPD; the United Front from Below was, fundamentally, a response to the fact that the party's "map" failed to correspond with the "terrain."

Of the absurdities produced by the KPD's exclusivist claims, the "social fascism" strategy was certainly the most destructive and, indeed, intensified splits within the KPD itself. Whatever Communist activists might share with the radical right in terms of ideas of manliness, warriorhood, and so on, a hallmark of authenticity for the majority was resistance to fascism. The party's failure to resist fascism by forging working-class unity—even while it staged performances, in a variety of media, of its role of leadership over the masses—was a major source of discontent in the movement. Strictures against cooperation between Communists and Social Democrats, as Klaus-Michael Mallmann has shown, were often ignored at the local level.[467] Even Communists who agreed with the party leadership's condemnation of Social Democracy often found themselves unhappy in the KPD. The tortured rationalizations and slavish adherence to the line coming out of Moscow, the failure to rationally analyze the German situation and make its policies accordingly, the overtures to the radical right, provoked resistance both within and without.[468] One disgusted ex-functionary who published a pamphlet criticizing the party leadership expressed the feelings of many Communists when he criticized the "pernicious revolutionary romanticism" of the party, its overtures to the radical right, and its attempt to foster "corpselike obedience" ("*Kadavergehöhrsamkeit*") among its members.[469]

Erich Wollenberg, who attended meetings of the KPD's central committee as leader of military operations for the *Rotfrontkämpferbund,* found the atmosphere "depressing. … The separation of the party leadership from the masses, the bureaucratization and the fixation on the obdurate party line—the main enemy was the social fascists, the social democrats."[470] Wollenberg went on to criticize the Stalinization of the party, especially the inability of party members to discuss real issues. He reported his dismay, and that of other leading Communists, about orders from Moscow that the KPD should participate with the Nazis in the referendum against the Social Democratic administration of the state of Prussia in August 1931.[471] This "*roten Volksentscheid*" was highly unpopular in the party, writes Wollenberg, and many KPD members refused to vote for it. He himself was disgusted by the sight of SA men and Red Front fighters carrying the same placards, and of Communist, Nazi, and *Stahlhelm* officials sitting at the same tables at the voting stations "under the swastika and the Soviet Star."[472] Such events contributed to what Wollenberg identified as a "difference in mood between the rank and file and the party leadership" with highly destructive consequences.[473]

The problems within the KPD were in part a consequence of an increased centralization and bureaucratization in the second half of the 1920s that affected both major left-wing parties.[474] Charges of excessive bureaucracy, of a leadership out of touch, of corruption, of a failure to effectively fight fascism, dogged the SPD as well. Moreover, in some ways, these complaints were not so different from those leveled by rightists against their leaderships—both grew out of a fundamental frustration with mass politics; and just as on the right, this frustration resulted in the founding of splinter groups aimed at protecting the purity of first principles threatened by the compromises of "politics." One of the most significant of the left-wing splinter parties of the Weimar Republic—the Socialist Workers Party (SAPD)—was aimed against the failings of both parties.[475] Founded out of a part of the left wing of the SPD after the fall of the party's last parliamentary coalition in 1931, the SAPD positioned itself as a *Sammlungsbewegung* aimed at collecting disappointed members of the two main left parties.[476] Its goal, in the words of one of the party's leading figures, was to "loosen up and blast open the rigid and paralyzed big parties."[477]

The SAPD criticized the failure of the SPD and KPD leaderships to seriously pursue a united front against fascism, and the lack of rank-and-file democracy in the two parties. It continued to make this charge as late as March 1933, singling out the KPD "bureaucracy" for special scorn.[478] The KPD especially was ruled, according to the SAPD, by a "dictatorial-centralist-bureaucratic organizational apparatus" that prevented it from responding to the needs of the situation or its own followers. One of the founders of the SAPD, Max Seydewitz, captured the general feeling in an epigram: "There is no democracy in the SPD and in the KPD there is a hundred percent less."[479] The KPD took the threat of the SAPD very seriously, holding party days in Essen and in the Wedding district of Berlin in the autumn of 1931 under the slogan "left SPD—The Main Enemy in the Camp of the Workers." In a revealing circular titled "The New Party—Their Arguments, Our Answers," the KPD responded to the SAPD's criticisms point by point. The charge that the KPD was undemocratic was answered, on the one hand, by the rather unconvincing assertion that the party was ruled by "Democratic Central-ism," and on the other, that the presence of a majority of workers in the party's councils ensured its democratic character. To the SAPD's rejection of the KPD's "playing at revolution," the KPD responded that the SAPD were "revolutionar-ies" the way the National Socialists were "socialists."[480] The KPD was stung in particular by the (accurate) charge that it was only interested in a "united front" under the leadership of the KPD.[481] In a speech in Bochum in December 1931, Seydewitz pointed out that in the Russian revolution, the Bolsheviks had not said "all power to Bolsheviks" but rather "all power to the Soviets," and that on the Soviets had sat Social Revolutionaries, Mensheviks, and so on. The statement of course ignored the extent to which Bolshevik allegiance to the Soviets had been a tactical maneuver but illustrates the way that the dispute over issues of demo-cratic participation in Russia continued to resonate in Germany.[482]

Similar issues informed the activity of other left-wing splinter groups. The "right opposition" of the KPD—the KPD-O ("KPD Opposition")—was formed by elements ejected from the KPD at the end of 1928 because of their opposition to the Social Fascism strategy and the increased meddling by the Comintern that it represented.[483] The KPD-O was aimed at eventually "winning back" the KPD, although this goal proved unattainable and the party split up in 1931–32.[484] A different strategy was elaborated by the Leninist Organization (aka "Die Org"). Founded in 1929 by Walter Löwenheim (code name "Miles"), the Leninist Or-ganization—later known as *Neu Beginnen* (New Beginnings) after Löwenheim's 1933 pamphlet of the same name—was a direct response to the KPD's Social Fascism strategy. Löwenheim criticized the inability of the two working-class par-ties to form a united front against fascism, arguing that the disagreement about whether or not it was possible to make a revolution at the present historical junc-ture had introduced an unnecessary and dangerous rift into the working-class movement. The SPD, Löwenheim argued, was too closely identified with the Weimar system to act effectively against it, while the KPD was a meaningless sect, prevented by a "false idea of its own role" from winning over the masses.[485] In the winter of 1929–30, Löwenheim and his brother Ernst started putting to-gether small independent groups to infiltrate the two large parties with the aim of creating a future unified working-class party.[486] Although these efforts ultimately came to naught, *Neu Beginnen* played a significant role in the socialist opposition to Hitler after 1933, competing with the SPD exile organization to speak for the Social Democratic underground in Germany and publishing its own counterpart to the SPD's Sopade reports, the *Miles Berichte*.[487]

The left-wing splinter groups of the Weimar Republic enjoyed limited electoral success—the SAPD, for example, polled very marginally in the two Reichstag elections of 1932.[488] But the importance of these groups lies elsewhere. First, in a broad sense, they were part of a larger dissatisfaction with official politics in the Weimar Republic. Like the splinter groups and factions of the radical right—but for more admirable ends—they sought to achieve a greater agency for themselves, creating an organizational space outside of the larger, less responsive parties. In this respect they prefigured the extraparliamentary opposition of the 1960s in West Germany, which reacted in a similar way against the reconstituted SPD's increasingly close identification with the system by working outside of parliament and outside of the party. More specifically, these groups demonstrated the failure of the left's two main institutional "cages"—the SPD and the KPD—to effectively embody the existing resistance to fascism in the Weimar Republic. Their existence was, in short, an expression of the disjuncture between institutions and social forces that, as has been argued elsewhere in this book, was characteristic of the politics of the Weimar Republic.

The centrifugal tendency represented by these groups (which, it must be noted, were ultimately in search not of splinter group activity for its own sake but a new and more responsive mass politics) was met by an opposite force, the tendency to lump under one umbrella the various groups and forces, to give them a common will and a common voice. For the SPD, this was, on one level, a matter of maintaining the status quo, for the SPD was a party of government with strong representation in the trade unions and factories, enjoying the allegiance of the majority of Marxist workers in Germany. Yet the SPD did have to try to respond to the pressure for action against fascism, particularly in its efforts to strengthen its paramilitary response through the Iron Front formed at the end of 1931.[489] It was the KPD, however, that had the greatest need to draw disparate elements under its umbrella. The foundational conceit of the party—its right to exclusive control over the masses—required that it do so. But unlike the SPD, the KPD was weakly rooted in the proletariat, meaning that it faced a greater burden of proof in making its claims. Indeed, the vehemence of the party's claims to represent the masses existed in inverse proportion to its actual representation among those masses. There were a number of reasons for the KPD's isolation in the Weimar Republic; the middle classes hated the party as a foreign threat, a bridgehead of property-devouring godless Russian Bolshevism; the majority of left-liberal intellectuals were "repelled by the [party's] aggressive collectivism and 'Soviet-ism'"; the working classes were locked up by the SPD and, increasingly—although the Marxist and Catholic milieus never completely broke down—attracted to the radical right.[490] The KPD did extend its membership dramatically from 1929, when the economic crisis helped it break somewhat out of its isolation; but even then, it was mainly a party of the urban unemployed, with weak representation in the factories that should, according to theory, have been its strongholds.[491] The party never had support commensurate with its exclusive claim over the masses, and this is one reason why the KPD had to try so hard to create—or at least perform—bottom-up participation.

The problem, however—and here we come to a key dilemma of Communism in the Weimar Republic—was that there was a fundamental tension between the party's need for bottom-up participation and its basic authoritarianism. This is the explanation for what Nancy Aumann has identified as the primacy of agitation over organization in the KPD's policies.[492] Unable to effectively organize— at least on a level commensurate with the party's claims—the KPD had to rely on winning over those it needed to organize; from here, it was but a small step to *depict* support in the hopes of making it a reality. Much of what was odd or infuriating about Communist policy in the Weimar Republic (above all, the Social Fascism strategy and the failure to seriously pursue a united front with the SPD until it was too late) and much of what has been undervalued or ignored (the overtures to the radical right and the provision of aid and comfort to fascism and fascist ideas through the creation of *Zersetzungsschriften*) can be better understood if we view it through the lens of the KPD's attempt to create semiotic evidence for its exclusive claim over the masses, that is, to perform that claim. The vision of a proletariat united under the leadership of the Communist Party was a fantasy. The SPD remained the majority party of the working class throughout most of the Weimar Republic, and when the SPD lost voters and members in the decisive period of the failure of German democracy, it lost them largely not to the KPD but to the Nazis. But if the KPD's vision could be named (through the titles given to newspapers and mass organizations); if it could be depicted (through photographs and drawings); if it could be staged as spectacle (through mass meetings designed to give an impression of greater numbers than the party really possessed); and if it could be placed onto the uniformed bodies of militants designed to depict the KPD's militancy and readiness for war—and occasionally, in isolated but highly revealing cases, a fusion of identities with the radical right (see below)—then the fantasy of the party's leadership role over the masses could be made a reality.

The KPD's attempt to speak for and in the voice of the masses was carried out in a broad range of printed matter, ranging from the daily *Rote Fahne* (Red Flag), *Die Welt am Abend,* and the glossy *Arbeiter-Illustrierte-Zeitung* (AIZ) to small local news sheets, fliers, postcards, and stickers.[493] Whereas papers such as the AIZ and *Die Welt am Abend* aimed at a level of mainstream acceptance, the small papers, news sheets, and leaflets were meant to carry the Communist message into the streets and tenement blocks, the schools and factories.[494] The primary means of visual communication for the KPD in the Weimar Republic, these papers covered every aspect of the party's activity, encompassing its paramilitary organizations, its school and youth groups, its factory and block groups, and its mass "antifascist" organizations. They were frequently local in provenance and reflected, to an extent, the influence of local activism. They were the "democratic voice" of the KPD, and the images in them tell us much about how the KPD saw itself and wanted itself to be seen. But they had a bigger function, which was to depict rank-and-file democracy. These sources were meant to illustrate that the masses *wanted* the KPD, and that the KPD in turn spoke for them. According to instructions published by the Central Committee of the KPD in July 1931, Communist newspapers in the factories, housing blocks, and villages were to appear *not* as the product of Communist cells but as the creation of the inhabitants or workers themselves. This was in part designed to confuse the police; but it was also meant to serve a semiotic function: the KPD's leadership role over the masses was stipulated by the masses themselves. The party placed great importance on a grassroots outpouring of propaganda. In the fall of 1931, in response to Chancellor Brüning's declaration of a state of emergency, the Central Committee demanded the production of a "flood" of new papers, which were to be created as quickly as possible at the local level using local resources and local funding. The product was to be distributed as quickly as possible, in spaces both hidden and public, such as "drawers, cloakrooms, and restrooms."[495] The KPD was caught between a desire to control its message and a lack of funds and organization with which to exercise this control; but this dilemma only mirrored a more fundamental one, between the party's democratic claims and its authoritarian aims.

This dilemma was played out as well in the party's creation of mass organizations. Groups such as the paramilitary (RFB), the KgdF, and the *Antifaschistische Junge Garde* played both a spatial-organizational and a semiotic role for the KPD. As "nonparty" organizations, they were an attempt, first of all, to cast an organizational net over the masses not directly organized in the party. They aimed at holding Communist supporters together in organizational "cages" into which the masses not directly under the control of the KPD could gradually be brought. Second, they were meant to perform the mass participation that would reinforce the appearance of the KPD's leading role over the working masses. The KPD was certainly not alone in affiliating itself with "nonparty" auxiliaries—the pro-Republican *Reichsbanner Schwarz-Rot-Gold*, although heavily associated with the SPD, was also "nonparty," being associated with the Catholic Center Party. But the KPD did differ in the way in which it attempted to establish organizations that gave the appearance of independence while being, in reality, closely tied to the party. In this way, the party tried to walk a narrow path, combining grassroots "democracy" with its (essentially authoritarian) leadership role over the masses.

Arguably the most important of the KPD's mass organizations, and the one most consistently involved in efforts to win adherents outside the relatively narrow confines of the KPD proper, was the RFB.[496] Founded in the summer of 1924, the RFB was intended from the beginning not to be just a street-fighting organization but a tool for enforcing the KPD's exclusivist claims. It had a number of interrelated tasks. First, it was to act as a rallying point for the politically apathetic, collecting those who "out of anger and disappointment with the course of the revolution" had given up on the political parties or trade unions to which they formerly belonged.[497] Second, it was to strengthen the KPD's insurrectionary capabilities, providing an organizational space for combat veterans who shared the KPD's goals and could bring their military expertise into the service of the revolution. Third, it was to act as a "counterorganization" against the nationalist and Social Democratic paramilitaries, denying to these organizations the allegiance of proletarians and "half proletarians" who rightfully belonged with the KPD. In a spirit that would become familiar a few years later with the advent of the Social Fascism strategy, a special task was to warn the working classes about the dangerous and pernicious character of the *Reichsbanner*. By playing both a military and an ideological role, carrying out "an ideological and physical struggle for the hearts and minds of … proletarian soldiers" wherever they might be found, the RFB was to act as a *Zwischenorganisation* linking the KPD to the masses.[498]

The RFB played two roles, acting as both organizational cage and a vehicle for organizing performances of the KPD's claims to represent the masses. The latter role required the maintenance of the fiction that the organization was independent of KPD control. *Die Rote Fahne* greeted the founding of the *Rotfrontkämpferbund* with respectful disinterest, extending the KPD's "sympathy and support" to the new organization and promising to encourage Communists to join it.[499] The Communist "fraction" within the RFB was to be the guarantor of the organization's ideological purity, preventing it from being hijacked by oppositional Communists, anarchists, or *agents provocateurs*.[500] In reality, everyone knew the RFB represented the interests of the KPD—Ernst Thälmann, after all, was its leader—although the RFB was involved in factional struggles within the party, and a portion of its membership did not belong to the party. The latter fact, however, was less a sign of genuine nonparty status than it was of the fact that a large percentage of the activists attracted to such organizations in the Weimar Republic had little patience for the niceties of ideology and were interested primarily in the opportunity to engage in manly struggle with their opponents. Crippled by chronic shortage of funds, persecuted by the police, and lacking any of the sympathy extended by society at large to their street-fighting counterparts on the extreme right, formations such as the *Rotfrontkämpferbund* faced an uphill struggle to gain members and pursue their objectives. The outlawing of the RFB after the events of 1 May 1929, supplied, for the KPD, the final proof of Social Democracy's treachery to the working class.[501] But any propaganda benefit derived from the events was more than outweighed by the very real effects on the RFB's operations. The KPD had hoped to retain 60 to 70 percent of the organization's membership after the ban, but in the event it maintained at best 50 percent.[502] In the wake of the ban, the RFB was reorganized with a view toward bringing the organization more closely under the control of the party, but, as will be seen, this goal, too, proved difficult to attain.

Even more explicit in its attempt to use "nonparty" status to cast the KPD's net around the masses was the *Kampfbund gegen den Faschismus* ("Fighting League Against Fascism") or KgdF. Founded in October 1930, the KgdF was part of the

KPD's alarmed response to the Nazi success in the Reichstag elections of September. Its chief goal, like that of the *Rotfrontkämpferbund,* was to "reclaim" the masses for the KPD. But now the Nazis were the main target. The KgdF was intended to blunt the increasing popularity of the Nazis among the working classes and, in particular, to prevent workers from cooperating with the factory cells of the NSBO.[503] Like the RFB, the KgdF was meant to appear as a "nonparty" formation. Speaking at one of a series of *Kampfkongresse* held in the Ruhr beginning in December 1930, the KPD's propaganda expert, Willi Münzenberg, urged "every honest worker, whether SPD or so far unorganized," to join "together with his Communist class brothers in this front."[504] The political police, well informed by spies within the new organization, identified a number of aims behind its founding. The KgdF was, first, to serve as a cover for the continuation of the banned *Rotfrontkämpferbund,* and, in this capacity, to strengthen the defense of working-class neighborhoods against the penetration of the Nazis.[505] Second, as a "nonparty" front organization, it was intended to diffuse responsibility for the party's illegal activities. But the KgdF's "nonparty" status had two more important aims. On the one hand, as Münzenberg's comment above suggests, it was an attempt to bring SPD (and other) workers into the KPD's sphere of influence as a preliminary to later conversion.[506] Speaking points for the *Kampfkongresse* of the KgdF called for the "widest possible application of the United Front from Below."[507] The KgdF was also seen as a vehicle for winning youth to the party, particularly members of the *Jungsozialisten* and SAJ who had shown a "stronger will" to fight fascism than their parent party.[508] On the other hand, and more fundamentally, it was meant to provide semiotic proof of the party's claim to represent the masses. Aware that it could not carry out its agitation "in the desired form" with the "heterogeneous elements" collected in the Kampfbund, the KPD leadership nevertheless hoped to use demonstrations of the Kampfbund to show that masses of workers not strictly affiliated with the KPD nevertheless supported the party's aims and accepted its leading role over the working classes. The KgdF thus served to resolve the dichotomy between the party's democratic claims and its authoritarian-conspiratorial aims.[509]

The KgdF played a central role in the "antifascist action" initiative begun in mid-1932, which aimed at combining a forceful revival of the United Front from Below strategy against the SPD with an extension of that strategy to Nazi workers.[510] The SPD rejected the KPD's call for a united front, suspecting—with some justification—that the KPD was operating in bad faith, that "the so-called 'Anti-Fascist Action' was in fact an 'Anti–Social Democratic Action.'"[511] The Anti-Fascist Action was not to be a "fixed organization" but a "movement." Its goal, in addition to gaining control over Social Democratic workers, was to bring proletarian and petit-bourgeois members of Nazi organizations into "open rebellion against the leadership."[512] The attempt to reach out to the Nazis was highly problematic, and not only for moral reasons; as Conan Fischer has persuasively argued, the strategy introduced a dangerous confusion into Communist ranks.[513] At the very moment at which the KPD appealed to Nazis to join a "united front of all working people," it was offering the "hand of brotherhood" to SPD and *Reichsbanner* workers for the fight against fascism amidst pages and pages detailing Nazi threats and abuses of the workers from around the country. The attempt to elide the distinction between the two sides reached absurd lengths, as in an article in the Communist press that placed quotations around "Nazi" and "Communist" as if the distinction was an invention of journalists looking for a sensational story.[514] As the *Vossische Zeitung* put it: "'The KPD is fighting a life or death struggle against capitalism and Versailles,' it reads across the entire width of the *Rote Fahne*—were one to replace the letters KPD with NSDAP, the sentence could go word for word in the *Völkischer Beobachter.*"[515] Police authorities familiar with planning for the initiative noted that the KPD had to emphasize that it was not a matter of fighting "together with members of the NSDAP against the *Reichsbanner* but the other way around, with *Reichsbanner* workers against the NSDAP."[516]

KPD, Class, and Nation

That this seemingly rudimentary point had to be reinforced was, of course, a consequence of the KPD's ceaseless agitation against the SPD; but the party's repeated forays into the ideological terrain of the radical right also played an important role. Communism and nationalism are, of course, far from mutually exclusive—they have been intimate bedfellows in the century just past. Internationalism was, by and large, a luxury afforded to Communist movements in countries with strong national traditions. In countries with nationalist deficits—as in those undergoing decolonization—Communist parties were, without exception, intensely nationalistic. It would therefore have been surprising if an attempt to elaborate an indigenous left-wing nationalism had not been undertaken in post–World War I Germany. Elements in the SPD urged a coming to terms with the issue of the nation, and such ideas were strong in parts of the Young Socialists and the *Reichsbanner.* The early KPD was not unaffected by Germany's postwar humiliation, nor by the questions it raised about the relationship between social and national liberation. The Hamburg National Communism of Heinrich Laufenberg and Fritz Wolffheim was an early expression of this concern. The revolution could only be accomplished through an alliance of the proletariat and the middle classes, it was argued, and that revolution could in turn only be defended through the creation of a People's Army capable of taking the fight to the encircling imperialist powers.[517] In an interesting twist on the *Dolchstoß* (stab in the back) legend current on the radical right, Laufenberg and Wolffheim argued that a bourgeoisie fearful of the armed proletariat had committed "blatant treason" against a German army still undefeated on the battlefield. Too effete to save Germany itself, the bourgeoisie needed to align itself with a "proletarian national" movement.[518] This attempt at elaborating a Communist nationalism in the German context was squelched by Lenin, who objected to it not on philosophical but on tactical grounds.[519] Laufenberg was dismissed by Karl Radek as a "National Bolshevik" (the first use of a term that would take on a number of different iterations) and both he and Wolffheim were expelled from the KPD.[520]

When the KPD picked up the demands it had formerly condemned, it was for tactical reasons. Beginning with Radek's "Schlageter Speech" in 1923, which sought to capitalize on patriotic resistance to the French occupation of the Ruhr, the KPD displayed a pronounced willingness to respond to nationalist sentiment. The Program for the National and Social Liberation of the German People of 1930 was, similarly, a response to both widespread outrage over the Treaty of Versailles and the rising electoral success of the Nazis. In both instances, the nationalism of the KPD rang hollow. There was another aspect to the KPD's nationalism, however, and this lay in its orientation toward the Soviet Union. While maintaining a formally internationalist position, the KPD affected what

Figure 4.2 "With the Red Army of the Soviet Union, defend the Socialist Fatherland." KJVD flier (no date). Bundesarchiv.

amounted to a "renationalization" of the socialist masses in an internationalist register, imagining a world community of the oppressed owing allegiance to the Soviet Union. This deep-structural or *fundamental* nationalism—as opposed to the tactical nationalism of the party's propaganda offensives against the radical right—was in some ways a natural consequence of revolutionary developments after 1917. The victory of Bolshevism in Russia, followed by the failure of the revolution to spread into Central Europe or elsewhere, would have more or less guaranteed, even if the meddling of the Comintern had not, that indigenous Communist parties such as the KPD would adopt a "patriotic" orientation to the USSR as the "Fatherland of the Working Class." Theoretically, the *tactical* nationalism of the KPD complemented its *fundamental* nationalism, since attempts to win over or disarm the German bourgeoisie by emphasizing the party's own patriotism served to protect the USSR from capitalist aggression (and indeed, were instigated for precisely this purpose by the USSR). In practice, however, they were in conflict, for it took complex gymnastics to convincingly represent the interests of Germany and those of the Soviet Union at the same time. The idea of "Red Germany" was an attempt to create a simulacrum of the USSR in Germany. The very qualities that made the KPD "anti-national" in the eyes of the German bourgeoisie—allegiance to the USSR and membership in an international community of struggle, the world proletariat—were the same that reinforced its own ersatz nationalism. The fundamental nationalism of the KPD worked at cross-purposes with its tactical nationalism, and in the end, the two cancelled each other out.

As far as the Communist relationship with National Socialism is concerned, the important point is that the KPD's nationalism was an expression of its need to break out of its isolation by embodying the widest possible notion of the "popular." If Communist workers were going to the Nazis or other radical right organizations in part because of their nationalism, then the KPD must find a way to reconfigure that nationalism in a Communist mode. As in the case of the party's assault on the right of the SPD to represent the working classes, this involved an attempt to "unmask" the nationalist claims of the Nazis. The Program for the National and Social Liberation of the German People placed the problem of "Germany's enslavement through the Peace of Versailles" on par with that posed by capitalist exploitation; and it argued that the KPD, rather than the NSDAP, was the true party of national revolution in Germany. "The Fascists (National Socialists) maintain that they are a 'national,' a 'socialist,' and a 'workers'' party," the program argued. "To this we reply that they are (on the contrary) a party hostile to the people and the workers, an antisocialist party of the utmost reaction, of the exploitation and enslavement of the working people [*Werktätigen*]." It was the KPD, backed by the power of the Soviet Union, that would really "tear up the ... Versailles 'Peace Treaty' and the Young Plan ... and annul all international debts and reparations payments laid on the working people of Germany by the capitalists."[521] The nationalist program was intended first and foremost to combat the NSDAP's growing success at the ballot box, but in its unmasking function it also came to play a major role in the ideological offensives of the KPD's mass organizations.

This Communist attempt at "unmasking" the NSDAP played an even more important role where Nazism's "left" claims were concerned. Both the KPD and the SPD stressed repeatedly the instrumental nature of National Socialism's revolutionary rhetoric. "The decisive motive for the flow of … the proletarian masses to the NSDAP," noted a set of speaking points designed for propaganda use by the *Rotfrontkämpferbund*, "[is the] sham-socialist demagogy of the Hitler party. We must realize that a great part of the Nazi-proletarians are misled workers who really believe that they are fighting against capitalism and for socialism."[522] In attempting to disabuse misled workers of this notion, the KPD emphasized not only that the NSDAP was not serious about socialism but also that, indeed, it was itself merely a gendarmerie for capitalism. The Communist press is replete with attempts to illustrate how National Socialism conformed to the vulgar Marxist definition of fascism as an inevitable product of capitalism. The classic Marxist definition, proposed by the Bulgarian Communist Georgi Dimitrov in his report to the Seventh World Congress of the Comintern in 1935, held fascism to be "the open terroristic dictatorship of the most reactionary, most chauvinistic, and most imperialist elements of finance capital."[523] A number of more nuanced definitions were elaborated by Communists already in the early 1920s, but the basic idea of fascism as a product of—or a front for—capitalism informed the KPD's response to National Socialism in the Weimar Republic. Images like that shown in Figure 4.3 were a staple of the Communist local and regional press.

Figure 4.3 Marxist fascism theory for young people in the pages of *Der Junge Antifaschist* Nr. 1. (no date). Bundesarchiv.

Soldiers of the Revolution

In attempting to win over Nazis, the KPD was able to draw on a number of commonalities related to the image of the revolutionary soldier. Efforts to win over workers and members of the lower middle classes belonging to the Nazi mass organizations focused heavily on aspects of the militaristic youth culture of the Weimar Republic. The KPD's youth wing, the *Kommunistische Jugendverbands Deutschland,* was intimately involved in efforts to proselytize on the radical right, and it put forward a vision of youth militarism based on a shared cultural content. *Die Junge Garde,* the official organ of the KJVD, regularly published articles detailing incidents of unrest in the Nazi movement and features on individual Nazi defectors.[524] Displaying a youthful militancy that bled over easily into celebration of warriorhood as an end in itself, Communist papers such as *Die Junge Garde* reconfigured iconography of right militarism as left militarism. Note how in Figure 4.4—the masthead from the *Rote Frontsoldat*—the space in the steel helmet occupied, in the mythology of the *Freikorps,* by the swastika (enshrined in the marching song of the Brigade Ehrhardt: "Swastika on steel helmet …") is now occupied by the raised fist of the Red Front. "Our generation is called to supply fighters for the greatest event the world has ever known," ran a characteristic slogan. "The proletarian class has begun to burst its chains."[525]

The sheer volume of the militarist Communist press was offered as semiotic proof of the commitment of the masses to the militant vision of the KPD (see Figure 4.5). The *Rotfrontkämpferbund* was especially proactive in theorizing its right to prepare for and celebrate the necessity of armed struggle. The RFB drew a distinction between an illegitimate "bourgeois militarism" on the one hand, and a legitimate proletarian attitude toward armed struggle on the other. It explicitly rejected "bourgeois and reformist pacifism" while defending the proletariat's right to organize militarily.[526] "It is no 'Red Militarism' when we march in file," insisted the author of guidelines for the RFB's military training, "but rather the spirit of proletarian military preparedness [*Wehrhaftigkeit*]."[527] As RFB guidelines put it, "As an organization of revolutionary front-soldiers, the RFB can adopt the worthwhile technical elements [*sic*] of militarism and make them useful for its

Der Rote Frontsoldat

ORGAN FÜR PROLETARISCHE WEHRPOLITIK

Figure 4.4 Masthead of *Der rote Frontsoldat*, Nr. 5, September 1932. Bundesarchiv.

Figure 4.5 The KPD's militarist credentials on display for a nationalist audience. *Aufbruch* Nr. 1, 3. Jg., January 1932. Bundesarchiv.

purposes." These things included, according to the guidelines, "tanks, airplanes, and [poison] gas."[528]

The potential of this militarism to serve as a bridge between the KPD and the Nazis came out clearly in the journal of military-political thought inspired by Richard Scheringer's defection to Communism. After his initial attempt to intervene on behalf of the KPD in the Stennes Revolt of April 1931, Scheringer became the centerpiece of a controversial "Scheringer line" aimed at winning

Figure 4.6 "Defend the Soviet Union." KPD flier (no date). Bundesarchiv.

recruits from the radical right. His prolonged imprisonment (extended by a new sentence, in April 1932, of 2½ years for Communist agitation while in prison) provided an additional propaganda opportunity, with a "Free Scheringer" campaign organized around a "Scheringer Committee" of "nonparty" signatories.[529] The magazine launched by Hans Kippenberger in the summer of 1931—

"Aufbruch. Kampfblatt im Sinne des Leutnant a.D. Scheringer"—represented yet another attempt to profit from Scheringer's credibility in militarist circles. It sought to capitalize on Scheringer's defection to attract militants of the nationalist right to the Communist cause, weakening the forces arrayed against the KPD and winning over technical experts for a future "Red Army."[530]

Aufbruch was aimed in the first instance against the NSDAP, and a number of high-profile National Socialist defectors and fellow travelers regularly contributed articles emphasizing—in accordance with the KPD's overall strategy of ideologically "unmasking" the NSDAP—the gap between the NSDAP's anticapitalist promises and its actual behavior.[531] The primary focus of *Aufbruch,* however, was the link forged between revolution and war, presenting military problems as "military-political" problems. This involved the creation of a "nationalist-militarist voice" capable of combining the language of masses and classes with the language of strategy, tactics, and military technology. The assumption behind *Aufbruch*—that Communism and radical nationalism had a common interest in issues of military preparedness—could draw on ample common ground.[532] Whether discussing military strategy and technique, mulling over the lessons of the Great War, examining the military-technical problems of the Red Army in Russia, or considering the tactical problems of the civil war in China, war provided considerable overlap in interest between Communist and nationalist militarism. China, particularly, supplied such a common ground, since the USSR was aiding the Chinese Communists, and German military officers served with the forces of the national Chiang Kai-shek in an advisory capacity.[533] *Aufbruch* was steeped in war, combining articles on revolutionary politics with articles on military tactics and technique in a way as to suggest that there was no fundamental contradiction between the two. And although it made no mention of the illegal interchange between the German and Soviet armies in the early 1920s, the magazine clearly sought to capitalize on the intense interest in the Red Army on the part of military observers in Germany.[534]

The particular milieu to which *Aufbruch* sought to appeal was symbolized by the participation of Beppo Römer, a radical nationalist and *Freikorps* leader active in the ethnic border struggles of the early postwar period,[535] who had afterward moved to the left, eventually joining the Communist Party in April 1932.[536] Römer's accession to the editorship of *Aufbruch* in May 1932 brought a dramatic increase in public interest, with his speaking engagements in Munich and elsewhere drawing large crowds.[537] Yet Römer's popularity—and Scheringer's—had less to do with their Communist message than with the aura of adventure and romance attached to warriors who had served in the postwar struggles for Germany. It also reflected a respect for militancy at a time when militancy was increasingly seen to be an end in itself. By the end of 1932, *Aufbruch* had a nationwide distribution facilitated by discussion circles in some thirty-two cities and a circulation of one hundred thousand.[538] Characteristically, the scene around *Aufbruch* was an artificial construction—an elaborate performance—that drew on and reordered elements of social reality. The journal counted on the participation of authentic *Grenzgänger,* activists who hoped to use the journal to pursue a Third Way between National Socialism and Communism. However, *Aufbruch* was by no means an independent voice of the National Bolshevik tendency in Germany; it was, rather, the KPD's attempt to create an artificial "National Bolshevism" under Communist control. *Aufbruch* was firmly integrated into the KPD's propaganda apparatus, its ideological content overseen by Theo Bottländer, the head of "Ressort C" (fascist organizations) in the party's *M-Apparat.* The publication of *Aufbruch* was linked to the creation of discussion circles, known as *Aufbruch-Arbeiterkreise* (AAKs), created to facilitate contact with likely recruits, above all "proletarianized" former officers and members of the right-wing intelligentsia known to be disappointed with Hitler.[539]

Dangerous Spaces

The fusion of "voice" and "institution" accomplished by the *Aufbruch* and the AAKs was carried a step further in the creation of Communist cells within enemy organizations. This cell building was part of a broad campaign aimed at disabling the military forces of the bourgeoisie, broadly defined. By infiltrating and subverting the forces of the government (army and police), "social fascism" (the Social Democratic *Reichsbanner*), and "national fascism" (the *Stahlhelm, Wehrwolf,* and the Nazis), the KPD hoped to break the power of the bourgeoisie to successfully resist the coming proletarian revolution. Again, however, there was more here than meets the eye, for attempts at cell building, and the propaganda with which they were associated, aimed not just at hindering the effectiveness of Communism's enemies but also at creating the appearance of Communist support. In this way, the campaign waged against Communism's enemies mirrored that waged among its friends; just as the KPD's own mass organizations were designed to illustrate Communism's foundational claim—the unity of party and masses—the Communist presence in the ranks of the enemy was intended to create, through semiotic trickery, the appearance of growing sympathy for the KPD's goals among the forces of order. Infiltration, not only of the right-wing *Verbände* but also of the armed formations of the state, had been a key part of Communist tactics from the early 1920s. One of the chief tasks of the KPD's secret *M-Apparat* involved the influence of opposing formations through espionage, infiltration, and internal agitation. The strategy of winning over the rank and file of enemy organizations, an outgrowth of the United Front from Below strategy directed at the SPD and its trade unions, was to be applied to all the armed forces of the bourgeoisie, whether official (army, police) or volunteer (right-wing and Social Democratic paramilitary groups).

The building of cells within the enemy organizations was a central element in the United Front from Below strategy and a crucial step in preparing the ground for the revolution. In order to capitalize on a revolutionary situation, the reasoning went, both the official and volunteer armed forces of the bourgeoisie must be weakened from within and their rank and file impregnated with sympathy for the revolution. In order to be successful at the decisive moment, the KPD must have worked to prepare the ground within these forces for a long time prior to the revolution.[540] Guidelines for work in the army and police envisioned that cells would "[bear] the agitation and propaganda within the troops and play a decisive role in the revolutionary mobilization of soldiers and police officials."[541] Beginning in October 1931, separate departments were created for each formation (i.e., one for the police, one for the army, etc.). "Active groups" of four to six men were to be formed to carry out the important work of propaganda creation and cell building. They were to be organized in every barracks, in every ship, and in every city district. Active-duty soldiers, sailors, and policemen were to be integrated into the "active groups" and would participate in the work of creating and distributing propaganda.[542] Although these efforts enjoyed only minimal success in the Reichswehr, the KPD does appear to have succeeded in infiltrating the *Schutzpolizei*. "By the end of the 1920s," writes Bernd Kaufmann, "there was probably hardly a large city in Germany in which the KPD was not anchored in the *Schutzpolizei* with illegal contacts or party cells."[543] A key element of the work in the *Schutzpolizei* was the creation of "Schupo newspapers," which were put together from information obtained by spies in or around individual units. The information thus obtained, containing a wealth of local detail, was played back with a Communist spin designed to resonate with the concerns of the target audience. These underground police newspapers were published in a number of cities.[544] A district conference of Red Schupo cells was organized in Berlin at the beginning of 1931.[545] The aim of this activity was portrayed in the characteristic image seen in Figure 4.7, in which a policeman marches shoulder to shoulder with the proletariat under the leadership of the KPD.

This sort of semiotic trickery, in which Communism adapted the voice and appearance of the enemy in order to more effectively play back its own claims, reached its ultimate expression in Communist work in the SA. Here, the Communist determination to speak for the masses—even the fascist masses—dovetailed with the shared cultural content that characterized the radical extremes in the Weimar Republic. Communist attempts to infiltrate the radical right organizations—primarily the *Stahlhelm*—were going on already in the early to mid-1920s.[546] These efforts reached a new pitch from 1930, focusing now on the rapidly growing Nazis. Appeals to working-class Nazis to abandon their leadership were a staple of the Communist press from 1930 on, as were reports of *Zersetzung* in Nazi ranks.[547] A profusion of fliers and local newspapers attempted to exploit Nazi discontent in the wake of the Stennes Revolt and to capitalize on the example of Richard Scheringer. Openly Communist papers such as *Der Rote Angriff*, published in Berlin beginning in early 1931, employed the Communist strategy of unmasking the demagogic claims of the Nazis while simultaneously emphasizing shared cultural content that could ease the transition of Nazis to Communism. On the cover of one issue, uniformed stormtroopers, hard-jawed and masculine, looked warily but respectfully at a heavily muscled and deter-

Heraus aus der Kaserne!
Fort mit der Militarisierung!

Figure 4.7 "Out of the Barracks!" The republican Schutzpolizei as it ought to be. "An die Polizeibeamten Deutschlands!" Flier (no date). Bundesarchiv.

mined worker, who called out to them: "*Her zu Uns!*" ("Here to us!") [see Figure 4.8].[548] Manliness, heroism, comradeship—the "virtues" of the trenches of the Great War—these, the cover illustration suggested, were the *real* connections between fighters of left and right. The cover of another issue depicted an automobile with Berlin *Gauleiter* Joseph Goebbels at the wheel, driving over the bodies of Berlin's workers, a self-satisfied Hitler sitting in the back seat next to a sack of money labeled "Jewish Finance Capital" (see Figure 4.12).[549] A crude example of the United Front from Below strategy aimed at the NSDAP, the cartoon "unmasked" the Nazi leadership as murderers of workers in the pay of capitalism. The crude Marxist interpretation of fascism—fascism as the extreme form of finance capitalism—was racialized with the reconfiguration of capitalism into "Jewish

Finance Capital." This attempt at turning Nazi anti-Semitism back against the Nazi leadership—which tried to link resentment against *Bonzen,* class resentments against capitalism, and racism all together—demonstrated a regrettable tendency on the part of the KPD to dabble in the basest forms of anti-Semitism to achieve tactical ends, a tendency denounced on more than one occasion by the SPD.[550]

Figure 4.8 "Come to us!" *Der rote Angriff aus dem Prenzlauer Berg,* Nr. 2. Institut für Zeitgeschichte.

Figure 4.9 "The Road to the Third Reich." *Der rote Angriff aus dem Prenzlauer Berg,* Nr. 1. Institut für Zeitgeschichte.

The *Zersetzungsschriften* were merely an extension of the same themes, offered now not by the KPD but by the "Nazis" themselves. A paper titled *SA-Mann Erwache!* ("SA Man, Awake!") was distributed in Essen by known Communist activists. "The content," noted the authorities, "is supposed to give the impression that [the flier] had been put out not by the KPD but by the SA and SS themselves. ... The text ... is completely adapted and suited to cause disintegration in the SA and SS."[551] Nuggets of information for these papers—styled as the product of the "Revolutionary Opposition in the NSDAP"—were obtained by Communist agents wearing the brown uniform. Nazi leaders in Berlin warned in September 1930 of attempts of these agents to "systematically and skillfully undermine the NSDAP from the inside out." Enemy operatives were, in particular, to express the view "that the party has become 'reactionary and is no longer revolutionary,'" to defame Nazi leaders as *'Bonzen'* and 'reactionaries,' and to make reference to the Communist press, especially the proclamation for the "national and social liberation of the working class [sic]".[552] The SA leadership called attention a year later to the presence of KPD agents in the SA, giving numbers of agents by city and noting that the agents possessed official NSDAP documents, stamps, and other forgery materials.[553]

The NSDAP appears to have made some attempts to combat the KPD using its own methods. Guidelines for the party's intelligence service called for the collection of all enemy propaganda publications and "a systematic monitoring of all enemy press productions."[554] The propaganda department of the NSDAP in Munich requested, in October 1931, that regional and local party groups identify former Communists in their groups for use in combating Communist propaganda. "In order to be able to combat the Communist agitation using so-called former National Socialists," it urged, "we are asking you to provide us with the addresses of as many as possible of the party comrades who have come over to us from the Communist camp."[555] Infiltration and internal subversion appear to have been attempted as well. Propaganda guidelines from late 1931 urged agents of the party's *Nachrichtendienst* working within Communist organizations to seek positions of influence from which they could function more securely and successfully.[556] The "number one political task" of this party intelligence service was the "immediate assimilation of collected material on cases of corruption, misconduct of enemy leaders, and Bolshevistic dirty tricks."[557] Such efforts, in contrast to those of the KPD, do not appear to have been particularly extensive.[558]

Reports from Communist operatives appeared in "NSDAP Weekly Reports" published by the KPD for internal use. The reports were aimed at assessing the effects of Communist propaganda and determining prospects for future work. Detailed inside information appeared in sections titled "From within the SA" and "Signs of Disintegration." Using these reports, Communist propagandists could learn, for example, that in the summer of 1932, stormtroopers of *Sturms* 44 and 45 in Berlin were openly talking amongst themselves of going over to the KPD: "the least we could do," one stormtrooper is quoted as saying to his comrades, "would be if we threw in our lot with the KPD and first cleaned house in Germany and solved the economic question—the rest can be discussed once everyone has work and bread again. Only the revolutionary KPD can help us in this."[559] Papers such as *Der Freiheitskämpfer* (Düsseldorf) and *Die Sturmfahne* (Hamburg) were produced with the help of SA junior officers using positions of authority to carry out Communist agitation.[560] *Die Sturmfahne* was produced at the initiative

KAMPFBLATT DER REVOLUTIONÄREN S.A.-MÄNNER D. STANDARTEN 20 U 39

| Nr 3 | Düsseldorf im August | Jahrgang 1 |

S.A. Männer meutern!

Fast kein SA und SS-Appell vergeht , bei dem wir SA/SS-Männer nicht zurecht (und zurück-)gepfiffen werden.Das Führerwort:"Die Geduld und Disziplin der SA/SS wird zwar immer auf stärkere Probengestellt,aber im Hinblick auf das Interesse der Partei...",das wir fast täglich von Neuem aufgetischt bekommen,wird schon von vielen SA-Männern auf den verständlichen "Proletenton" gebracht.Aus dem"Interesse der Partei" wird dann "jiddeln um die Ministerposten,und aus"Geduld und Disziplin", machen immer mehr Kameraden:"Die da oben verfetten und verbonzen,die.wollen ja gar keinen Kampf mehr gegen das System...",die verschachern die Revolution"

Jawohl Kameraden!Es sieht immer mehr danach aus,als ob es auch mit der "Machtübernahme"Scheise wird.Wie oft hat man uns,"Hitlers treueste Kämpfer", nun schon genarrt! Erst sollten wir am 13.März "Hitler an die Macht bringen" dann am 4.April-- Zurückgepfiffen!Und dann kam der "Sturm auf Preussen"--Wieder zurückgepfiffen!Dann sollten wir am 31.Juli. endlich marschieren! "SA Halt!!Anstatt Marschbefehl Appelle,SA Dienst,Bereitschaft mit Vertröstungen und Versprechungen:auf die "legale Machtübernahme".Hinter den Kulissen aber schacher-

Was geht in der Gauleitung vor sich? Gaudirektor Overdiek als Schwerverdiener Fliegerleutnant Rudi

Seite: 3

ten unsere Führer mit der Reaktion um 2 oder 3 Minidterposten,genau so wie ether die schwarzroten System parteien."Der Führer fordert vom Reichspräsidenten die ganze Macht!" sagte man uns.Und was wurde daraus? Der Führer liess sich von Hindenburg und Papen heimschicken wie einen dummen Jungen,während wir zum wievielten Male auf den Marschbefehl warteten.

Statt Marschbefehl --SA-Urlaub !

Anstatt uns marschieren zu lassen beurlaubt uns der Führer und als"Ersatz" dürfen wir Sonntag Morgen Stuba-Appells machen und dann einen Film ansehen und "Heil Hitler" brüllen.Ist es da ein Wunder,wenn die Disziplin sich lockert,wenn die Unzufriedenheit in den SA/SS Stürmen wächst? Ist es ein Wunder,wenn so viele bei denAppells fehlen und keinen Dienst

Halt mit dem Posten Schacher!

Figure 4.10 *Alarm!* Another Communist Zersetzungsschriften aimed at the SA. Jg. 1, Nr. 3, August 1932, Düsseldorf. Compare the iconography with that in Figure 4.11. Bundesarchiv.

Figure 4.11 SA cigarette advertisement from *Der Angriff* 39, 20 February 1932. Bundesarchiv.

of the treasurer of a Hamburg SA formation who was active, simultaneously, in a *fake* opposition group working at the behest of the Communist *M-Apparat* (the so-called *Sturmfahne* group) and a *genuine* Nazi opposition group calling itself the "League of National Socialist Front-Soldiers" [!]. The latter group, made up of former and active-duty SA and SS men, included supporters of both Walther Stennes and General Ludendorff, as well as a spy who reported on the group's meetings to the NSDAP. The spy was well aware of the presence of the operative from the *Sturmfahne* group, whom he reported as possessing "the most intimate connections to the KPD."[561]

Papers appearing throughout Germany relied on a more or less standard set of claims and rhetorical techniques.[562] Their main focus was on unmasking the socialist claims of the Nazi leadership. This unmasking was closely tied with criticism of *Bonzen*, employing the concepts of symbolic social class to make the style of bourgeois *Bonzentum* associated with the party leadership synonymous with that represented by the system. "Not only we revolutionary SA men," claimed an article in *Die Sturmfahne*, "have recognized that our movement, according to the will of our *Führer*, is an instrument for the protection of the existing system of goldsacks and corrupt *Bonzen*." The government, it continued, had nothing to fear from Hitler because he had proven himself willing to suppress "all true revolutionaries" in the Nazi movement.[563] They focused heavily on corruption, which allowed them, simultaneously, to play on and intensify local grievances (e.g., between local SA and party leaders) and to play into the sense of moral outrage against the system, *Bonzen*, and so on. The *Sturmfahne* came closer than any of the KPD's other *Zersetzungsschriften* to making explicit its Communist affiliations, calling on dissatisfied Nazi stormtroopers to vote for the KPD's Ernst Thälmann in the presidential election of March 1932: "Our opposition group will vote for the candidate ... who will fight against the system—the candidate of the Commune! We are not completely in agreement with the Commune, but we nevertheless see in this candidacy the (only) truly active fight against the system."[564] In a rather bizarre application of the United Front from Below strategy, *Die Sturmfahne* appealed directly to the rank and file: "to you, and not to Adolf Hitler, we swear our oath of loyalty, to remain with you until the day when we can [unfurl] our banner [over] the united front of all revolutionary workers." *Die Sturmfahne* urged stormtroopers not to leave the Nazi movement but rather to fight for the revolution from within the SA:

> We summon you also to fight, to range yourselves around our banner. ... Don't leave the ranks of the SA! Join together with all oppositional comrades of your *Sturm*. Be careful, so that the *Sturmführer* will not be able to send any spies into your ranks. He who searches for us as a sincere fighter will know where to find us!!! A triple Heil to the German Revolution![565]

Here, the KPD clearly intended not merely to sow discord in the SA but to transform the SA from within into a sort of "Red SA," a goal it continued to pursue well after January 1933.[566]

Along with social class, *Die Sturm-fahne* also performed race and gender. Adolf Hitler was depicted in a pose both effeminate (see Figure 4.12) and vaguely "bourgeois" (note the sagging belly and prominent rump, implying lack of physical fitness and life behind a desk), suggesting, again, the opposite of the "revolutionary," who had by definition to be both "manly" and "proletarian." The southern German flourishes (note the socks) were meant to call to mind Hitler's alien, "Catholic" (i.e., South German) nature, playing into one of the key complaints against Hitler in North German opposition circles. Hitler as "effeminate bourgeois Catholic" was, the image was meant to suggest, unfit to lead revolutionaries in struggle against the system. *Der SA Kamerad,* published in Cologne, complained about a "gay *Sturm*" in the local SA, asking, "what business do SA workers have with this gay riff-raff?"[567] These papers also used the stereotyping, essentializing language of the Nazis to demonize enemies. Papers such as the *Freiheitskämpfer* tried to turn the anti-Semitism of the stormtroopers against the party by printing bizarre rumors about the NSDAP's involvement with

Figure 4.12 "Our Leader Adolf." *Die Sturmfahne,* Nr. 8, Jahrgang 1932. Bundesarchiv.

"the Jews." The authors wondered whether "the Jews" had used their "financial control" over the movement to dampen its revolutionary spirit, alleging that "the Jews" had so little to fear from the NSDAP that Jewish merchants even capitalized off of the movement by selling Hitler postcards (see Figure 4.13).[568] *Die Sturmfahne* from Hamburg printed anti-Semitic caricatures such as the bizarre image of the "Nazi Jew" in Figure 4.14, meant no doubt at one level to suggest that "the Jews" were in control of the Nazi movement, and in this sense, making up some of the same "unmasking" strategy employed by both sides.[569] *Das Sprachrohr* from Berlin, in the process of appealing to stormtroopers unhinged from the NSDAP in the wake of the Stennes Revolt, complained about the Jewish influence in film and journalism. *Das Sprachrohr* criticized the newspapers of Nazi fellow-traveler Alfred Hugenberg, which employed Jewish editors yet hypocritically dabbled in anti-Semitism when it fit their political purposes.[570] The clear implication

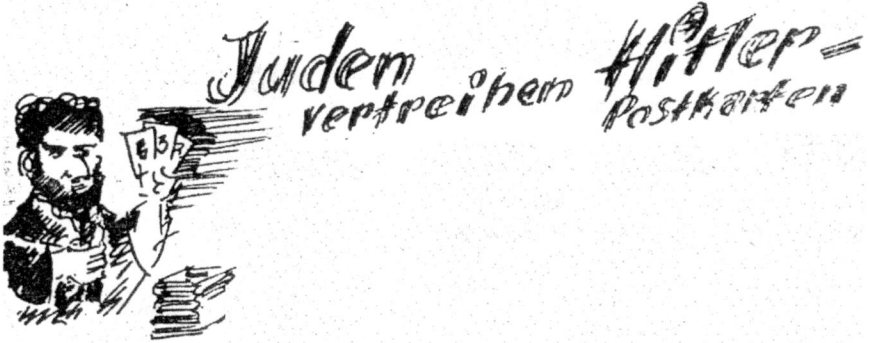

Figure 4.13 "Jews sell Hitler Postcards." *Der Freiheitskämpfer,* no. 2. NSDAP Hauptarchiv, Hoover Institution Microfilm Collection.

was that the Nazis and their conservative allies—conservative allies who were in any case overwhelmingly rejected by the SA as insufficiently radical—were not "really" anti-Semitic and therefore not really "revolutionary." Anti-Semitism functioned in this instance as a mark of authenticity for the true revolutionary, defined in Nazi terms. Here again, the Communists were disputing, at one semiotic remove, the right of the Nazi Party to speak for the stormtroopers.

The class analysis underlying the production of *Das Sprachrohr* came out clearly in the way in which the paper tried to exploit class sensitivities, linking them to broader suspicion of the party. Rank-and-file SA men, it was argued, took it as a given that they would be treated poorly by party bureaucrats in the *Gau* or party offices, especially—it was taken pains to point out—if they appeared dressed in working-class garb. This contempt for the workers in the movement was part of a larger contempt of the party for the SA, as demonstrated by the "feudal" relations between them.[571] A new, successful revo-

Figure 4.14 "Heil Israel!" *Die Sturmfahne* Nr. 11, Jahrgang 1932. Bundesarchiv.

lution of the SA, argued *Das*

Sprachrohr, must come from "the simple SA men in the *Sturms* and the [party] activists in the sections."[572] In an "appeal to the expellees" kicked out in the wake of the Stennes Revolt, *Das Sprachrohr* invoked, in the language of soldierly pathos, the masculine, proletarian self-image of the stormtroopers:

> SA comrades, party comrades! You have been expelled. Yesterday you still belonged to the pride of Hitler, to the best of the Brown Battalions. Yesterday you were still the rough fighters … for the Third Reich. Today you have been kicked out, expelled … separated from comrades with whom only yesterday you marched. Today you are criminals in the eyes of Hitler and his company. *You are expelled from the party and the SA, but you are not expelled from the fight for Germany and its liberation from the yoke of the Young-slavery. Hitler has outlawed you, not the German people. Goebbels has spit on you and thrown garbage on you and not us!*

Appealing to the pride of self-proclaimed revolutionaries, the authors continued: "We activists in the SA and party … call you to work together with us. We see in you not renegades and criminals. For us you are revolutionary freedom fighters who have taken the first step on the path of decision."[573]

These papers represented an attempt at semiotic trickery that tried to blend Nazi and Communist concerns, drawing simultaneously on the very real cultural elements they had in common. Attempting to erase the boundary between the proletarian militancy of Communist supporters on the one hand, and (as it was hoped, the proto-Communist) proletarian militancy of Hitler supporters on the other, they performed identities that made sense to both sides, blurring the distinctions between the radicalism of left and right. The charges in these papers were delivered using language that everyone understood—the language of soldierly virtue and revolutionary honor. Faithful, honest (*ehrliche*) revolutionaries, willing to suffer and die for a cause, were contrasted with greedy and insincere "civilian" party leaders who paid lip service to the revolution while scrambling to position themselves for material benefits. "We would be traitors and cowards," reads a characteristic passage, "if we left you comrades in the lurch and gave you away to the demagogy of our leaders."[574] The gulf between the manly and virtuous "soldiers" and the effeminate and corrupt "civilians" was summed up succinctly in the rhetorical question posed in another paper: "Or is one supposed to deny that there are, in Hamburg, fat bankers in the party?"[575]

Communist *Zersetzungsblätter* attempted to erase distinctions in another way as well, for in employing the same imagery, claims, concepts, and language of openly Communist papers such as *Der Rote Angriff*—which themselves used the language of soldierly militancy and did not shrink from employing anti-Semitic stereotypes—they helped create a sort of transinstitutional "underground press" meant to demonstrate a dovetailing of Nazi and Communist concerns. The significance of this underground press—as a supposed expression of the voice of the rank and file—was amplified by notices in the *official* Communist press, which reported on signs of *Zersetzung* in the Nazi movement as if they were real. *Aufbruch,* for example, gave prominent attention to the papers of the "Nazi opposition." Numerous appeals urged the stormtroopers to follow Scheringer's path to the KPD, and every small sign of their disaffection was reported and exaggerated.[576] *Aufbruch* published internal Nazi memoranda dealing with problems in the SA—gained through intelligence contacts within the Nazi organizations—and used every opportunity to emphasize the growing signs of *Zersetzung* in the NSDAP.[577] Here again, elements of the real were blended together with the fake to reinforce the KPD's claims about the inevitability of socialist revolution. Communist cell activity and the production of *Zersetzungsblätter* were not very successful in terms of provoking mass defections to the KPD, but there does appear to have been a significant degree of dovetailing between Communist and Nazi radicalism at the rank-and-file level. Conan Fischer relates, for example, that members of *Standarte* 76 in Hamburg were taken to task by Nazi officials for singing a slightly altered version of the *Internationale* as a marching song, prompting orders prohibiting the singing of "forbidden songs";[578] and it is this same unit—*Standarte* 76—that was home to the "circle of oppositional SA comrades" that claimed responsibility for publishing *Die Sturmfahne*.[579]

There is, furthermore, evidence that papers such as *Die Sturmfahne* were read with interest by rank-and-file Nazis. Writing during the same period when *Die Sturmfahne* was being published in Hamburg, the police president in Cologne called attention to orders prohibiting the "reading [of] any kind of enemy newspapers," which accompanied the expulsion of numerous individuals from the

Zeitungen der revolutionären SA.-Opposition

Figure 4.15 "Newspapers of the SA Opposition." *Aufbruch*, 2. Jg., Nr. 9, December 1932. Bundesarchiv.

NSDAP and SA. "In the recent period," Nazi leaders in Cologne are quoted as saying, "the KPD has ... again expanded the *Z-schrift* 'Der SA Kamerad' and now publishes *Z-schriften* in the individual city districts. SA leaders have to work immediately against these activities. The papers are to be confiscated, the identity of the disseminators is to be ascertained." Junior SA leaders were called upon to dispute the "lies" contained in these papers at meetings with the rank and file.[580] Even after 1933, the Gestapo reported a good reception of Communist *Zersetzungsblätter* in parts of the SA.[581] This phenomenon does not suggest that Nazi stormtroopers stood ready to embrace Communism but instead signaled the extent to which the claims of the two radical extremes could overlap in the minds of rank-and-file activists. Indeed, the provenance of Communist *Zersetzungsblätter* occasionally seems to have confused not only the KPD's Nazi audience but also the police and even Communist activists themselves. In one case a Communist activist learned through a contact that an entire Hitler Youth unit had been supplied with "Hitler Youth opposition" letters. "The Hitler Youths really believe," he noted with some astonishment, "that the letter comes from an oppositional colleague." Not completely sure himself, he asked parenthetically: "from [our people]?" Even more significant, in terms of blurring the line between the "authentic" and the "fake," was that the provenance of the letter did not even really matter: "In any case," the activist concluded, "the letter is being discussed [by everyone]." The task now was to "carefully verify the mood" of the Hitler Youth and answer the original letter with new letters of Communist origin.[582] If Communist efforts to turn SA activism in an explicitly Communist direction could never be truly successful, bound as they were to founder on the rocks of the SA's visceral hatred for a KPD owing allegiance to Moscow and ruled by "Jewish Marxists," the KPD's efforts to portray a blurring of Communist and Nazi radicalism at the rank-and-file level do not appear to have been entirely created out of whole cloth.[583]

This commonality of interests was a guiding assumption of the strategy of person-to-person agitation pursued by the KPD in the final Weimar years. It is no accident that it was the *Rotfrontkämpferbund* and its successor organization, the KgdF, that were charged with the responsibility not just of combating Nazis in the streets—itself demanding a degree of bloodthirsty élan—but of carrying out the ideological struggle among the stormtroopers. On the very eve of the Nazi seizure of power, the RFB was urging activists to seek out *Reichsbanner* and SA fighters in their pubs and hostels, to carry out personal discussions and hand-deliver *Zersetzungsschriften*.[584] Activists of the KdgF were engaged in this work as well. "Guidelines for discussions with comrades of the SA" instructed militants on how to approach and debate with stormtroopers. "Widespread agitation [in the SA] over the 'treason of the leadership'" was to be exploited in order to carry out "'offensive' discussions with the working [*Werktätigen*] members of the SA." Communists were urged to take account of the special character of the SA: "We know from experience that in political questions the SA is very unclear and poorly informed; therefore present the issues ... as primitively as possible. Link up with their feelings and sensitivities." This political missionary work was the task of every Communist: "Every comrade must be ready to pursue the ideological campaign among the SA and party proletarians with intensified vigor." The weight placed on this activity—and the startling lack of realism behind it—comes out clearly in the tag line: "For us it depends not on the defection of single individuals but the subversion of entire [units]."[585]

This "street-level," person-to-person missionary work was integrated into the larger Communist propaganda apparatus. Stormtroopers were to be urged to create resolutions and declarations of support for the KPD, which activists were then to submit for publication in the Communist press. Questions for discussion were to include: "Is Hitler leading a fight against this system, against [reparations] and the emergency decree?" Reference was to be made to Hitler's positive comments to the foreign press regarding reparations as proof that he was "prepared to be the slave of German and international finance capital." These points were summarized in a propaganda sheet published by the *Kampfbund* for distribution to SA men. The sheet also took up the case of Richard Scheringer—who only days before had been sentenced to a renewed prison term of 2½ years for treason (now for his propaganda on behalf of the KPD)—contrasting his revolutionary martyrdom with Hitler's betrayal. Asking rhetorically why Scheringer had been sentenced to more prison time, the leaflet answered: Because "Scheringer is really an enemy of the system. He is serious about the fight for the social and national liberation of the working people [*Werktätigen Volkes*]." The leaflet invited SA men who agreed with this assessment to join in the real struggle on the side of the KPD.[586] The existence of common concerns in these dialogues was taken as a given. It is clear that Nazi and Communist paramilitary fighters always had their eye upon one another and were influenced by each other.[587] The two sides were familiar in many cases on an individual level, knew each others' symbols, greetings, and songs.[588] Just as the Nazis had their own version of the "Internationale," the RFB had its version of the Nazis' "Horst Wessel Lied" ("make way for the red storm troops").[589] Sentiments like such as the one captured in another of the RFB's marching songs—"We are the front ranks ... we will be liberated when the bourgeois bleed"—could just as easily have come from the SA.[590]

The emphasis on fighting as an end in itself—just one part of a continuity of ideas based not only on a more or less vague anticapitalism and hatred of the system but also on the idea of the revolutionary soldier—was potentially dangerous from the KPD's perspective. Like the NSDAP, the KPD had trouble keeping its fighters in line and worried about their ideological reliability. Only about 50 percent of RFB fighters actually belonged to the party.[591] The KPD expressed concern about the RFB, and RFB leaders struggled in turn with issues of discipline and control.[592] "The man we *don't* need," observed the author of a memorandum for internal RFB use, "is the loudmouth who [brags] in every pub about 'the actions he carried out,' who always complains that one must 'do something,' but who at the decisive moment always has some kind of excuse."[593] In ideological training instituted for the illegal RFB in the fall of 1930, the Communist leadership was chagrined to discover—much like the leaders of the SA's *Reichsführerschule*—that material on the "Foundations of the Class Struggle" and the "Materialist and Idealist Worldview" produced far less interest among the students than military-political instruction, weapons training, and jujitsu.[594] RFB fighters were instructed to demonstrate through "iron discipline" that they were "the truest soldiers of the revolution, of socialism, of the party, and of the Soviet Union," but the reality is that those most interested in fighting were often those least interested in ideological niceties.[595] Indeed, the potential for this changing of sides was so openly accepted that it was enshrined in the RFB's version of the Nazi "Horst Wessel Lied": "And should we see each other once again, be it in Berlin or on a Baltic Sea beach, if you've become a Nazi pig, I'll proudly pass you by."[596]

Conclusion

Communist subversive work in the SA was the ultimate performance. By actually "becoming" SA men, Communist operatives bore in the very bodies and uniforms the "communization" of the SA they hoped to bring about. Yet the potential for defections to the NSDAP was increased, rather than decreased, by the policy of infiltration and publication of *Zersetzungsblätter*.[597] This chimerical attempt to forge a united front with Nazi proletarians "from below" reached its ultimate expression in the creation of so-called *Scheringer Staffeln* from units of the banned *Rotfrontkämpferbund*, whose members sported Soviet armbands with their SA uniforms.[598] But this did not fuel significant defections from the NSDAP to the KPD.[599] To be sure, as we have seen, the common fund of symbols with which they played meant that such activity raised interest in the SA. But when SA men and other Nazis did sometimes defect to the KPD, it was usually an act of protest against the embourgeoisement of the Nazi movement rather than a sign of a conversion to Marxism-Leninism.[600] The campaign built around Richard Scheringer neither provoked a mass defection from the SA nor succeeded in building a significant bridge between the militarist bourgeoisie and the KPD.[601] The KPD's nationalist rhetoric was less convincing to potential converts from the right than the Nazis' social revolutionary rhetoric was to those from the left, and Communist success in infiltrating and building cells within the Nazi mass organizations came nowhere close to what the KPD hoped for or would have needed to make its strategy work.[602] The illusion, shared by Scheringer and others, that the SA was a "valuable force," a hopeful symbol for Germany's future—an illusion possible in the first place only for those blinded by militarist fantasies and willing to ignore the fundamental chauvinism and racism of the Nazis—was brutally shattered in January 1933, when the stormtroopers unleashed by Hitler's victory turned their fury not on the capitalists but on the organizations of the working class.

The KPD's strategy of semiotic trickery had several causes.[603] It was, in the first instance, the product of an ends-justify-the-means approach to politics; anything—the repetition of Nazi charges against the Jews, promises of a future war against the Western powers—was allowed if it furthered the ultimate goal of revolution. Second, it was a direct outgrowth of the thinking behind the Social Fascism strategy; as Franz Borkenau pointed out, if the SPD was fascist, and the workers organized by the SPD were under the control of fascists, and if these misled workers needed to be won away from their fascist leaders, then there was no reason not to speak for Nazi fascists as well.[604] Third, at a more fundamental level, the strategy was an outgrowth of the Communist need to achieve a total voice: the *Zersetzungsschriften* produced by the KPD were part of the blanketing of written propaganda designed to show that everyone—even the police, the *Reichsbanner,* and the Nazis—all were beginning to come around to what they *must,* eventually, realize: that the party was right in its analysis of the situation and justified in its claims to lead the working classes (and, increasingly, the middle classes as well). In this sense, the campaign was part of a totalizing approach to politics that tried to inhabit every space in society. But the KPD could not accomplish this in Germany the way Communists were able to in the USSR or in Eastern Europe after 1945. A total "voice" could only be achieved by total control of the repressive powers of the state. And after 30 January 1933, it was National Socialism, and not Communism, that gained the opportunity to shape and portray the nature of the revolution.

The other part of the KPD's United Front from Below strategy, that aimed at the Social Democratic workers, had scarcely more chance of success, for most potential converts were repelled when the meaning of "alliance" with the KPD became clear. There was, however, very significant support for the fight against fascism on the part of the German working class. The *Kampfbund gegen den Faschismus,* for example, began quite promisingly. Police authorities in Westphalia noted, for example, that while the *Rotenmassenselbstschutz* was too weak to bother banning, the KGF was quite another matter. According to the police, the KgdF carried on a "lively political existence" in the province. Its meetings were strongly attended, and its propaganda effect—"in the sense of the United Front tactic"—was considerable.[605] On the other hand, police authorities in Berlin estimated that less than a year after its founding, the KgdF possessed approximately one hundred thousand members in Germany as a whole. Only about half that number paid dues. The organization was somewhat weaker in Berlin than in the provinces, and in the judgment of the police, the KgdF had largely failed to achieve its goal of breaking into the ranks of the "unorganized" working class. "The ideological mass struggle against fascism" remained weak "because a large portion of the members know neither the program of the Communist International or the goals of the KPD, and possess only nebulous and weak ideas of Socialism, Communism, and the Five-Year Plan of the Soviet Union."[606] This might be taken as evidence of a lack of ideological acumen on the part of militants, but it might also be seen as evidence that many workers found the specific obsessions of the KPD irrelevant to the fight against the Nazis.

The Nazi "seizure of power," affected in the wake of Hitler's appointment as Reich Chancellor on 30 January 1933, might have been thought to have put a stop to this sort of intermixing of signs, identity, and personnel characteristic of the late Weimar Republic. Indeed, the opposite is the case, for the performative politics of the Weimar Republic were now set to go into high gear. Even in the face of mass anti-Communist violence and with their enemies, the Nazis, holding the levers of power, the KPD continued in its efforts to infiltrate the Nazi organizations, and indeed, the blurring of identities in some ways reached its ultimate expression in the first year and a half of the Nazi regime. The concept of the Beefsteak—"brown on the outside, red on the inside"—is a term not of the Weimar Republic proper, but as will be seen in the next chapter, of the transitional period between democracy and dictatorship in the spring and summer of 1933. The unfolding of this dynamic occurred, however, in a very different way than had been imagined by Communist strategists.

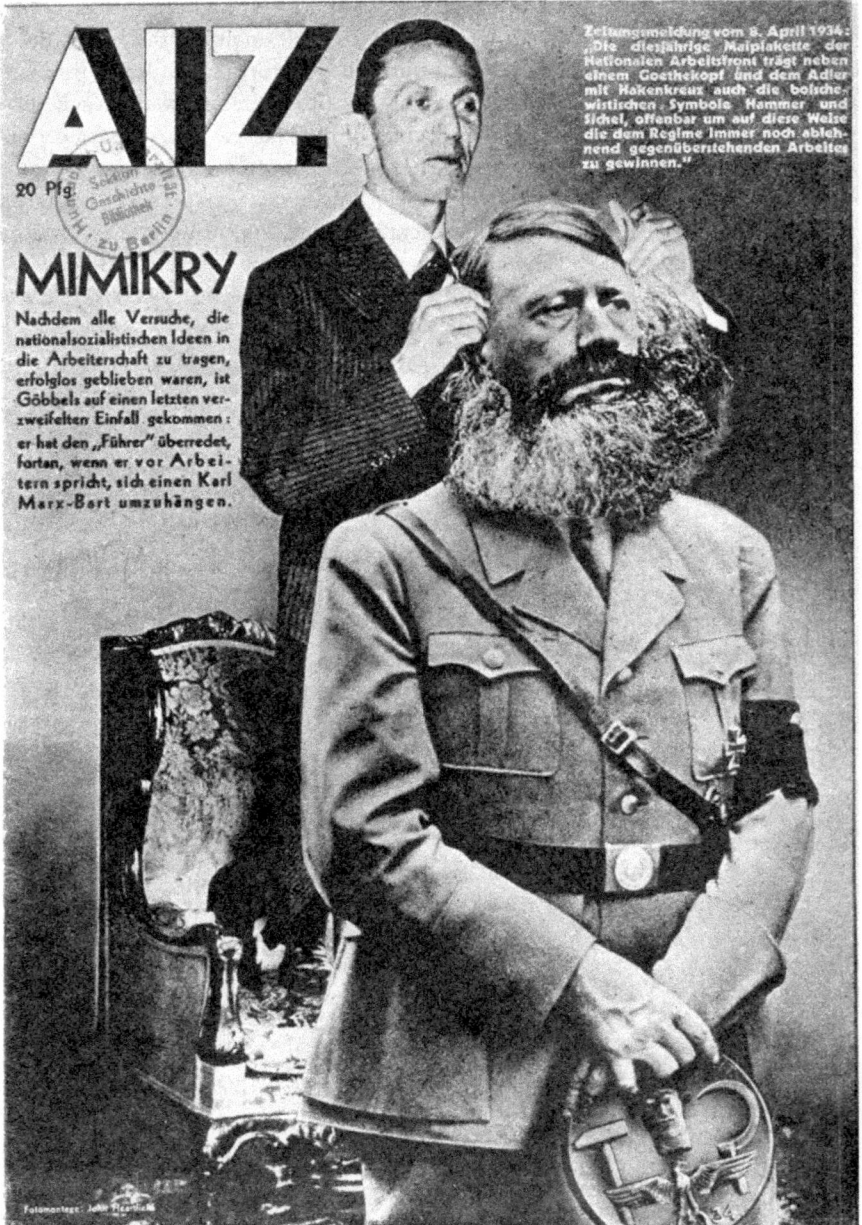

Figure 5.1 "Mimikry," *AIZ*, May 1934. Bundesarchiv.

Chapter 5

BETWEEN *GLEICHSCHALTUNG* AND REVOLUTION

*I*n the summer of 1935, as part of the Germany-wide "Reich Athletic Competition," citizens in the state of Schleswig-Holstein witnessed the following spectacle:

> On the first Sunday of August propaganda performances and maneuvers took place in a number of cities. They are supposed to reawaken the old mood of the "time of struggle." In Kiel, SA men drove through the streets in trucks bearing ... inscriptions against the Jews ... and the Reaction. One [truck] carried a straw puppet hanging on a gallows, accompanied by a placard with the motto: "The gallows for Jews and the Reaction, wherever you hide we'll soon find you."607

Other trucks bore slogans such as "Whether black or red, death to all enemies," and "We are fighting against Jewry and Rome."608 Bizarre tableau were enacted in the streets of towns around Germany. "In Schmiedeberg (in Silesia)," reported informants of the Social Democratic exile organization, the Sopade, "something completely out of the ordinary was presented on Sunday, 18 August." A notice appeared in the town paper a week earlier with the announcement: "Reich competition of the SA. On Sunday at 11 a.m. in front of the Rathaus, *Sturm* 4 R 48 Schmiedeberg passes judgment on a criminal against the state." On the appointed day, a large crowd gathered to watch the spectacle. The Sopade agent gave the setup: "A Nazi newspaper seller has been attacked by a Marxist mob. In the ensuing melee, the Marxists set up a barricade. The SA has the task of restoring order." The action unfolded as follows: "The barricades were set up on the

122 | *Weimar Radicals*

lead car [of the parade]. The SA drove up in a truck. The barricades were stormed with flags flying. … One of the Marxist criminals was seized and immediately condemned."[609] A procession was staged in Hamburg in front of the house of a long-arrested Communist: "The criminal (a straw puppet) was hanged and then drawn up to the roof. An SA man then appeared in the window and cut the rope, so that the puppet fell to the pavement. The 'condemned' was then bound to the radiator of a truck and driven around the city and surrounding areas." Afterward, an SA leader gave a speech praising the stormtroopers for the splendid way in which they had done their duty, noting that their demonstration had shown that "the old fighting spirit of the SA" was still alive and well. Scenes like these were repeated all over Germany during the days of the "Reich Competition." "Barricades" were stormed in a number of cities.[610] In the Neukölln district of Berlin, "a truck full of SA men dressed as Communists drove through the streets. The SA-Communists sang the *Internationale* and at intervals shouted 'Red Front!' Fifty yards behind them came another truck full of SA men with swastika flags. This procession was supposed to demonstrate to the population how it was before, and how it is now."[611] In at least one instance, living victims were employed in these bizarre charades. "On Sunday, 25 August," noted a Sopade report,

> the Lausitz SA arranged a "propaganda parade" through town and country. One of the trucks carried a cage containing a Jew and a Marxist through the streets. Behind the Marxist and the Jew stood an SA man holding a revolver in firing position. A second vehicle full of SA men explained the meaning of the procession via megaphone. Fortunately, the majority of the population turned away from this atrocious display.[612]

Such was the way in which National Socialism chose to represent its version of the revolution, choreographing the living bodies of its followers (and in at least one case, its victims) into a dance of meaning designed to channel revolutionary energies into purely formal spectacle. The ideological content of the competition materials reinforces the point. Correct orientation was "not just a matter of book knowledge" but of "inner and outer attitude. … Our inner attitude is to be understood as: comradeship, reliability, and willingness for self-sacrifice. Our outer attitude [is to be displayed in] the appearance of our formations, our readiness for action, and order in our private and public life." The set of questions published for stormtroopers preparing for the ideological competition reveals the extent to which the Nazis attempted to place the cult of the *Führer* above everything else. Questions for consideration—all fifty-seven of which contained the word "*Führer*"—included: "When was the *Führer* born?" "Where was the *Führer* born?" "What was the occupation of the *Führer*'s father?" "Which blow of fate hit the Führer the hardest?" "Why did the *Führer* not become an artist?"[613] The caricature of the "National Socialist revolution" presented in the *Reichswettkampf* mythologized the activism of the *Kampfzeit* (time of struggle), portraying a victorious fight against the left that, as Gerhard Paul has pointed out, did not actually take place until after 1933, when the NSDAP had all the powers of the state at its disposal.[614] More importantly, it presented the revolution as a defensive struggle against internal enemies, eliding the social aspirations that had been a part of National Socialism's appeal. If this fictive version of the National Socialist revolution suggests that the meaning of the revolution had been controlled, the real version of the revolution was much more complicated; indeed, it saw the debates of the Weimar Republic—about nationalism, socialism, and revolution—continue to be played out.

"The NSDAP has seized the entire initiative"

Like other National Socialist euphemisms, the term *Gleichschaltung* ("coordination" or "synchronization") bears a heavy weight of meaning.[615] On a practical level it refers to Nazism's assault on the centers of political and administrative independence in Germany during the opening phase of the regime—the destruction of the Weimar party system, the purge of the civil service, the centralization of state authority at the expense of the *Länder,* and the co-optation of the trade unions. More broadly, *Gleichschaltung* represented the attempted Nazification of all aspects of German culture and society. The journalist Ernst Erich Noth, a keen observer of the process, dubbed these two aspects of *Gleichschaltung* the "organizational-technical" and the "ideological-mythical."[616] The first, accomplished by a combination of legal measures, intimidation, and violence, went largely unchallenged; the second presented somewhat greater difficulties. Noth employed the metaphor of "digestion" to describe the process; he argued that the difficulties of the NSDAP—more profound than the stage-managed totalism of its propaganda let on—were a result of its excessive appetite: the more National Socialism succeeded in swallowing up its opponents of both left and right, the more it enfolded within itself elements inclined to criticism and rebellion.[617] *Gleichschaltung,* for Noth, entailed the destruction of those revolutionary elements that had stood in the zone of conflict between the extremes of left and right, by which he meant those that had resisted incorporation into the totalizing performances of Communism and National Socialism, but this is only partially correct; the process was not merely one of destruction but of subsumation, in which the distinctive radicalism of these elements flowed into and helped fuel the dynamism of National Socialism.[618] It was not just those who opposed National Socialism who presented the problem—not merely the "Black Marxists" with whom, as will be seen, the regime was obsessed—but those who, excited by the idea of the National Socialist revolution, had their own ideas about what it meant.

Where Nazism's opponents and fellow travelers were concerned, *Gleichschaltung* resembled nothing more than a massive "Flucht nach vorn"—a "flight to the front" in German military parlance—aimed at winning temporary safety and gaining tactical initiative. From the *Völkisch* splinter groups to the large paramilitary *Wehrverbände;* from the *Bündisch* youth to the National Revolutionaries; from the followers of Otto Strasser to the underground activists of the KPD; all who had opposed the Weimar Republic while resisting or holding themselves aloof from National Socialism now found themselves forced to react to National Socialism's totalizing demands. "The NSDAP," as *Bündisch* leader Eberhard Koebel resignedly put it, "has seized the entire initiative."[619] Difficult decisions now had to be made about the extent to which it was desirable or possible to work around or within the mass organizations of National Socialism. The decision to work from within—one, as we have seen, already made by Communists and others before 30 January 1933—was justified in part by the belief in the ephemeral nature of the Nazi regime. It was not just the notoriously myopic KPD that saw the "Nazi revolution" as a passing phase; the belief that Hitler would make a quick exit was general. This is one reason why, during the early phase of the regime, Communists and others could, despite the atmosphere of violence and intimidation, continue to work toward the goals they had pursued before 30 January 1933. The period up to the so-called Night of the Long Knives of 30 June–2 July 1934, if not for some time afterward, represented not just the consolidation phase of the Third Reich but the end phase of a "Long Weimar Republic" in which the battle over meaning characteristic of the Weimar continued. The playing field was no longer level, however, for what Hitler received alongside his chancellorship was not just access to the levers of power in Germany but also the opportunity to settle, once and for all, the questions—about the meaning of "socialism," of "revolution," and of the relationship of these two to the "nation"—that had characterized radical politics in the Weimar Republic and that, initially at least, seemed to remain open. One of the most fascinating, if little examined, aspects of *Gleichschaltung* is that its peculiar dynamism came not just from those who welcomed National Socialism but from those who opposed it. Indeed, the hopes of many Nazis for a "second revolution"—a demand associated especially with the SA—dovetailed with the revolutionary aspirations of those, such as the Communists, who believed that "Nazi Germany" was but a prelude to "Soviet Germany," and many activists of the Youth Movement, who came to believe that their ideal of a *Volksgemeinschaft* combining nationalism and socialism might yet be realized through the pressure of the ranks in the National Socialist mass organizations.[620]

When Hitler was named Reich Chancellor on 30 January 1933, at the head of a conservative coalition of "national concentration," he was only one in a series of (apparently temporary) chancellors appointed by the aging president Paul von Hindenburg. Only two Nazis held cabinet posts: Wilhelm Frick (Minister of the Interior) and Hermann Göring (initially Minister without Portfolio, subsequently acting Prussian Minister of the Interior);[621] Hitler ruled at Hindenburg's pleasure, and his powers were far from absolute. Franz von Papen's famous quip regarding Hitler—"we have hired him"—expressed well the mistaken optimism of the conservatives. The steps by which National Socialism gained its ascendancy—among them the state of emergency in the wake of the Reichstag fire of 27 February 1933, and the Enabling Act following the Reichstag elections of 5 March; the intimidation of opponents both external and internal culminating in the Night of the Long Knives; and, after the death of Hindenburg in August of that year, Hitler's assumption of the combined powers of president and chancellor—are well known. Yet Nazism's success in clearing space for the "National Socialist Revolution" left open the question of what type of revolution this would be. Hitler's appointment released the dammed-up forces of Nazi radicalism, which expressed themselves in an orgy of violence against enemies real and perceived. The chief targets of this violence were the Marxist parties, above all the KPD. "No Red Front man who had ever beaten or made fun of an SA man during the 'time of struggle,' observed Rudolf Diels, first head of the Gestapo, "now escaped the personal vengeance of the victorious 'Browns.'"[622] Special brutality was reserved for stormtroopers who had defected to the KPD before 1933.[623] The wave of terror escalated dramatically in the wake of the *Reichstag* Fire of 27 February 1933. Four thousand Communists and other alleged opponents of the regime were arrested over the night of 27–28 February 1933, when Communist premises were raided and the party's presses closed.[624] President Hindenburg signed an emergency decree on the 28th granting extensive powers of repression to the new state. Now with the complete backing of the state authorities, the stormtroopers unleashed a reign of terror against Communists, Social Democrats, and other perceived enemies, settling old scores and giving free reign to their pent-up rage and frustration. Impromptu jails were set up where SA men beat and tortured their victims. There were at least 150 of these so-called wild SA concentration camps in Berlin alone.[625]

The violent wave of the first months of 1933 was only the tip of the iceberg of a spontaneous outburst of popular radicalism.[626] Aimed in the first instance against the organizations and institutions of the working class (and targeting, where regionally appropriate, Catholic organizations and youth groups), this uprising was, simultaneously, fueled by a fascist rank and file motivated by a vaguely defined but powerful concept of a revolutionary "national socialism," the content of which was both unclear and evolving. The widespread nature of the revolutionary hopes invested in National Socialism was noted by a number of contemporaries. Ernst Erich Noth emphasized it,[627] as did the KPD's propaganda expert, Willi Münzenberg, who argued that the Nazis had been forced to emphasize their social-revolutionary intentions by pressure from below.[628] Herbert Crüger, one of the followers of Otto Strasser who went over to the KPD in 1931, spent the early months of the regime in a National Socialist student home in Berlin, where he was greatly impressed by the atmosphere of revolutionary excitement. The students there, members of the National Socialist German Student Association (NSDStB), some of whom Crüger knew from his Hitler Youth days, were obsessed, he wrote, "with ideas of an egalitarian *Volksgemeinschaft*, … a socialism in which the concept 'German' occupied a central position."[629] The French anarcho-Marxist Daniel Guérin, traveling in Germany during the early months of the regime, detected the same attitudes. Struck by the extent to which everyday Germans he met—on the road, in the youth hostels, at meetings—invested social revolutionary hopes in the NSDAP, Guérin was shocked and frustrated by the way in which left-wing demands had become intertwined with the ethnic nationalism of the Nazis. He cites the example of a young worker, a Communist with a deep emotional attachment to Ernst Thälmann, who complained bitterly to him of the "betrayal" of the two working-class parties in the Weimar Republic. They "should have forged unity in action," he said, "[but they] didn't want to." He went on: "We'll have to make our revolution alone. While waiting for the International to exist, we have to think about the present. First of all, to liberate ourselves from the *Diktat* of Versailles, to free our oppressed comrades in Silesia, in the Saarland, in Austria, in the Sudetenland, in Memel and Danzig ... to found a German workers' state!"[630] Another young worker announced to Guérin that he had quit the NSDAP, explaining:

> I'm not satisfied. It's no longer a revolutionary party; it hasn't got any teeth. I want *real socialism*. For fourteen years, the Social Democratic party had the chance to build it, but what did it do about it? I'm not a Communist, because I'm a German first and I don't want to be treated like a Russian *moujik*, but I respect the Communists and feel closer to them than the rest. ... So long as they all betray socialism, I will remain without a party.[631]

"There are thousands like him," wrote Guérin, "mixing up their confused demands for socialism with a fanatical sentiment born of national humiliation. And it is more so among the youth than the adults." A speech witnessed by Guérin in a working-class dance hall in Leipzig was particularly revealing. "Our Revolution, *Volksgenossen*, has only begun," proclaimed a local party activist. "We haven't yet attained any of our goals. There's talk of a national government, of a national awakening. ... What's all that about? It's the *Socialist* part of our program that matters. ... We have now but one enemy to vanquish: the bourgeoisie."[632]

Hopes and expectations like these rather quickly began to be referred to under the rubric of the Second Revolution, a term that "came to stand for the deeply ingrained feelings in the party of anticapitalism, anticonservatism, and general radicalism."[633] These hopes carried with them the potential for great disappointment, a potential increased by the transformation of National Socialism into a mass movement.[634] Charges about the embourgeoisement of the movement, which had been current before 1933, became even more pronounced as bandwagon jumpers—derisively labeled *Märzgefallene* by Joseph Goebbels—crowded into the NSDAP. Simultaneously, the rise of what Ernst Erich Noth called a "new type of *Bonzen*"—even hardier and more ubiquitous than the old—gave rise to a growing anger.[635] The picture of creeping discontent sketched out by Noth is confirmed by reports from the intelligence services of the underground KPD, the exiled SPD, and the NSDAP itself. Characteristic was the comment of an SS *Sturmführer* at a meeting in Krefeld in June 1934, recorded by a Communist agent: "Hitler must call for struggle against the *Bonzen*, then we will be with him. If he doesn't do it, then he'll be buried together with the other *Bonzen*. We must conquer the old Communists for our side; they are guys that you can really start something with. The washerwomen who are coming over to us now aren't worth a penny." He concluded by calling for Germany to follow the example of the Soviet Union: "In Russia it is good. Everything there goes from the bottom up, not the way it is here where everything comes down from the *Bonzen*. In Germany we have to get rid of the *Bonzen* and create a Reich that will really show Russia something."[636] An SA man in Cologne announced to a group of SA and SS men, "We were promised that twenty-four hours after we were in power, there would be no more department stores or banks. Now you don't hear anything about it."[637] Another threatened, "It's not going to last much longer, then the whole splendor is going to be over. My comrades say it, too; we've been swindled. Hitler doesn't attack capital like he promised; therefore we will have to move against him."[638] Attitudes like these prompted a Communist spy to note in April 1934: "The expectations that the SA men had attached to the seizure of power, and which have not been fulfilled, have allowed a very violent mood of opposition to come out among the old SA men."[639] Agents of the SA's own intelligence service detected similar attitudes. Typical were the comments of one SA man who said, "Now as before, the capitalists have the power, and people such as Thyssen, Krupp, and so on, remain war profiteers, even if they join the NSDAP en masse. In one and a half years, the *Verbonzung* [bigwigification] in the party and in the government has taken on the same form that it had in the Weimar state." Of Göring and other Nazi leaders he concluded, "I would take part in a Communist uprising myself, just to be able to do away with [these] people."[640]

This picture of simmering discontent is confirmed by the reports of the Sopade, the intelligence agency of the exiled SPD. "The proletarian SA men ... ," noted a report in early summer 1934, "really believed that with the carrying out of the Second Revolution, the large banks and the princes of the stock exchange, heavy industry and the department stores, would be nationalized."[641] Other reports emphasized the role played by such attitudes in ongoing SA violence. Noted one:

> The revolt of the SA on May 1 [1934] in Bremen, the fight ... against the police and the eventual occupation of the Brown House ... was accompanied by great tumult on the streets. Between seven and eight o'clock in the evening, the rebellious SA formations moved through the streets and stormed the ... department store Karstadt. Several large display windows were smashed, [and] the SA men raised fifteen giant swastika and black, white, and red flags ... from the roof. ... The police advanced against the Nazi revolutionaries [and] there was much brawling and many arrests.[642]

Assaults like this on "capital" were accompanied by violence against reactionaries accused of watering down the movement. Earlier on the day of the Bremen Karstadt attack, SA and SS men became involved in a raging battle with members of the *Stahlhelm*, the *Wehrwolf*, and the *Jungdo*, leading to thirty arrests.[643] A few weeks later, members of the Hitler Youth attacked the motorcade of Hitler's labor minister, Franz Seldte of the *Stahlhelm*. A British journalist described the incident:

> A regiment of Hitler Youth lads yesterday ambushed Major Seldte, leader of the German Steel Helmets, and Minister of Labour in the Nazi cabinet, attacked him with sticks, fired

revolvers, and reluctantly let him escape with his life. This extraordinary incident is the climax of months of hostility between the Nazi Storm troops and Hitler Youths—who consider the Nazi revolution has by no means gone far enough—and their former allies, the Steel Helmets, who are hated as reactionaries, monarchists, and Junkers. ... The seriousness of the affair is evident from the fact that all news of it is withheld from the public. Major Seldte was returning from a meeting which he had addressed near Magdeburg when his car was held up by a Hitler Youth regiment 200 strong. Insults were shouted at him ... and furious young Nazis rushed at him with upraised sticks.

The cause of this event, he continued, was anger over Seldte's reference

to the Nazi revolution as a "phenomenon of puberty." Since then the youth of Germany have been after Major Seldte's blood. Their publicity chief, Herr Staebe, has been rushing from one end of the country to the other, addressing mass meetings of Hitler Youth and calling for vengeance. "Strike the reactionaries wherever you find them," he cried yesterday, in a speech at Hannover. The Hitler Youth shouted with applause and carried Staebe triumphantly on their shoulders through the streets.[644]

Such events were by no means isolated. The Sopade noted in June 1934: "There exist reports from various parts of the country about fighting between SA men, between the SA and the SS, between the SA and the *Stahlhelm,* between the SA and the Labor Service, the SA and the army, etc., etc."[645] A French journalist estimated in June 1934 that there had been at least sixty SA revolts in the preceding three months.[646]

"Our socialism...is the exact opposite of Marxism"

Nazi authorities were understandably nervous about the Pandora's box of radicalism they had helped open. Dangerous expressions of radicalism were blamed on the influence of "Black Marxists" working within the NSDAP, a problem exacerbated by the integration of the working classes into the mass organizations of the regime. Officials in Hannover noted in April 1934 that the

indiscriminate admission of workers into the NSBO and SA as well as other organizations has made the agitation of the KPD ... easier, and the (work) of official agencies more difficult. Not only can Communist slogans be brought directly [into the organizations] under the pretense of membership in the NSBO and the SA, but the Communists have even succeeded occasionally in influencing entire NSBO staffs so that Communist demands come—unknowingly or purposefully—to be supported by the NSBO functionaries.

Factory owners were complaining, the report went on, that

functionaries of the NSBO or members of the SA not only demand special rights that disrupt the factory, but some of them make demands that can presumably be traced back to Communist influence. In very many cases office holders [in the factory councils] are confirmed who only a year ago were still fanatical opponents of the present system. These are exactly the people who have become ... extraordinarily arrogant ... and ... demand a revolutionary renewal, or they are, after the Communist slogan "red on the inside, brown on the outside," the best pioneers for the KPD.[647]

Worries like these were based partly on imagination, partly on essentializing ideas about the permanence of class convictions.[648] But they were also based, as we have seen, on a recognition of the potential for a dovetailing of Nazi and anti-Nazi radicalism.

Such fears were fueled especially by the dramatic growth of the SA, which expanded from a number of some 400,000 in 1932 to more than 2 million in the first few months of 1933.[649] The doors to SA membership were more or less thrown open in June 1933, and the SA increased further in size with the incorporation of the *Stahlhelm* into SA Reserve I in November.[650] By the beginning of 1934 there were some 2,950,000 men enrolled in the SA.[651] Nazi authorities took a number of measures to police the radicalism of the rank and file. At the beginning of 1933 Hitler prescribed "sharpest surveillance, cool treatment" for those "radical elements [in the SA] that because of their social origins are easily inclined to Marxism." Hitler's order further stipulated that nonproletarian SA men were to be protected from comrades still under the influence of Marxism, if necessary by shipping the latter off to work programs in the countryside.[652] The head of the Berlin SA, Karl Ernst, established a sort of secret police within the SA, "Department IE," which had the task not only of undertaking special missions against Jewish intellectuals and others targeted for revenge or extortion but also of catching Communist infiltrators among the stormtroopers.[653] The SA also established throughout the Reich its own *Feldpolizei* (field police), which had the task of surveilling both SA and party members.[654] Worry about the orientation of new SA men was reflected in orders stipulating a six-month probationary period for new recruits established in the summer of 1933.[655] A few months later, Hitler ordered local SA leaders to conduct house searches of all stormtroopers who joined the SA after 30 January 1933.[656]

At the beginning of 1934, the Gestapo began to observe and collect material on the SA. Observing the SA was one of the first tasks accorded to the SS security service, the *Sicherheitsdienst* (SD). The man responsible for the reorganization of the SD in southern Germany, Dr. Werner Best, oversaw the creation of a special department within the SD for this purpose.[657] The overall effect of these controls was limited, and they were far outweighed in their effect by the massive growth of the SA.[658] Best later argued, in justifying the strike against the SA leadership in June 1934, that "the admission of millions of former Marxists, the unclear proclamation of 'socialist' goals, [and] the phrases of the 'Second Revolution'" could have given rise to a sort of "Brown Bolshevism."[659] Best made these comments in postwar West Germany, where they would have resonated with official anti-Communism. Yet there seems little reason to doubt that they accurately reflect the concerns of the time. Röhm warned that the revolution would be carried through with the *Spiesser*, "or if needs be, against them," and as we have seen, there is much evidence that his demands for a Second Revolution—understood as a call for a necessary "socialist" revolution to follow the national revolution of early 1933—resonated with those of the rank and file.[660] Even during the wave of terror against the left in the first months of 1933, stormtroopers in Breslau had to be reminded by their commanding officer that they were forbidden to debate with Marxists. The stormtroopers were urged rather to convince them that "Marxism is played out in Germany."[661]

Röhm's murder in the Night of the Long Knives was, in the first instance, a product of institutional-political power struggles, and above all a product of Hitler's fear of alienating the army leadership threatened by Ernst Röhm's demands to use the SA as the basis of a revolutionary army. It was also, however, the product of real fears brought on by the success of *Gleichschaltung*, of the knowledge that enemies really were at work, that Hitler supporters expected promises to be fulfilled, and that as a result, enemy agitators had something substantial to work with. Above all, as Gerhard Paul has argued, it was a product of the need to control meaning.[662] The Night of the Long Knives was important because it cleared the way for the Nazis to define the National Socialist revolution. Just as the party used violence against the left to eliminate leftist voices, it used violence against its own movement to eliminate those voices. Violence and performance were two sides of the same coin. It was only after the Night of the Long Knives, as Gerhard Paul has argued, that National Socialism could present its "theater spectacle" without interruption. The continued radicalism of National Socialist militants, especially violent disturbances involving the SA, were a threat to the creation of this performance, and it was to eliminate this threat, Paul argues, that the SA was tamed by the regime. June 30, in other words, cleared the way so that the bodies of National Socialism's followers could be choreographed into spectacles such as the propaganda parades of the *Reichswettkampf* with which we began this chapter.

Police measures aimed at controlling indiscipline that threatened the propaganda spectacle of National Socialism were, however, only a small part of the disciplinary project associated with *Gleichschaltung*. Alongside these now came an emphasis on aspects of Nazi ideology that had remained more or less in the background during the *Kampfzeit*.[663] Nazi leaders called for discipline repeatedly over the course of 1933–34, and each of these calls was subtly linked with attempts to direct the activism of the stormtroopers. Especially important was the attempt to link SA radicalism with the goals of the state, to decrease the impetus of action from below and reinforce the importance of central direction from above. On 10 May, during the SA's reign of terror against Nazi enemies in the wake of the Reichstag fire, Hitler expressed his concern in a speech to the SA and SS. "The national government has executive power in its hands," he noted, and "the further carrying out of the National Revolution must therefore be systematic and directed from above." Leaving no uncertainty about the direction the revolution must take, Hitler continued, "You must, my comrades, take care that the National Revolution of 1933 will not go down in history as something comparable to the Revolution of the ... Spartacists in the year 1918. Don't let your-selves ... be torn away from our slogan! It is: The destruction of Marxism." Hitler warned of "conscience-less individuals, principally Communist spies, [who] are attempting through individual actions to compromise" the position of the party. "In particular," he continued,

> attempts are being made, by molesting visitors in cars with foreign pennants, to bring the party, and by extension Germany, into conflict with foreign countries. SA and SS men! You must yourselves immediately regulate such individuals and call them to account. You must ... immediately give them over to the police, no matter who they say they are. [664]

Joseph Goebbels employed a similar tactic in a speech to the SA in Leipzig on 15 May. Referring to the SA as the "battalions of discipline," Goebbels tried to lay the problems not on the Communists but on the bourgeois latecomers to the movement. Playing on the SA's hatred of the bourgeoisie by blaming the so-called *Märzgefallene,* Goebbels noted that the radicalism of people who had been in the movement for only two or three months was not the radicalism of true revolutionaries but of "overexcited *Spießbürger.*" Making sure that he was not misunderstood, Goebbels continued: "We know very well the distinction between party comrades who came to us before 30 January, and those who came to us after 30 January. To come to us beforehand was difficult; to stay away from us afterward was also difficult."[665]

Like Hitler's attempt to blame excessive SA activism on Communist infil-trators, Goebbels's attack on the *Spiesser* entering the movement was aimed at strengthening the connection between the SA and the party by blaming sources of tension on outsiders. Simultaneously, it represented an attempt to direct the anger of the SA into a dead end. The goal of enforcing discipline in the SA, of which this strategy was a part, was linked, at the same time, with the attempt to define the revolution in ways that both served a useful political purpose and rein-forced the authority of the Nazi leadership. The connection between public order and the carrying forward of the revolution was explicitly drawn by Goebbels in his speech before the Leipzig SA. "The legality that we are practicing today," he noted, "is something completely different than the legality of Müller and Stre-semann and Brüning. We are revolutionary legalists, or put another way, legal revolutionaries."[666] By emphasizing Nazism's break with the democratic past and drawing an explicit connection between seemingly antagonistic aims ("revolu-tion" and "legality"), Goebbels attempted to reinforce the revolutionary credibil-ity of the NSDAP while simultaneously urging restraint on the party's militants.

A key component of the Nazi effort to shape and define the revolution was the ideological offensive against Marxism. Nazism, and not Marxism, was to be sold as the legitimate vehicle of the German revolution. In his very first public speech as Reich Chancellor, Hitler blamed Marxism for all the negative developments that had afflicted the German people since 1918. Promising to never deviate in his struggle to eradicate the parties and ideology of the class struggle, he posed the choice in stark terms: "Either Marxism or the German people."[667] In a proclamation for the 1 May 1933, proclaimed by the Nazis as the Day of German Labor, Goebbels pronounced the death of Marxism: "Marxism lies smashed on the ground. The organizations of the class struggle are beaten. We have not led the fight against the culture-threatening danger of Bolshevism for reactionary, antipopular, or antiworker reasons. German Marxism must die, so that a path toward freedom can be opened up for German labor."[668]

Before an assembly of the Berlin NSBO on 21 May, Goebbels argued that Nazism, not Marxism, was the bearer of working-class militancy in Germany, noting that the Nazi revolution was, in the truest sense of the word, a workers' revolution. Alluding to the fact that enemy forces were operating within the movement, and linking their defeat to the carrying out of the "real revolution," Goebbels continued: "Don't let the movement be adulterated! Don't allow a camouflaged Commune or a hidden bourgeoisie to enter the movement. The movement is revolutionary and must remain revolutionary!"[669] The character of this revolution was still in doubt, but now the Nazi leadership was in a position to monopolize the way in which it was defined. Socialism was to be created not by Marxist class war, not by undisciplined radicalism flying off in every direction, but by top down, centrally directed leadership.

Speaking before an assembly of the "Young People for German Socialism" in December 1933, Goebbels assured his audience that Nazism had not simply used "socialism" as a catchphrase in order to achieve power: "Socialism is not just an over-and-done-with affair, not just a … parade horse that we rode while fighting for power, and from which we are now going to dismount because we've come into power. Socialism is a conviction that the people have to fulfill, that doesn't have anything to do with bourgeois prejudices." Making sure that his young audience did not misunderstand the form that Nazi socialism was going to take, Goebbels continued: "Our socialism, as we understand it, is the best of our Prussian inheritance. We inherit it from the Prussian army, from the Prussian civil service." He went on to link Nazism with the greatness of the German past: "It is the socialism that enabled the great Frederick and his army to withstand seven years of war. It is the socialism that gave a starved and exhausted Prussia, after this seven years of war, the strength to rebuild not only its old but also its new provinces." This was a socialism, Goebbels continued, that had "something soldierly … about it." Drawing a connection between socialism, militarism, and the needs of Germany as a nation, Goebbels stated, "What socialism is within the nation, nationalism is to the outside world. The distinction is no longer between classes … but between values." Goebbels summed up his argument as follows: "Our socialism … is the exact opposite of Marxism."[670]

In his very first public speech as Reich Chancellor, Hitler spoke of the "restoration of cleanliness" in German culture as a prerequisite to German national rebirth.[671] But the rebirth of culture narrowly defined was only a small part of Hitler's vision. In a speech to SA leaders a few months later, Hitler spelled out his vision of the far-reaching implications of the Nazi revolution. In the words of the correspondent from the *Vossische Zeitung*, Hitler began by outlining for the assembled stormtroopers his view of the nature of revolution. Revolution was not an end in itself but "a means to a higher goal." There were, Hitler continued, "two types of revolution known to history: that of the idea, and that of pure violence." The higher form, the "revolution of the idea" (*weltanschaulichen Revolution*), must have as its goal the "the education and forming of man" to correspond to "the ideal which gave this revolution its meaning." This would amount to nothing less than the creation of a "new man," and the task of the SA leadership would be to contribute to the birth of this "new man" by bringing up the people in the spirit of National Socialism. The revolution was not to be socioeconomic but cultural, biological, and above all racial. The race problem was the key: "The question of leadership, of socialism, of authority, etc., all go back to the same root: blood and cultural identity." For Hitler, the true meaning of the "socialism" in National Socialism, and, by extension, of the Nazi revolution itself, was drawn not from Marx but from Darwin: "Socialism is nothing other than the natural order of a people according to its inherent capabilities."[672]

"I wear the brown uniform only for appearances"

In Leni Riefenstahl's film of the 1934 Nuremberg party rally, *Triumph of the Will,* the NSDAP's socialism is depicted as a function of the masses coordinated under the will of one man, with workers, peasants, and soldiers willingly submitting themselves to the greater good of Germany. When Ernst Röhm's replacement as SA chief of staff, Victor Lutze, says in the film, "We SA workers will always be true only to the *Führer,*" he is not only affirming the allegiance of the SA to Hitler in the wake of the Röhm purge but also setting the final seal on the definition of socialism achieved by the regime.[673] Yet the battle over the meaning of socialism continued, and ferment within the National Socialist mass organizations gave hope to those who hoped to still capitalize on the atmosphere of revolutionary change. It is fitting that the first film produced under National Socialism, *Hitler Youth Quex* (1933), took as its subject the death of Herbert Norkus, the Berlin Hitler Youth killed by Communists and renegade National Socialists under the command of Walther Stennes.[674] In the film, Stennes's stormtroopers are absent; in their place are bloodthirsty Communists. Joseph Goebbels considered this distinction important enough to return to in a major speech almost two years after the release of the film: "When Norkus, who was a member of the Hitler Youth, was stabbed by some communist brutes the *Rote Fahne* barefacedly declared that Norkus was killed by a Nazi spy; so that the Nazis were alleged to have murdered a seventeen-year-old member of their own party."[675] In reconfiguring the death of Norkus into a pure act of Communist aggression, eliding the participation of self-styled National Socialists, not to mention the NSDAP's cooperation with the Communists in the BVG strike later that same year, the film aimed not only to erase uncomfortable memories but also to further a cult of martyred youth so important in National Socialism.

In this sense, it was part of the NSDAP's broader attempt to take over the mantle of the youth movement.[676] The fate of this movement under National Socialism is indicative, for in many ways, it willingly submitted to *Gleichschaltung*. Before 1933 there were about one hundred thousand of both sexes in *Bündisch* groups. The majority of these went more or less voluntarily into National Socialist organizations. The phenomenal growth of the Hitler Youth would otherwise have been impossible. At the end of 1932, the Hitler Youth had 108,000 members. A year later the figure was 2.3 million, and after another year, more than 3.5 million. As with other sectors of society, there was a wave of opportunistic joinings of the NSDAP from the *Bündische Jugend*. These joinings ran in parallel with attempts to preserve autonomy. The *Freischar Schill* disbanded itself, enthusiastic about 1933 but also worried about the threat posed by the Hitler Youth.[677] In late March 1933 a *Großdeutscher Bund* was formed, encompassing some seventy thousand members of various *Bünde*. The leaders of these groups hoped to incorporate themselves into the National Socialist movement while preserving "*bündisch* living space."[678] The *Bund* was outlawed by Baldur von Schirach, the new Nazi national youth leader, on the day he took office (17 June 1933). But as Mathias von Hellfeld has pointed out, von Schirach lacked any real authority within the regime at this time, making his prohibition of the *Bund* more symbolic than real.[679] The ambiguous attitude of the *Bündische* toward the Nazi revolution was captured well by Eberhard Koebel. While challenging the idea that the mass *Wehrverband* offered a more "militarily effective" model than the small elite *Bündisch* group, Koebel concluded that in the end, both the *Großdeutscher Bund* and the Hitler Youth were so thoroughly infiltrated by the personnel and spirit of the *Bündische Jugend* that the distinction between them hardly mattered. "To dispute the complete victory of the NSDAP," he wrote, "to diminish it, to take advantage of the potential for reaction against it, leads from the real world away into a world of illusion, into a naive private world. The *Bünde* will disappear. We won't shed any tears for them."[680]

The Reich Youth leadership wanted to bring as many people as possible into its mass organizations, yet simultaneously worried about the possible effects of success.[681] "The leaders of the *Bünde* ... are today still to an extent active in the old sense," complained the authorities; "a portion of them have let themselves be taken into the Hitler Youth and there attempted to build cells."[682] The attempt of *Bündisch* figures such as Eberhard Koebel and Karl Paetel to seek influence in the Hitler Youth represented a special source of concern.[683] Koebel joined the Hitler Youth in Berlin in order to continue his *Bündisch* activities, prompting Hitler Youth leaders to warn of attempts by his supporters to infiltrate the Hitler Youth and *Deutsche Jungvolk*.[684] They cited, for emphasis, the example of a local group of the *Deutsche Jungvolk* in Erfurt, which held "tea evenings" and sat on pillows "like Indians or Chinese." No brown shirts were worn, all the works of Tusk were on hand, and a d.j.1.11 flag hung on a wall. In Magdeburg, an activist reported that a "strong Communist attitude" ruled in the local Hitler Youth.[685] During the initial period of the regime, older loyalties ran in parallel with new. A follower of

Tusk in the Berlin district of Kreuzberg remembers that he could still publicly appear in the uniform of the *Bündische* as late as 1934.[686] The last of Koebel's Red-Gray Garrisons, in Danzig, survived until 1939.[687] Hitler Youth and *Deutsche Jungvolk* leaders continued to worry about the influence of the *Bündische* well into the mid-1930s.[688] But under the illusion that they could continue to pursue their radical ends inside what they saw as a revolutionary movement, *Bündisch* activists were already contributing to their own *Gleichschaltung* and adding the force of their aspirations and energy to National Socialism. They did this because in some ways they had little choice, but also because they believed in broad goals that—as in the case of Eberhard Koebel and many others—might be pursued first on the left, now on the right, and because they were not at all unused to marching, drill, commands, flags, and songs. In this way, the integration of the *Bündische* was the end result of the process of self-militarization that had taken place in the Weimar Republic. In the end, as Ernst Erich Noth wrote, the youth of his generation "returned to the barracks almost willingly."[689]

* * *

Whereas many of the *Bündisch* groups were largely interested merely in protecting the autonomy they had sacrificed in joining or being integrated into the mass organizations of National Socialism, the Communists and some of the various National Bolshevik or National Socialist splinter groups still hoped for revolution.[690] The KPD was without a doubt the greatest victim of the early phase of the Nazi *Machtergreifung*. The party was officially banned on 6 March 1933. By the end of the year, some sixty to one hundred thousand Communists had been arrested or sent to concentration camps.[691] Although the Politburo of the KPD escaped immediate arrest, much of the middle-level leadership was wiped out in the repression. Communists who were not arrested fled or went into hiding. The KPD estimated that the party lost two-thirds of its membership in the first ten months of 1933.[692] Nevertheless, the party was able to rebuild its organization in many parts of Germany in the first few years, and many party members managed to remain active even at the height of the repression. In March 1933 one official of the *M-Apparat* in Berlin still maintained contact with Communist district leaders in Berlin-Brandenburg, Hannover, Hamburg, Halle-Merseburg, Leipzig, Thuringia, Middle-Rheinland, and Danzig.[693] Authorities in Düsseldorf noted that Communist activity remained lively in September 1933.[694] The KPD in Kassel began to be rebuilt in October 1933, the district leadership bringing out its own paper, *Der Kämpfer*.[695] In Hamburg and surrounding districts, the Communist Party organization was reconstructed from the end of 1934.[696] In Düsseldorf the party organization under the leadership of Hugo Paul was able to distribute fliers denouncing Nazi outrages against the workers, like the raid on the working-class suburb of Gerresheim on 5 May 1933.[697]

Zersetzungsblätter for the SA and police continued to be produced during the Spring of 1933 and into 1934–35.[698] In Cologne the KPD published *Der SA Kamerad* (see Figure 5.3). In Essen Communist operatives were able to create and distribute a number of different leaflets; one operative arrested by the Gestapo in late 1933 was found to have examples of fifteen different pieces in his apartment. Among these were fliers designed specifically for the SA and SS. One of them, the aforementioned "*SA-Mann Erwache!*" contained calls for stormtroopers to organize opposition cells in every *Sturm*, to renounce acts of terror against the workers, to demand the right to criticism of the party leadership, and to fight with the workers for real socialism. The leaflet, designed to look as if it was created within the SA, was signed, "The leadership of the opposition group in the Ruhr."[699] In Franconia, where a revolt of the SA under Walter Stegmann had only recently been contained, the KPD released a flier titled "SA Proletarians! Open Your Eyes! Finish the Job!" It sought to convince the stormtroopers that they had nothing to gain by following anti-Nazi rebels but must take their revolt to its logical conclusion by joining the KPD.[700] In Berlin *Der SA Sturmbanner* ("Organ of the Mutinous Berlin SA") tried to dampen the enthusiasm of SA men for the new Nazi government by noting the government's inclusion of conservatives such as von Papen and criticizing Hitler's failure to immediately improve the economic situation.[701]

The official party press, now operating underground, continued to publicize the activity of the "SA Opposition." "We reproduce here a call by rebellious SA [men]," read an article in *Der Kämpfer*, "to which we have added nothing."

> SA and SS comrades! National Socialists! More than thirty SA and SS comrades have been taken to the Papestraße concentration camp. Why? Because they demanded the carrying out of the socialist revolution. Our *Sturm* 4 was dissolved, because it mutinied over Hitler's betrayal of socialism. Three of our comrades were shot during this action by SS men who had been incited [by their leaders].

Two other *Sturms* had been dissolved, the flier continued,

> because they refused to take action against Communist workers until Hitler carries out the socialist revolution. In the tavern at Kulmannstraße 17, SA men, with Hitler's betrayal before their eyes, sang the Internationale. ... We revolutionary SA men ... in agreement with our Communist comrades, with whom we've been discussing things, say the following: We won't give our weapons up. We will remain in the SA and build cells there. Long live the socialist revolution, the Red Front! The Communist cell in *Sturm* 4.[702]

In cities where the KPD had been strong before January 1933, surviving Communist functionaries were able to rebuild some of the party organization and continue their activity under cover.[703] To an even greater extent than before 1933, the KPD continued to focus on its strategy of infiltration.[704] The size of the Communist presence in the SA, SS, NSBO, and other Nazi organizations has, for obvious reasons, been difficult to quantify. As far as the SA is concerned, a significant portion of new recruits is known to have previously belonged to the KPD.[705] Rudolf Diels, the first head of the Gestapo, estimated that in Berlin, 70 percent of new SA recruits after 30 January were former Communists. In some cases,

Gegen Reaktion — für Arbeit, Brot und Freiheit am 5. März für die Liste der Kommunisten!

Figure 5.2 An SA man proclaims his allegiance to Communism. A Reichsbanner man declares his support for the antifascist front. *AIZ* Nr. 7, February 1933. Bundesarchiv.

wrote Diels, entire units of the RFB went over to the SA en masse.[706] Peter Longerich has questioned Diels's frequently cited 70 percent figure as exaggerated, and although he must certainly be right that the figure is too high, he appears himself to have erred in the other direction.[707] According to Diels's subordinate Gisevius, at least a third of the post-1933 SA was made up of former Communists for

DER S.A. KAMERAD

Das Urteil von Beuthen

I. Jahrgang | Mitteilungen der Opposition in der SA, SS, NSDAP Köln August 1932

Die Säulen des 3. Reiches

Der schwule Sturm 24/III/16

"Neue Gesittung wächst nur aus den Wurzeln nationalen Volkstums."

".. ein neues Land, das auf den Säulen des Dritten Reiches aufsteigen wird über der Fäulnis der Welt."

(Westd.Beobachter 27/28.8.)

So eine Klappe riskieren sie und wenn man sich die "Säulen des Dritten Reiches" näher ansieht, steht man nicht vor den Säulen sondern vor den Säuen des Dritten Reiches!

Und wir wollen sie, Kameraden der SA, in dieser Nummer ganz gründlich besehen.

Tatsachen - SA Männer - Tatsachen:

Den Sturm 24/III nennt man offen in der Stadt den "schwulen Sturm". Er liegt in Lindenthal und der Sturmführer heisst

Graf von der Schulenburg.

Es fehlt ihm ein Buchstabe. Er ist nämlich Graf von der Schwulenburg! In Lindenthal wohnt auch der Leiter des Nachrichtendienstes Walter Frielingsdorf und sein Liebster, der Geschäftsführer der Lindenthaler Ortsgruppe, Riemann. Sie sind ständige Gäste in der Schwulenkneipe "Traube". Wir können uns nicht allzulange mit ihnen beschäftigen, es gibt wichtigere Dinge. Aber: Was haben SA-Arbeiter mit diesem schwulen Gesocks zu tun?

Wieso kämen wir dazu, uns von diesem verkommenen und degenerierten Gelichter führen zu lassen? Wohin kann uns sowas schon führen?

Solcher und ähnlicher Mist schlägt auch über den Köpfen unserer Oberführer zusammen. - Bei den Appell, an den Sturm- und Truppabenden warnt man uns vor den "Zersetzungsversuchen" der Kommune. Was heisst hier Kommune? Wir fragen: Wahr oder nicht wahr!

SA-tran - an die Wahrheit!

Der SA Kamerad spricht die Wahrheit.

Vor etwa 14 Tagen wurden uns grossartige Ehrenerklärungen für den Lumpen Palm und für seinen ganzen Stab vorgetragen. Es wurde gesagt, dass sich diese Leute des Vertrauens und der Wertschätzung der Obersten SA-Führung und des Führers erfreuen. Die Oberste SA-Führung wird auch danach sein. In der vorigen Woche, am 22. August musste nämlich in einem Rundschreiben der Gauleitung das uns von einem Kreisleiter, der zur Opposition gehört, zur Verfügung gestellt wurde, folgendes bekanntgegeben werden:

"Gegen die Pgg. Palm, Baur u. Klotsch mussten erneut Gau-Uschla-Verfahren eingeleitet werden. Während der Dauer der Untersuchungen sind die genannten Pgg. von jedem Parteidienst beurlaubt."

Was heisst das, SA-Kamerad? Das heisst, dass wir Euch die Wahrheit sagten und dass die ganze Gauleitung und der ganze Stab der Standarte 16 und der Untergruppe Köln-Aachen

eine verlogene Bande

sind!

Wir schrieben in der zweiten Nummer des "SA-Kamerad", dass Palm und Baur Standartengelder unterschlagen haben. Wir sagten, dass sie die Beitragsgroschen der SA-Männer noch neben ihrem Gehalt von 600 Mark im Monat verpulvern!

das sind Tatsachen, die nun heute auch von den "Säulen des Dritten Reiches" zugegeben werden müssen! Sie stehen nun ganz klein und erbärmlich da.

Nur die Einheitsfront aller Werktätigen vernichtet das Ausbeutertum!

Figure 5.3 Der SA Kamerad. Mitteilungen der Opposition in der SA, SS, NSDAP. August 1932, Cologne. Bundesarchiv.

whom "the popular phrase ... was 'Beefsteak Nazis'—Brown on the outside, red inside.'"[708] A leading functionary in the KPD's Red Sport organization gave a figure of 20 percent.[709] The SA itself gave a figure of 55 percent.[710] Internal SA memoranda, the surviving files of the Gestapo, and reports from the KPD's own intelligence apparatus all contain evidence of a significant Communist presence in the SA.[711] Reports from individual SA units in the spring and summer of 1933 even listed the names of individual Communists.[712] One activist retained membership in the KPD while serving as an agent in the SA intelligence service.[713] In a number of cases Communists occupied mid-level leadership positions in the SA and SS. In an SS intelligence platoon in the Altona district of Hamburg, thirty to thirty-five out of fifty members were former Communists, including the unit commander's right-hand man. A Communist functionary in contact with members of the unit noted: "The comrades report unanimously that the tone of the SS men is 'rosy,' and each one assumes the other is a 'Beefsteak' (brown on the outside, red on the inside)."[714] The presence of former Communists in the SA was sufficiently taken for granted that Rudolf Hess could write to Ernst Röhm in September looking for stormtroopers willing to testify against their former comrades in the Reichstag fire trial.[715]

The idea of the Second Revolution supplied a ready myth for a continuation of the United Front from Below of the Weimar years.[716] Herbert Crüger, a former Strasser supporter who had gone over to the KPD before 1933, was recruited by the KPD's *M-Apparat* to agitate on behalf of the KPD in a succession of National Socialist student homes to which he belonged. Crüger joined in frequent debates about the nature of the coming Second Revolution, in which he urged his fellows to "a critical posture toward the Nazi leadership, which in its practical politics had backed away from much of what it had up until then promised."[717] Crüger distributed papers designed for the SA with the help of some of the SA men in the home.[718] The articles in these papers, wrote Crüger, "picked up on current opinion in the SA, ... asked what the goals of the second wave of National Socialist revolution must be, and demanded to know who the real enemy was, the Communist workers, or the big capitalists."[719] Another Communist, a member of an SA *Sturm* in Berlin, reported in April 1934:

> A few weeks ago I was sitting in the afternoon with a few comrades in the *Sturmlokal*. ... After a while two SA men from the *Sturm* came in and told us that they had received the [*Zersetzungschrift*] *Rote Standarte* in the mail. ... One said: "The Commune is right about a lot of things. ..." Four others also came in and read the paper. The son of an official said: "The Commune is baiting us again. You must give the paper to the *Stuf* [*Sturmführer*] and don't let everyone read it." I am of the opinion that the others took pleasure in the content.[720]

Even after the purge of 30 June 1934, some KPD leaders were hopeful. As during the Stennes Revolt of 1931, unrest in the SA was interpreted in terms of impending revolution. "In the SA ... ," wrote one Communist official, "revolutionary, antifascist, and Communist propaganda is more and more widely noticeable. The entire SA seems to be contaminated."[721]

Even the purge of the SA that began on 30 June was interpreted as a hopeful sign. The KPD distributed a flier titled "The Revolutionary SA Man," which read: "SA Comrades! The SA has been sent on leave because it is no longer needed, the SA leadership hit from behind. We revolutionary SA men had nothing in common with Röhm, but we don't want to have anything in common with Hitler and Göring, either. Hitler has betrayed the SA and delivered it to its enemies."[722] Some in the KPD appear to have deluded themselves into believing that the party's agitation had caused the events of 30 June. "Under the pressure of our revolutionary work among the masses before the 30th of June," argued the *Reichsleitung,* "the disintegration in the SA has grown. ... In recent weeks there have been new examples every day where SA men and NSBO members, together with our comrades, have taken up the fight against their employers and been fired; a portion have been sent to concentration camps." In order to take advantage of the situation, the party was to intensify its efforts at building cells and producing *Zersetzungsblätter.* A list of demands for revolutionary SA men were drawn up and subsequently published in an "SA opposition sheet." They included:

> 1. Revenge against the comrade-killers Hitler and Göring. 2. [The SA opposition] does not recognize the dictatorially appointed commissars and leaders. 3. The SA opposition demands the free election of SA leaders from *Truppenführer* to *Stabchef.* 4. We demand the disbanding of the Field Police, the Department Ie, that is, the spy-formation in the SA and patrol duty. 5. We demand the suspension of arrests, persecution, torture, and murder of oppositional SA men and revolutionary antifascist fighters. 6. We demand the release of all SA men and revolutionary worker-comrades arrested because of their revolutionary opinions. 7. We refuse to allow ourselves to be used against the workers and working people. 8. We demand the free supply of uniforms [and] footwear. 9. We demand free expression of opinion, freedom of discussion in the *Sturms,* control over the use of contributions, and the right of SA men to publish their own *Sturm* newspapers.[723]

Guidelines advised Communists on how to calm the fears of prospective recruits in the SA in the event of the coming Communist takeover [!]. In an article titled "SA-man Schulze asks, we answer him," propaganda guidelines were provided in the form of a hypothetical conversation between a Communist and an SA man. "SA man Schulze," whose hunger has given him second thoughts about the Nazi regime, says:

> I realize that you Communists have turned out to be right, that the working class, including the SA, [has been hoodwinked]. My comrades know that as well. But we are afraid of the day that you Communists come to power, because then you will make a bloody reckoning with us, because it was [through the work of SA men] that Communists were murdered. Give me an answer to the question: What would you do with us SA men who haven't beaten or murdered any Communists?[724]

* * *

The KPD's belief that Hitler was temporary and revolution imminent was shared by Strasser's Black Front.[725] "Hitler is only a transition," argued Strasser; "after Hitler comes not Bolshevism but German Socialism."[726] Strasser emphasized the importance of infiltrating the SA to carry on revolutionary work from within.[727] Black Front propaganda guidelines urged activists to collect enemy addresses for direct-mail campaigns, a tactic actively pursued by both the Black Front and the KPD, and one that reflected the united front tactic: "Especially desirable are the addresses of SA, NSBO, and *Stahlhelm* members, as well as those of decent former Marxists." As the emphasis on address collecting suggests, the chief focus of Black Front activity in the NSDAP was intelligence gathering and the distribution of propaganda. Both were supported by the forging of personal contacts and the attempted building of cells.[728] The interrogation records of Black Front activists captured and tried for treason provide a view into this work. Wilhelm Zander belonged briefly to the NSDAP in 1932, before quitting to join the *Revolutionäre Freiheitsbewegung* led by the former Hitler Youth leader Wilhelm Kayser, which affiliated itself with the Strasser movement in December 1932. Zander seems to have felt, as his codefendant Hans Bauer put it, that the NSDAP was "not adequately utilizing the socialist momentum" of Nazism and would, "in the event of an eventual seizure of power, [sell out] to big business."[729]

In April 1933 Zander joined the SA in hopes of "strengthen[ing its] fighting spirit." As *Wehrsportreferant* for *Sturmbann* I/240 in Cologne, he was responsible for training some eighty junior officers of the unit. According to the Gestapo, "Zander reported regularly to … Kayser and other members of the Cologne group of the Black Front about events in the SA, the SS, the *Stahlhelm,* and other organizations of the National Socialist state." He was able "repeatedly to give … Kayser SA *Gruppenbefehle* that had to do with the affairs of the SA and its relationship with other organizations, as well as disagreements within these organizations."[730] Material gained in this way was used in the creation of a series of propaganda fliers produced between June 1933 and July 1935. The fliers created from this material were duplicated for the most part in Zander's apartment on a hectograph machine that he obtained for use in his SA service. Kayser, Zander, and the others produced ten to twelve different propaganda fliers. These included multiple issues of the *Antifaschistischer Rundbrief,* as well as titles like "Differences between Chief of Staff Röhm and Hitler," "Against alarmists and fault-finders!?" and *Der Sozialistische Stoßtrupp.* Each flier was produced in an edition of five hundred and mailed to addresses in Cologne, Elberfeld, Remscheid, Soligen, Düsseldorf, Duisberg, and Essen.[731] In addition to producing fliers, the group around Kayser compiled its own intelligence reports, which were dutifully smuggled to Strasser in exile abroad. Information from these reports were used in Strasser's publications, which were sent into Germany, passed hand to hand among activists, and then distributed as propaganda.[732]

Another Strasser activist, Erwin Simon, had been a member of the KPD from December 1931 through May 1932. Attracted to Communism by the example of Richard Scheringer, Simon became disenchanted with the KPD and joined the Black Front in November 1932. In April of the following year, he joined the SA, assuming the rank of *Rottenführer* in *Sturm* 52/36 in Halle. Simon reasoned that since every other party or group fighting for "German socialism" had been banned, the NSDAP was now the only party "out of which something could develop." In a letter to a friend (used in evidence against him at his trial) Simon wrote: "The work continues underground. ... Much has changed, but the goal remains the same. ... The socialist longing lives, even in the SA. I can testify to that because I'm hiding right in the middle of it. The only thing that has changed is [the composition of] the boss-strata, the owners of the gravy train." Explaining his decision to join the SA, he continued: "Everything is *Gleichgeschaltet*, including the socialists. [Therefore] everything today must be achieved through the SA, the SS, and the Labor Front. What counts today is alertness and personal connections, and in addition, attaining positions of leadership in the SA. Every revolutionary must become at least a *Sturmführer*." Giving voice to a widely held view, Simon concluded: "The revolution will come from the inside out, from within the party."[733]

Such assessments were not unique to the KPD and the Black Front. Ernst Niekisch, already in 1933, noted the discontent in the Nazi movement and attached great meaning to what he saw as the beginning of a mass exodus from the NSDAP.[734] Even an informed observer such as Ernst Erich Noth, writing on the eve of the purge of the SA in June of the following year, saw the growing tension in the NSDAP as a sign that the "true fighters" were beginning their revolt, a revolt in which the KPD would "yet play a role."[735] Agents of the Sopade and *Neu Beginnen,* less prone to wishful thinking and revolutionary inflationism than the Communists and the Strasserites, were quick to point out the dangers of false hopes. A *Miles Bericht* from the spring of 1934 criticized what it called the "strong overestimation of the amount and worth of opposition voices ... characteristic of Communist or Communist splinter groups and sects." The Communists, it continued, are constantly speaking "of a 'new beginning' or a 'revolutionary uprising' in a moment where ... more than 40 million people have been brought into line behind Hitler."[736] *Neu Beginnen* warned in particular of false hopes in the wake of the Night of the Long Knives: "It is not true that the Nazi Party no longer exists, as has been said. On the contrary, it is stronger than ever."[737]

Yet the overly optimistic assessments criticized by Social Democratic agents were more than simple wishful thinking; they represented a continuation of the same beliefs about Nazi radicalism—the same superimposition of "socialism" (variously understood) over Nazi radicalism—that characterized the Weimar Republic. There was a widespread revolutionary feeling that the Communists, Strasserites, and members of the Youth Movement rightly identified, and it did have anticapitalist elements that the KPD could (mis)identify as "Bolshevistic." Ironically, all of these groups tried to "coordinate" themselves so as to more effectively *resist* coordination, to operate as individuals within the mass. But "massification" had its own logic. As Hans Bernd Gisevius, a member of the Gestapo, put it, "everyone, whatever his name, whatever his nature, men and women, old and young, lukewarm and enthusiasts, opportunists, defeated opponents, and rough-and-tough SA men—all were forged into a molten mass of human beings capable of reacting only as a mass."[738]

Some former members of the Marxist working-class organizations appear to have gotten into the spirit of the National Socialist revolution. This had sometimes been the case even before 1933. The Communist propagandist Willi Münzenberg wrote of meeting, in the fall of 1932, old Communists who had already gone over to the SA: "You Communists are taking too long," they told him; "Adolf will do it faster. If he betrays us, we'll hang him. We are the SA, and ... we'll be able to create the socialism Adolf promised us."[739] There were a variety of motives for defections after 1933. Many Communists joined the SA in order to avoid arrest. One of these was Peter Kramer, the former leader of the KPD Ortsgruppe in the Ruhr, who made the mistake of gloating to a Gestapo spy: "If they only knew who I was."[740] For every Communist or other previously anti-Nazi militant who kept the faith and continued to agitate for his old party after 1933—or, in contrast, embraced National Socialism—there were many others for whom old and new identities coexisted. As one SA man put it in 1935, in a moment of drunken candor that got him in a lot of trouble: "I'm no SA man; I've been a member of the Communist Party for thirteen years and I wear the brown uniform only for appearances."[741] The daughter of a Berlin Communist recalled years later:

> The desertion was unstoppable. Hitler had won. Everyone, the most unlikely and the most good-natured, was a potential informer. The only way to survive, to get a job, to keep a job, to keep out of prison and avoid being beaten up, was to leave the KPD and the SPD and to keep quiet. It was more sensible still to join the Nazi Party and pin a swastika on your lapel.[742]

She further recalled:

> One defector from the KPD was Fritz Walter. ... This pleasant, quite ordinary man of about thirty worked in a factory and had been a good member of the Communist Party. But even before Hitler took over, he had gone to my parents' flat and "talked like a different man"; the next time, he turned up in a Nazi uniform. ... The *Führer*, he insisted, was good for Germany and good for the German people. My parents were disgusted and afraid.[743]

The willingness of many Communists to join the Nazi movement is hardly surprising, as Conan Fischer has pointed out, given the ways in which the KPD purposefully attempted to blur the lines with the radical right in the final years of the Weimar Republic.[744]

Lines also became blurred when criminal elements from the SA and the Red Front converged under the cover of the National Socialist revolution. A landlord in Düsseldorf-Gerresheim experienced this fact personally in the summer of 1933, when he was confronted in his home by several dozen SA men demanding to conduct a house search. When he refused to let them in, he recounted, the stormtroopers broke down the door and ascended the stairs with drawn revolvers. Once inside, they began to brutally beat the occupants, shouting, "We are the Commune, we are in power." They smashed the apartment's furnishings, roughed up all the occupants, and beat the landlord and his friend with fists, boots, cudgels, and rubber truncheons. This "action" only came to an end when a police official appeared more than an hour later and explained to the stormtroopers that independent initiative of this sort was no longer allowed. In his letter of complaint to the SA leadership, the landlord noted that the stormtroopers were frequent associates of some of his renters, "ill-tempered" men whom he knew to be Communists. "As far as I could find out," he wrote, "the greater portion of the SA men who took part belonged as recently as 5 March to the KPD. For weeks a lively traffic between SA men and these renters has been noticeable." Both the renters and the SA men were actively involved in party work, he added, noting indignantly that "an SA man in uniform even distributed fliers for the Communist Party." These stormtroopers, the landlord concluded melodramatically, were "Communists in the truest sense of the word, and only crept into the SA in order … to be able to continue carrying out their dark intrigues."[745]

The anti-Communist hysteria and denunciatory self-policing of this account aside, there is little doubt that the lawless atmosphere of the spring and summer of 1933 allowed formerly competing conceptions of "revolution" to dovetail. An SA man in Duisberg-Hamborn, Adolf Hess, had formerly been a member of the KPD and the *Kampfbund gegen den Faschismus*. Hess joined the SA at the beginning of March 1933 with a number of other Communists from his neighborhood. Once in the brown uniform, according to the Gestapo, Hess and his comrades

> repeatedly … undertook independent actions [house searches] in the Josefskolonie [a working-class district] without having been ordered to do so by the party or anyone else. Through this terror [Hess] earned the hate of various Communists and had to flee. Since this time he has stayed far away from Hamborn. In the meantime he has been in the Saar where he … took part in demonstrations of the Communist Party. Hess … has not given up his Communist point of view, and it was probably his intention to advertise for the idea of the KPD within the SA.[746]

Despite his zealous persecution of his former comrades, Hess failed to win the trust of his fellow stormtroopers. "In the legal period," another report noted, "Hess was the greatest agitator against the NSDAP, then [he] suddenly gives in to the NSDAP the day after the seizure of power, puts on the SA uniform, and behaves like the most zealous defender of the National Socialist idea."[747]

Even principled Communists who joined the National Socialist organizations for purposes of infiltration were at risk. The so-called Scheringer groups, formed from members of the Berlin "Young Workers" organization for purposes of subversion of the SA, are a case in point. They possessed only weak connections to the KPD, and their activities were discouraged as too dangerous for young activists in any case.[748] The police president in Hannover noted: "The KPD is attempting by all possible means to penetrate the national socialist organizations, especially the SA. ... The party has shown success, however, in only a few individual cases, because the vast majority of people entrusted with this task take the ideals of the [Nazi formations] as their own and refuse any further activity for the KPD." The situation was so bad that young Communists entering the SA for purposes of subversion were charged with the task of not only winning over the stormtroopers but also winning back Communists who had preceded them into the SA. "Repeatedly this tactic has worked out to the detriment of the KPD," the police president continued, because the defecting agents passed their knowledge of KPD organization along to their new comrades.[749] A Communist activist belonging to the SS in Hamburg complained that the connections he had painstakingly forged had been ignored by the Altona party organization, which, in his opinion, "placed no worth on a systematic cultivation of the enemy in his mass organizations." He added indignantly that a young Communist whom he had advised to follow him into the SS had accused him of "strengthening fascism." Nevertheless, the functionary continued, the local party possessed good and many-sided connections in the SA and SS, although most of these activists had joined these formations on their own accord.[750] The party's unwillingness or inability to take advantage of the situation was especially frustrating, he noted, because "in almost every ... *Sturm* there are individual comrades I spoke to who are ready to work with and for us." Although this functionary maintained excellent connections within a recently formed SS intelligence platoon, which he estimated was made up of 60 to 70 percent former Communists, he was unable to turn the situation to advantage. His main contact, the "right-hand man" of the unit commander, kept in regular contact with him personally, because the party never used the reports it received. Acknowledging that activists like these could easily be lost to the KPD, he concluded revealingly: "I only uphold this contact so as to keep the people from 'swimming away.'"[751]

Ironically, the process of *Gleichschaltung* of former enemies proceeded apace with a precipitous decline in revolutionary élan. A growing mood of defeat comes out clearly in Social Democratic and Communist intelligence reports over 1934–35. A Communist report noted in April 1934: "In many SA formations ... there remain only about 1 percent 'old fighters,' above all people who joined after January [1933]. For the most part poor human material, unpolitical."[752] A Communist agent in an SA *Sturm* in the Neukölln district of Berlin noted: "Our *Sturm* is 175 men strong, two-thirds workers and one-third employees and sons of small tradesmen. The *Sturm* is made up of 80 percent *Märzgefallene*, and they have only joined either in order to maintain their position or to get a job. ... At the most only about 30 percent are convinced National Socialists, and they are the ones for whom it is going well financially."[753] A Sopade agent in Bavaria similarly estimated that only 20 percent of the SA members there were fanatical Nazis.[754] "The most noticeable thing to me," noted a Communist agent in Hamburg in the spring of 1934, is that the streets are no longer ruled by the masses of Brownshirts like they were six months ago, and that the SA and SS men one sees are entirely new people. The "old" [activists] are hardly to be seen at important demonstrations. Some of them are now employed, leaders of work details, students in the indoctrination courses, or in the police; many have drawn back from active service.[755]

Even before 30 June 1934, there are indications that the morale of the SA was slackening. Disappointment with the course of the Nazi revolution, anger over the failure of the regime to improve their lot, and exhaustion stemming from the punishing regimen of drill and maneuvers had a negative effect on the élan of the SA, especially that of the "old fighters," leading to discipline problems and loss of interest.[756] Sopade linked this situation to an increased suicide rate among SA men, as noted in a report from the spring of 1934: "The number of suicides is growing alarmingly. In the last six weeks, eighteen men in the Berlin SA have killed themselves. Even SA men in well-paid positions commit suicide."[757] A *Sturmführer* in Berlin noted the disappointment and bitterness in his *Sturm* in November 1934: "I had to kick out twelve 'old fighters,' the [most experienced] people that I had. I was sorry about it, but they were so embittered and full of rage that they were simply no longer usable." The *Sturmführer* expressed what was probably the opinion of many when he concluded: "We've become soldiers of the second rank. Now all I need is a good, steady job, and then I'll leave the SA with an honorable discharge."[758] The same 1934 Sopade report noted: "Reports [from all over Germany], for example from Berlin, Schleswig-Holstein, and Saxony, agree … that a change in mood is occurring in the SA and SS. Discipline is slackening and punishment must be increased." The report also stated, "Morale in the SA is noticeably giving out. The men are furious about the countless limitations that are ever more being placed on them (most recently they have been prohibited from beating up pastors). They are [upset] with the stupid military drill and strenuous maneuvers, especially the night exercises."[759] One SA man in Munich, when asked why he was not participating in a march marking the fifteen-year anniversary of the Versailles treaty, answered: "I just don't like it anymore. It's always the same. That the peace treaty has been nullified I already know. But I've had enough of the eternal marching around for nothing."[760] The lack of meaningful activity, combined with the punishing routines of service, began to sap whatever ideological character the SA had possessed. Noted another Sopade agent: "A certain weariness produced by the harshness of service is becoming noticeable in the SA. That the SA discusses the problems of socialism can thus far not be observed."[761] In the Rheinland, noted the Sopade,

> the dissatisfaction in the lower ranks of the Nazi movement … is taking … serious forms. The SA in the West is practically in disintegration. … For a long time now the SA men play hooky from inspections, curse the *Bonzen,* and criticize the system. They feel themselves betrayed, and today no longer stop at criticizing Hitler. … In certain SA formations it has gone so far that when someone is greeted with "Heil Hitler," the SA men put their heads together and whisper: "Lick my …"[762]

Conclusion

The KPD continued in its revolutionary pipe dreams well into 1935 and beyond,[763] as did the Black Front.[764] The groups of the Youth Movement and the nationalist *Wehrverbände* were incorporated, some more quickly or willingly than others, but all nevertheless, into the mass organizations of National Socialism. It is a paradox that it was precisely this "self-*Gleichschaltung*," and in particular the attempts to retain a space for autonomy (as with the Youth Movement) or to actively work toward subversion (like the KPD and the Black Front, and to an extent also the *Bündische*), that gave force to National Socialism. But in allowing themselves to be *gleichgeschaltet* into the Nazi organizations in order to resist *Gleichschaltung* on behalf of those activist forces that they sought to save for the coming revolution, they ultimately only helped the Nazis. Hans Bernd Gisevius rightly divined the interplay between this surge of the masses and the revolutionary aims of the leadership, noting that it was "this sudden, obscure pressure from below in the victorious movement that lent fresh courage to the new rulers, that strengthened their own drives and inspired them with the ultimate audacity they needed to go all out."[765] It was precisely the involvement of the masses that made it a revolution, however confused or varied the impulses behind their involvement:

> Only [these] interacting impulses … , only the irrational turbulence in the souls of the people, can explain the total *Gleichschaltung* that took place in that summer of 1933. It was accomplished by vigorous thrusts from the Party, but it was also voluntary and spontaneous. People worked themselves up into a wholly unwonted revolutionary excitement, and in their irrational and malleable mood they helped to swell the power of the revolutionaries.[766]

The vague revolutionary hopes that motivated members of the SA and other Nazi organizations, which accounted in part for the willingness of people to "coordinate" themselves, to continue working inside like the Communists—the "from below"—did not come to pass. In their place came a revolution from above. The truth is that all the groups that embraced or hoped to profit from or control the Nazi revolution (including, ultimately, many Communists) believed in the same things—enough of the same things at any rate—to take any real force out of the opposition to Nazism. All of them later wanted to be seen as resisters against Hitler, from the KPD, to Richard Scheringer, to the various figures of the "National Revolution," to the *Bündisch* youth groups, to the more-or-less anti-Nazi youth gangs of the Nazi period.[767] Much worthwhile work has been done documenting this resistance, and the intention here is not to downplay the risks taken by those who, although they shared aspects of the Nazi worldview, refused to go along with the regime when the time came. The point here is not to assign blame for the catastrophe of Nazism but to point out that the extent to which Nazism as a mass movement drew on a widely shared world of ideas, and that the widely shared nature of these ideas is one of the things that gave National Socialism its force.

The other side of the coin of self-*Gleichschaltung* was the violence carried out by the regime. It was violence that gave National Socialism the opportunity to establish the meaning of the 1933, to determine the content of terms such as "socialism," "revolution," and *Volksgemeinschaft.*" The Marxist parties were driven underground, and figures who, in one way or another, had attempted to stand between the radical extremes accommodated themselves or faced exile, prison, or death. The significance of oppositional activity should thus not be overstated. It took place within mass organizations acting as means of social control, "caging" the various types of radicalism feeding into the regime. This control was supplemented by a system of police terror and denunciatory self-policing highlighted by recent scholarship.[768] Walther Stennes fled the country after being released from Gestapo custody through the intervention of Hermann Göring. Those who tried to pursue Third Way politics after 1933, National Bolsheviks and figures of the Youth Movement such as Beppo Römer, Ernst Niekisch, Eberhard Koebel, Harro Schulze-Boyson, and others, faced exile, prison, or death. Various figures of the *Bündisch* and National Revolutionary camps either fled the country to continue their activity in exile or ended up in concentration camps.[769] Eberhard Koebel was arrested on 18 January 1934, and beaten in Gestapo custody. He fled the country after his arrest.[770] Richard Scheringer returned to the army, serving in the campaigns in Poland and Russia. Scheringer simultaneously maintained clandestine ties with Communists in Bavaria, while remaining close friends with his comrade from the Ulm trial, Hanns Ludin.[771] Ludin was executed as a war criminal in 1947 for his involvement, as German ambassador to the puppet Tiso regime in Slovakia, in the deportation and murder of Slovakian Jews.[772]

Much of the activity of resisting National Socialism revolved around trying to disrupt the performance staged by the new regime. But smuggled literature and leaflets strewn in public lavatories were no match for the mass media controlled by a modern state ruled with dictatorial powers. And many of the very people who most hoped to disrupt the performance, as we have seen, were often directly and enthusiastically involved in it. The monopoly of meaning, just as important as the monopoly of violence, allowed Hitler to set out on an ambitious agenda, beginning with a reversal of the outcome of 1918 and moving on to complete the racialization of the revolution, which had only been latent before 1933. George Mosse was quite correct in noting how the Nazis "modified ... the social aims of the Youth Movement"—which, as we have seen, were similar to those of many Nazis—"by directing the revolution against the 'enemy within' rather than against the existing class structure."[773] It was the success of the Nazis in doing this that finally rendered meaningless the activities of opponents and fellow travelers.

CONCLUSION

*T*wo competing ideological incursions—one by Communism seeking to be "national," the other by Nazism attempting to be "social"—achieved nothing like a convergence at a hypothetical point labeled "National Socialism." Even if elements of shared ideology were created by the KPD's self-destructive attempt to remold itself along radical nationalist lines in 1923/1930, and even if defections from one side to the other did occasionally create a literal area of overlap at the grass roots, the space between the two movements is to be seen less as an area of overlap than a space in which the two movements played with the meaning of symbols in an effort to win over militants and masses. The *Zersetzungsschriften* created by the KPD were, in this sense, more than marginal expressions of a little-known aspect of the KPD's battle against Nazism, but a pure distillation of the larger battle of symbols between the radical extremes. The fact that contemporaries were frequently unsure of the provenance of such papers only reinforces the extent to which the radical extremes in the Weimar Republic formed a "semiotic community" capable of understanding and playing with the same symbolic language.[774] The symbolic battle being carried out between the two mass parties of the radical extremes was part of a bigger battle in the Weimar Republic around ideas such as nationalism and socialism. But the struggle to redefine symbols that characterized the symbolic warfare between the KPD and the NSDAP was carried out within those movements as well, and was, indeed, a key feature of their politics; symbols were deployed not only by the parties to dispute the opponent's control over the masses but within the movements to dispute the official narrative passed down by the movement's leaders.

Seen in the widest view, the radical popular movements of the Weimar Republic were attempts to forge meaningful self-determination in the face of the insufficiencies of parliamentary democracy and capitalism. There can be little question that the anticapitalism of the radical right was widespread and authentic. It would have made little sense, after all, for a movement directed against the system not to reject capitalism—or at least aspects of it—when that very system was based on capitalism. The mass movements of the radical extremes, and the various smaller groups in orbit about them, were revolutionary, inasmuch as they thought of and positioned themselves as fighters for popular interests against oppression. The division between "progressive" and "entrenched" forces derived from the French revolution is clearly inadequate to describe the split between fascism and Communism, both of which saw themselves—and won followers—as "parties of movement." Nor is the more recent association of the left with "socialism" and the right with the "nation" of any help. In the particular conditions of the Weimar Republic, the multiplicity of crises threw the traditional concerns of "left" and "right" into disorder; the right struggled to assert itself on the "social question" as the only hope for the creation of a "true" nationalism; the left, faced with intractable patriotic chauvinism, found itself forced to grapple with the question of the nation. Both movements were fed by popular radicalism, both faced, for different but related reasons, splintering tendencies, and both faced the challenge of how to channel popular radicalism into particular directions. National Socialism and Communism each strove to produce the appearance of popular participation and, to an extent, actually achieved that participation; as a *Volkspartei* with cross-class appeal, possessing an ideology susceptible to multiple interpretations and capable of drawing on disparate sources of radicalism, National Socialism was rather more successful in this undertaking. Ultimately, however, with the consolidation of the regime, the popular had to be given decisive shape, the radicalism of Hitler's followers, above all those in the SA, tamed and directed. As the primary institutional expression of National Socialism's nationalization of the masses—at least until the NSDAP had the opportunity after 1933 to directly shape the lives of Germany's workers—the SA became a key site in the battle over meaning between the radical extremes. Competing interpretations of the meaning of SA activism and SA revolt mirrored larger patterns of meaning creation, the KPD attempting to position SA activism in terms of class struggle, the Nazis in terms of ethnic-racial struggle with class functioning symbolically; but each attempted to channel radical energies using the concepts and vocabulary of young warrior manhood. On both ends of the spectrum, there was a powerful tension between the authentic activist impulses of the rank and file—the "from below"—and the version of rank-and-file activism created "from above."

Nazism possessed important advantages in the struggle to define and shape the radicalism of its followers. Unlike the KPD, whose attempts at profiting from the strength of German nationalism ran up against its allegiance to a foreign power, and whose attempts to embody values of revolutionary warriorhood in its mass formations—sometimes disputed within its own party—conflicted with the impulse to fight against Nazism as the ultimate expression of a militaristic German society, the NSDAP enjoyed the support of important elements in that society, profiting from the interest of those who, though they might not care to give their entire allegiance to Hitler, were in basic agreement with much of what he had to say. In embodying warrior virtues in a way that resonated, rather than conflicted with, the beliefs and interests of conservative elites and the representatives of militarism in officialdom and civil society, the Nazis enjoyed what Roger Eatwell has termed "syncretic legitimation," giving them a decisive advantage in the struggle with their opponents on the revolutionary left.[775] A further advantage enjoyed by the Nazis was that in contrast to the KPD, which tended to stifle rank-and-file activism and prohibit realistic assessments of the tactical situation, the NSDAP, armed with vague goals such as the creation of a *Volksgemeinschaft*, generally allowed a wide latitude to its activists in "working toward the *Führer*," that is, in working toward the goals that they themselves had attached to the mythological person of Hitler.[776]

National Socialism and German Communism (or speaking more generally, fascism and Bolshevism) should not be seen as two sides of the same totalitarian coin—they were not the same; but both did pursue a mythological politics (which was also, simultaneously, an enlightenment politics of human perfectibility), which meant that they possessed certain common characteristics, including shared ideas of victimhood and attempts to regain agency in the face of modernity. Opposing narratives—of the struggle to save Germany from Bolshevism, or the victory of the German proletariat in alliance with the Soviet Union—ran in parallel with shared narratives of valor, sacrifice, the struggle of good against evil, and the necessity of social warfare—with the concomitant essentialization, demonization, and extermination of enemies—to achieve a human rebirth. This latter impulse is one that the next wave of popular upheaval in Germany, the New Left of the 1960s, attempted to dispense with (although in the event, especially in the left-wing terrorist groups of the 1970s, it fell pray to some of the same problems). Characteristic of the radical politics of the Weimar Republic was the disjuncture between social aspiration and political institution. There was a widespread desire for new forms of participation, even—or especially—as we have seen, in the antidemocratic movements. It was characteristic of the times that people looked to mass solutions to society's problems, more often than not militaristic solutions; but it is equally characteristic that they looked for agency in the midst of their mass participation. To be sure, if not for mass unemployment, loss of career prospects, and the breakdown of social and political institutions, people—above all young men—would not have been available for extremist projects such as those offered by the NSDAP and the KPD. In this sense, Weimar radicalism was heavily contingent; but the impulse behind it was a latent one in modern societies. After 1945, people once again grappled with the problems of socialism, nation, and revolution, largely, but not entirely, rejecting antidemocratic solutions. Fascism has largely discredited itself, even if it still appeals to young men sometimes—particularly in the depressed areas of the former East Germany—and occasionally gains representation in state parliaments, as has happened in recent years with the National Democratic Party in Germany. Very few, however, regard fascism as a promising new millennial movement as they did between the world wars; and one effect of the Holocaust was to largely discredit racism on the radical right, forcing its adherents in many cases to adopt the language of cultural pluralism and difference to disguise their true aims.[777]

At the same time, one of the hallmarks of the New Left of the 1960s, and of the New Social Movements and network politics that grew out of it, is that they rejected Stalinism and Bolshevism, the politics of manliness and war, and the creation of a "New Man" (although, here again, in the latter case, not always completely). But the key thrust of these movements was to attempt, once again, to create more responsive structures of participation, to create new methods of political activism, to make the content of politics match up to the form of politics. It is characteristic as well that one of the hallmarks of the radicalism of the 1960s was the creation of a multifocal underground press that, in contrast to the KPD's news sheets of the Weimar Republic, actually did spring from below, and actually did represent the authentic voice of rank-and-file militancy.[778] The attempt to overcome the disjuncture between institution and content—and the distrust of official institutions with which it is connected—continues to the present day.[779] In this sense, although the street battles between uniformed adherents of totalizing mass movements strike us an inalterably foreign and distant, the political struggles and conceptual categories of the Weimar Republic continue to echo, faintly but insistently, in the political life of Europe at the turn of the twenty-first century. It is surely indicative, however, that in contemporary Germany, it is now the radical right that seeks to imitate the radical left and not the other way around. Right-wing extremists in the streets of Berlin and other cities adopt the clothing styles and the rhetoric of the left—the Palestinian *kaffiyeh,* for example—styling themselves as allies with the Third World against "U.S. imperialism."[780] They do this because since the end of World War II, and the moral disaster of fascism, and especially since the 1960s, it is the left that has held the moral ascendancy in the radical milieu, not only in terms of its overall radicalism but also in the sense that it responds to the issues of the day. It is now the *left* that is seen to have the ideas—local self-determination, environmentalism, anti-imperialism—that must be included in any program.[781] *These* are the ideas of this epoch, just as surely as ideas of combining socialism and the (ethnic) nation were the ideas of the interwar period. However, these ideas are no longer played out through the antinomy between elite and mass, for the age of the masses is over. That this is so is partly a matter of scale: the map of radical right aspiration has shrunk, as Diethelm Prowe has pointed out, from the world to the individual apartment block;[782] and for both left and right, the discourse on anti-imperialism and local/cultural autonomy has brought in its train a privileging of the local, connected, in turn, with a focus on the individual and local activism.[783] Left-wing millenarianism modeled on Bolshevism or similar movements seems to have disappeared, for the moment anyway, but discontent with an ever more managed society is latent and perhaps growing, largely unnoticed. The radical right, on the other hand, has changed its tactics to gain admission to state parliaments, and may gain in influence if or when cultural struggles over the transformation of Europe into a multicultural society heat up. But these struggles will be fought out over a different landscape, and in very different terms, than the ideological battles of the Weimar Republic.

NOTES

1. NSDAP Hauptarchiv (hereafter HA) 17/325, SA Gruppe Nord-West to OSAF, 16 June 1931.
2. *Der Freiheitskämpfer,* no. 2, June 1931, HA 17/325.
3. See chapter 3.
4. The phrase comes from a Communist spy in the SS after January 1933; BA-SAPMO, I 2/705/25, 16.3.34, p. 4; it appears in a slightly different form in Hans Bernd Gisevius, *To the Bitter End* (Boston: Houghton Mifflin, 1947), 105. See chapter 5.
5. For example, at a meeting of the *Kampfbund gegen den Faschismus* (KgdF) in Cologne in October 1931; PP Köln to RP Köln, 13 October 1931.
6. "Liebe Freunde!" reads the note typed at the top of a sheet of text for a fake SA flier intended for KPD regional subgroups in late 1933. It continues, "In the following a rough draft of a flier for the SA. With regards to the distribution, it is especially important to take care that the flier gets into the hands of Nazi supporters, especially SS and SA people. Greetings, R.L. (Reichsleitung)"; "An alle UBL," October 1933, Nordrhein-Westfälisches Hauptstaatsarchiv Düsseldorf-Mauerstrasse (hereafter NWHStA), R34. The text of the flier is signed "Die Leitung der Oppositionsgruppe in der SA und SS." Such efforts (discussed in chapter 4)—before and after 1933—were later justified in the historiography of the German Democratic Republic as a necessary part of the struggle against fascism; see Edgar Doehler and Egbert Fischer, *Revolutionäre Militärpolitik gegen faschistische Gefahr. Militärpolitische Probleme des Antifaschistische Kampfes der KPD von 1929 bis 1933* (Berlin: Militärverlag der Deutschen Demokratischen Republik, 1982).
7. This campaign is discussed in James J. Ward, "'Smash the Fascists...': German Communist Efforts to Counter the Nazis, 1930–31," *Central European History* 14, no. 1 (1981): 30–62; see also Hans Coppi, "'Aufbruch' im Spannungsfeld von Nationalismus und Kommunismus—eine Zeitschrift für Grenzgänger," in Susanne Römer and Hans Coppi, eds., *Aufbruch. Dokumentation einer Zeitschrift zwischen den Fronten* (Koblenz: Verlag Dietmar Fölbach, 2001), 50.
8. See Ward, "'Smash the Fascists,'" 61.
9. See Conan Fischer, *The German Communists and the Rise of Nazism* (Basingstoke, UK: Palgrave Macmillan, 1991).
10. See Pamela Swett, *Neighbors and Enemies: The Culture of Radicalism in Berlin, 1929–1933* (Cambridge: Cambridge University Press, 2004); see also Eve Rosenhaft, *Beating the Fascists? The German Communists and Political Violence, 1929–1933* (Cambridge: Cambridge University Press, 1983).
11. See Swett, *Neighbors and Enemies.*

12. The issue of "side-switching" is discussed in Timothy S. Brown, "'Beefsteak Nazis' and 'Brown Bolshevists': Boundaries and Identity in the Rise of National Socialism," paper presented at the Annual Meeting of the American Historical Association, San Francisco, January 2002. See also Swett, *Neighbors and Enemies,* chapter 4.

13. Swett, *Neighbors and Enemies.*

14. See chapter 4.

15. Helmuth Plessner, *The Limits of Community: A Critique of Social Radicalism* (Amherst, N.Y.: Humanity Books, 1999).

16. See Peter H. Merkl, *Political Violence Under the Swastika: 581 Early Nazis* (Princeton, NJ: Princeton University Press, 1975); Rosenhaft, *Beating the Fascists;* Richard Bessel, *Political Violence and the Rise of Nazism: The Stormtroopers in Eastern Germany, 1925–1934* (New Haven, CT: Yale University Press, 1984); Richard Bessel, "Politische Gewalt und die Krise der Weimarer Republik," in Lutz Niethammer, ed., *Bürgerliche Gesellschaft in Deutschland. Historische Einblicke, Fragen, Perspektiven* (Frankfurt am Main: Fischer Taschenbuch Verlag, 1990); Dirk Schumann, *Politische Gewalt in der Weimarer Republik: Kampf um die Strasse und Furcht vor dem Bürgerkrieg* (Essen: Klartext, 2001); Sven Reichardt, *Faschistische Kampfbünde. Gewalt und Gemeinschaft im italienischen Squadrismus und in der deutschen SA* (Cologne: Böhlau Verlag, 2002).

17. See Otto-Ernst Schüddekopf, *Linke Leute von Rechts. Die nationalrevolutionären Minderheiten und der Kommunismus in der Weimarer Republik* (Stuttgart: W. Kohlhammer Verlag, 1960); see also Otto-Ernst Schüddekopf, *National-bolshewismus in Deutschland 1918–1933* (Frankfurt am Main: Ullstein, 1972).

18. Other than a doctoral dissertation from the early 1980s (Nancy Aumann, "From Legality to Illegality: The Communist Party of Germany in Transition, 1930–1933" [Ph.D. dissertation, University of Wisconsin–Madison, 1982]) and the piece of GDR scholarship cited above (Doehler and Fischer, *Revolutionäre Militärpolitik*), the present volume is the only work to give this campaign serious attention.

19. On the idea of the *Volksgemeinschaft* see the discussion in Claus-Christian W. Szejnmann, *Nazism in Central Germany: The Brownshirts in "Red" Saxony* (Providence and Oxford: Berghahn, 1999), 118–22. On the *Volksgemeinschaft* idea after 1933, see Gerhard Paul, "Die widerspenstige 'Volksgemeinschaft.' Dissens und Verweigerung im Dritten Reich," in Peter Steinbach and Johannes Tuchel, eds., *Widerstand gegen den Nationalsozialismus* (Bonn: Bundeszentrale für Politische Bildung, 1994), 395–410; and Bernd Stöver, *Volksgemeinschaft im Dritten Reich. Die Konsensbereitschaft der Deutschen im Spiegel sozialistischer Berichte* (Düsseldorf: Droste Verlag, 1993).

20. See Fischer, *German Communists.*

21. See Timothy S. Brown, "Richard Scheringer, the KPD and the Politics of Class and Nation in Germany: 1922–1969," *Contemporary European History* 14, no. 1 (August 2005): 317–46.

22. The concept of totalitarianism, long out of favor for its association with Cold War anti-Communism, has made somewhat of a comeback in recent years. See the discussion of this issue in Ian Kershaw, *The Nazi Dictatorship: Problems and Perspectives of Interpretation* (London: Hodder Arnold, 2000), chapters 2 and 10; the concept, as Kershaw points out, is rather less useful for the study of movements than it is for the study of regimes. For an analysis of the latter see Ian Kershaw and Moshe Lewin, eds., *Stalinism and Nazism: Dictatorships in Comparison* (Cambridge: Cambridge University Press, 1997); see also Henry Rousso, ed., *Stalinism and Nazism: History and Memory Compared* (Lincoln: University of Nebraska Press, 1999).

23. On the importance of noninstitutional actors in the propaganda of fascism, see Roger Griffin, *The Nature of Fascism* (New York: Routledge, 1991).

24. Klaus-Michael Mallmann, *Kommunisten in der Weimarer Republik. Sozialgeschichte einer revolutionären Bewegung* (Darmstadt: Wissenschaftliche Buchgesellschaft, 1996).

25. A point made by Gerhard Paul in *Aufstand der Bilder. Die NS-Propaganda vor 1933* (Bonn: Dietz, 1990), 11.

26. Noteworthy exceptions are Fischer, *German Communists;* Christian Striefler, *Kampf um die Macht. Kommunisten und Nationalsozialisten am Ende der Weimarer Republik* (Berlin: Propyläen, 1993); and Swett, *Neighbors and Enemies.*

27. David Schoenbaum noted several decades ago that German fascism and the Hitler movement were not coterminous; "Germany was full of ideological fascists," writes Schoenbaum, "'conservative revolutionaries,' 'national Bolsheviks,' *Bündische Jugend.* All of them could have communicated with Charles Maurras or Mussolini. Communicating with Hitler was not so easy, either before 1933 or after." See *Hitler's Social Revolution: Class and Status in Nazi Germany, 1933–1939* (Garden City, NY: Anchor Books, 1967), xv. The implications of this observation for understanding the radical scene in the Weimar Republic have largely not been followed up.

28. See the discussion in Kershaw, *Nazi Dictatorship,* 262ff; see also Hans Mommsen, "National Socialism: Continuity and Change," in Walter Laqueur, ed., *Fascism: A Reader's Guide* (Berkeley: University of California Press, 1976), 184.

29. Paul, *Aufstand der Bilder,* 11.

30. Michael Mann terms these the "idealist" and "materialist" schools; see *Fascists* (Cambridge: Cambridge University Press), 4–5.

31. Walter Benjamin, "The Work of Art in the Age of Mechanical Reproduction," in *Illuminations* (New York: Schocken Books, 1968), 217–51.

32. See the discussion of this issue in Kershaw, *Nazi Dictatorship,* chapter 2.

33. See Jürgen Falter, *Hitler's Wähler* (Munich: Beck, 1991); Jürgen Falter, "How Likely Were Workers to Vote for the NSDAP?" in Conan Fischer, ed., *The Rise of National Socialism and the Working Classes in Weimar Germany* (Providence and Oxford: Berghahn, 1996), 9–45; Thomas Childers, *The Nazi Voter: The Social Foundations of Fascism in Germany, 1919–1933* (Chapel Hill: University of North Carolina Press, 1983); Thomas Childers, "The Social Bases of the National Socialist Vote," *Journal of Contemporary History* 11, no. 4 (1976): 17–42.

34. For an excellent brief summary of the history of the debate about National Socialism's social makeup, see Detlef Mühlberger, ed., *Hitler's Voice: The Völkischer Beobachter, 1920–1933,* vol. 2 (Bern: Peter Lang, 2004), 105–8.

35. See Conan Fischer, "Class Enemies or Class Brothers? Communist-Nazi Relations in Germany, 1929–33," *European History Review* 15, no. 3 (July 1985): 259–79; and the following exchange in the journal *Social History:* Richard Bessel and Mathilde Jamin, "Nazis, Workers, and the Uses of Quantitative Evidence," *Social History* 4 (January 1979): 111–16; Conan Fischer and Carolyn Hicks, "Statistics and the Historian: The Occupational Profile of the SA of the NSDAP," *Social History* 5 (January 1980): 131–38. See also Peter Baldwin, "Social Interpretations of Nazism: Renewing a Tradition," *Journal of Contemporary History* 25, no. 1 (January 1990): 5–37. Conan Fischer has given the percentage of working-class stormtroopers as 50 percent for Germany as a whole, and other scholars give similar figures; see Detlef Mühlberger, *Hitler's Followers: Studies in the Sociology of the Nazi Movement* (London: Routledge, 1991), 116–20; and Michael H. Kater, "Ansätze zu einer Soziologie der SA bis zur Röhm-Krise," in *Soziale Bewegungen und Politische Verfassung, Industrielle Welt: Schriftenreihe des Arbeitskreises für moderne Sozialgeschichte* 62 (1975): 339–79; Mathilde Jamin, *Zwischen den Klassen: Zur Sozialstruktur der SA-Führerschaft* (Wuppertal: Hammer, 1984), 371. The percentage of working-class stormtroopers was undoubtedly significantly higher than 50 percent in some large cities. The lower middle classes were also heavily represented, but as Peter Merkl has pointed out, the usefulness of strict class delineations in a period of social upheaval, widespread poverty, and unemployment is doubtful; see Peter H. Merkl, *The Making of a Stormtrooper* (Princeton, NJ: Princeton University Press, 1980), 153, and Merkl, *Political Violence,* 75–76.

36. Sheila Fitzpatrick, *Tear Off the Mask! Identity and Imposture in Twentieth-Century Russia* (Princeton, NJ: Princeton University Press, 2005).

37. Juan J. Linz, "Some Notes Toward a Comparative Study of Fascism in Sociological Historical Perspective," in Walter Laqueur, ed., *Fascism: A Reader's Guide* (Berkeley: University of California Press, 1976), 4.

38. "First they stole the colour red," wrote Ernst Bloch, "stirred things up with it. ... [Then] the posters gradually grew paler and paler so that they no longer frightened the financial backer." See "Inventory of Revolutionary Appearance" (1933) in *Heritage of Our Times,* trans. J. Cummings (1933; Cambridge: Polity Press, 1991), 64–67.

39. William H. Sewell, Jr., "The Concept(s) of Culture," in Victoria E. Bonnell and Lynn Hunt, eds., *Beyond the Cultural Turn: New Directions in the Study of Society and Culture* (Berkeley: University of California Press, 1999), 49.

40. Ibid., 56.

41. Mann, *Fascists,* 3.

42. Ronald Grigor Suny, "Back and Beyond: Reversing the Cultural Turn?" *American Historical Review* (December 2002), 1494–95.

43. This process was exemplified by the history of revolt in and around the Nazi movement (the focus of chapter 3), by Communist attempts to turn this revolt in an explicitly left-wing, anticapitalist direction (explored in chapter 4), and by the various actors—from the Youth Movement, the "National Bolshevik" scene, or left- or right-wing splinter groups—existing in the conflict zone in between (discussed throughout).

44. Mann, *Fascists,* 3.

45. See Jeffrey Herf, *Reactionary Modernism: Technology, Culture, and Politics in Weimar and the Third Reich* (Cambridge: Cambridge University Press, 1986).

46. Thomas Meyer, *Die Inszenierung des Scheins. Voraussetzungen und Folgen symbolischer Politik* (Frankfurt am Main: Suhrkamp, 1991).

47. See chapter 4.

48. John Gray, *Al Qaeda and What It Means to Be Modern* (New York: The New Press, 2003), 3.

49. Benjamin, "The Work of Art in the Age of Mechanical Reproduction," 241.

50. François Furet, *The Passing of an Illusion: The Idea of Communism in the Twentieth Century* (Chicago: University of Chicago Press, 1995), 4.

51. Point 24 of the 25-point program of the National Socialist German Workers' Party, reprinted in Gottfried Feder, *Hitler's Official Program and its Fundamental Ideas* (1920; New York: Howard Fertig, 1971), 43.

52. Furet, *Passing of an Illusion,* 18.

53. The goal of extremist mass movements, then, was to offer their followers precisely these new and more authentic forms of collectivity, that is, an ideal version of *community.*

54. See the discussion of the performative turn in Vikki Bell, *Culture and Performance: The Challenge of Ethics, Politics, and Feminist Theory* (Oxford: Berg, 2007).

55. Sonya O. Rose, *Limited Livelihoods: Gender and Class in Nineteenth-Century England* (Berkeley: University of California Press, 1992), 8.

56. On the concept of authenticity see Charles Taylor, *The Ethics of Authenticity* (Cambridge, MA: Harvard University Press, 1992).

57. See Detlef Siegfried, "White Negroes. Westdeutsche Faszinationen des Echten," in Michael Rauhut and Thomas Kochan, eds., *Bye Bye, Lübben City. Bluesfreaks, Tramps und Hippies in der DDR* (Berlin: Schwarzkopf & Schwarzkopf, 2004), 333–344, 334.

58. On the life and career(s) of Richard Scheringer, see Brown, "Richard Scheringer."

59. Gordon A. Craig, *The Politics of the Prussian Army, 1640–1945* (Oxford: Clarendon Press, 1955), 427–28.

60. Thilo Vogelsang, *Reichswehr, Staat und NSDAP. Beiträge zur deutschen Geschichte 1930–1932* (Stuttgart: Deutsche Verlags-Anstalt, 1962), 82.

61. Alan Bullock, *Hitler: A Study in Tyranny* (New York: Bantam, 1953), 131; Craig, *Politics of the Prussian Army,* 434.

62. Quoted in Bullock, *Hitler,* 131. The speech was given in Munich in May 1929.

63. Craig, *Politics of the Prussian Army,* 434; Francis L. Carsten, Reichswehr *und Politik, 1918–1933* (Cologne: Kiepenheuer & Witsch, 1965), 341.

64. Carsten, Reichswehr *und Politik,* 341–33; Vogelsang, *Reichswehr,* 82.

65. Scheringer's superior, General Ludwig Beck, testified to this effect at the trial; see Hans Mommsen, *The Rise and Fall of Weimar Democracy* (Chapel Hill: University of North Carolina Press, 1989), 424.
66. Ibid. See Groener, "Einleitung eines Verfahrens wegen Vorbereitung zum Hochverrat," 17 March 1930, and other correspondence in Institut für Zeitgeschichte (hereafter IfZ) Fa 70.
67. This formulation appeared in an anonymous flier titled "The spirit of the army is dead!" Vogelsang, *Reichwehr*, 83.
68. Carsten, Reichswehr *und Politik*, 343.
69. Richard Scheringer, *Das Grosse Los. Unter Soldaten, Bauern und Rebellen* (Hamburg: Rohwolt, 1959), 191.
70. Ibid., 192. Two of the three later belonged to the SA themselves; Wendt joined even before the treason trial began. He quit with the outbreak of the Stennes Revolt, which he called the "revolution of the German working people"; see *Vorwärtz*, 5 April 1931. Ludin assumed a leadership position in the SA after the Leipzig trial.
71. The details of the case against Scheringer are discussed in "In Namen des Reichs," IfZ 1827/56.
72. The Young Plan, formulated by the American politician and economic advisor Owen Young, set the reparations payments required by the Treaty of Versailles at 121 billion Reichsmarks, to be paid in fifty-nine yearly installments. Reparations were suspended under the Treaty of Lausanne in July 1932.
73. Vogelsang, *Reichwehr*, 92.
74. Ian Kershaw, *Hitler, 1889–1936: Hubris* (New York: W. W. Norton, 1998), 337.
75. Dr. Otto Strasser (1897–1974) had been a member of the so-called Nazi left and coeditor, with his brother Gregor, of the Berlin-based *Kampfverlag*, a left-wing National Socialist press. The last holdout of this Nazi left after its defeat at the Bamberg party congress in 1926, Strasser came into repeated conflict with Hitler over the course of the movement and finally quit the NSDAP altogether in July 1930. Declaring that "the socialists are leaving the NSDAP," Strasser went on to form his own organization, the *Kampfgemeinschaft Revolutionäre Nationalsozialisten* (KGRNS). See the sketch of Strasser in Patrick Moreau, "Otto Strasser: Nationalist Socialism versus National Socialism," in Ronald Smelser and Rainer Zitelmann, eds., *The Nazi Elite* (New York: New York University Press, 1993), 235–44; see also Patrick Moreau, *Nationalsozialismus von Links. Die "Kampfgemeinschaft Revolutionärer Nationalsozialisten" und die "Schwarze Front" Otto Strassers 1930–1935* (Stuttgart: Deutsche Verlagsanstalt, 1984); Günther Bartsch, *Zwischen drei Stühlen. Otto Strasser. Eine Biographie* (Koblenz: Verlag Siegfried Bublies, 1990); Kurt Gossweiler, *Die Strasser-Legende* (Berlin: edition ost/Neues Berlin, 1994); and the relevant sections in Louis Dupeux, *Nationalbolshewismus in Deutschland 1919–1933. Kommunistische Strategie und konservative Dynamik* (Munich: Verlag C. H. Beck, 1985).
76. Scheringer, *Das Grosse Los*, 218.
77. Bullock, *Hitler*, 130–31, 134.
78. Joseph Goebbels was delighted with the result of Hitler's appearance at the trial: "The echo in the press is magnificent." See *Die Tagebücher von Joseph Goebbels. Sämtliche Fragmente. Teil I. Aufzeichnungen 1924–1941. Band 1. 27.6.24–31.12.1930,* ed. Elke Fröhlich (Munich: K. G. Sauer, 1987), entry for 26 September 1930.
79. Walther Stennes (1895–1983), former Great War officer and Berlin police captain, held the post of OSAF Stellvertreter Ost (deputy to the higher SA leadership–East). See Moreau, *Nationalsozialismus von Links*.
80. Scheringer, *Das Grosse Los*, 227.
81. While in prison, Scheringer was exposed to the Communist Manifesto and learned Russian with the help of a Communist fellow prisoner, Heinrich Kurella; see Coppi, "'Aufbruch,'" 30. For an account of this period of Scheringer's development from a Communist fellow prisoner, see Fritz Gäbler, "Erinnerungen an meine Festungshaft in Gollnow und meine erste Bekanntschaft mit Richard Scheringer," in *Beiträge zur Geschichte der deutschen Arbeiterbewegung*, 1961 Heft I-IV pp. 621–635.

82. Scheringer, *Das Grosse Los,* 237; Goebbels mentions the trip in his diary, observing of Scheringer: "He's concerned above all with the social question." See Goebbels, *Tagebücher, Teil I, Band 1,* entry for 26 February 1931.

83. Quoted in Scheringer, *Das Grosse Los,* 237.

84. Thilo Vogelsang, "Der Sogenannte 'Scheringer Kreis,'" in *Gutachten der Institut für Zeitgeschichte, Bd. 2* (Stuttgart: Deutsche Verlagsanstalt, 1966), 470.

85. Scheringer, *Das Grosse Los,* 192.

86. For a detailed discussion of the press coverage, see Herbert Holst, "Richard Scheringer. Ein Beitrag zur Biographie," BA, Nachlass Scheringer NY 4037–50, pp. 48–59.

87. Quoted in "Der Leutnant von Ulm. Richard Scheringer 70 Jahre alt," *Süddeutsche Zeitung,* 14–15 September 1974.

88. *Augsburger Post,* 21 March 1931.

89. "Das Echo der mutigen Tat Scheringers," *Die Rote Fahne,* no. 79, 4 March 1931.

90. *Die Tagebücher von Joseph Goebbels. Sämtliche Fragmente. Teil I. Aufzeichnungen 1924–1941. Band 2. 1.1.1931–31.12.1936,* ed. Elke Fröhlich (Munich: K. G. Sauer, 1987), entry for 22 March 1931.

91. Conan Fischer, *German Communists,* 112. Karl Radek's so-called Schlageter Speech of June 1923, celebrating the death of a young nationalist militant executed by the French occupation authorities, signaled an early willingness on the part of the KPD to make common cause with nationalist extremists. See Karl Radek, "Leo Schlageter, der Wanderer ins Nichts," in Karl O. Paetel, *Versuchung oder Chance? Zur Geschichte des Nationalbolshevismus* (Göttingen: Musterschmidt-Verlag, 1965). For a detailed treatment of the "Schlageter line" from a contemporary/participant, see Ruth Fischer, *Stalin and German Communism: A Study in the Origins of the State Party* (Cambridge, MA: Harvard University Press, 1948), 268–87.

92. The full text of the "Programmerklärung zur nationalen und sozialen Befreiung des deutschen Volkes" is reprinted in Hermann Weber, ed., *Der deutsche Kommunismus. Dokumente* (Cologne: Kiepenheuer & Witsch, 1963), 58–65.

93. BA-SAPMO RY 1/ I 2/3/22.

94. See *Die Rote Fahne,* 24 August 1930. The program was a response to both the startling electoral success of the NSDAP in the state and local elections of 1929 and the signs of disarray in the Nazi camp signaled by the departure of Otto Strasser in July 1930; see Coppi, "'Aufbruch,'" 20. The program is usually attributed to Heinz Neumann, writing at the instigation of Stalin; see Vogelsang, "'Scheringer Kreis,'" 469; Fischer, *German Communists,* 106–7; Adolf Ehrt, *Totale Krise—totale Revolution? Die "Schwarze Front" des Völkischen Nationalismus* (Berlin, 1933), 201; Georg Schwarz, *Völker hört die Signale. KPD bankrott* (Berlin, 1933), 201; Babette Gross, *Willy Münzenberg, Eine politische Biographie* (Stuttgart, 1968), 224; Hans Coppi questions Neumann's involvement, noting the fundamental similarity between the Program for the National and Social Liberation of the German People and the declaration of the fight against National Socialism drafted by the Central European Secretariat of the Comintern in April 1930. See Coppi, "'Aufbruch,'" 20.

95. Ward, "'Smash the Fascists,'" 61.

96. Coppi, "'Aufbruch,'" 23. The nationalist program was followed by the publication of a *Bauernhilfsprogram* in early 1931; see Vogelsang, "'Scheringer Kreis,'" 469.

97. Coppi, "'Aufbruch,'" 21; Fischer, *German Communists,* 48.

98. BA-SAPMO, RY 1//I/2/1/78, Bl. 120. Protokoll der Sitzung des Zentralkomitees 14–15 May 1931. See also Schüddekopf, *National-bolshewismus,* 294–95.

99. Scheringer, *Das Grosse Los,* 227. See the remarks in Gäbler, 621–35.

100. Coppi, "'Aufbruch,'" 41–42; see also Ward, "'Smash the Fascists,'" 52. After 1925, the propaganda and intelligence work of the *M-Apparat* was divided along lines of competency that included the SPD and *Reichsbanner* (in some localities also the Center Party); the right-radical organizations: NSDAP, SA, SS, *Stahlhelm, Deutschnationale Volkspartei* (DNVP); the police; the armed forces; factories and government agencies; and counterintelligence, subdivided into

offensive (police, judiciary, enemy intelligence) and defensive (uncovering of spies, traitors, and provocateurs) sections. The attempt to win converts among the social revolutionary elements in the NSDAP was the responsibility of Ressort C. Bernd Kaufmann et al., *Der Nachrichtendienst der KPD 1919–1937* (Berlin: Dietz Verlag, 1993), 227. Kippenberger contributed a chapter on the military lessons of the Hamburg fighting to a Comintern text—*Der bewaffnete Aufstand* ("The Armed Insurrection"); see James J. Ward, "Revolution in the Revolution? Ideas of Armed Struggle in the German Communist Movement, 1929–1933," paper presented at the History Conference of Hudson Valley Colleges and Universities, Bard College, 27 October 1983, 6–7.

101. "In Namen des Reiches …" IfZ München, 1827/56, p. 8.

102. IfZ München MA 644, "Aus dem Brief des Oberleutnant a.D. Scheringer an den kommunistischen Abgeordneten Kippenberger."

103. *Erwachendes Volk—Briefe an Leutnant Scheringer* (Berlin: Agis-Verlag, 1931).

104. Leon Trotsky, *The Struggle Against Fascism in Germany* (New York: Pathfinder Press, 1971).

105. Carl von Ossietzky, *Sämtliche Schriften. Band VI. 1931–1933. Texte 969–1082*, ed. Gerhard Kraiker, Gunther Nickel, Renke Siems, and Elke Suhr (Reibeck bei Hamburg: Rohwolt, 1994), 134–35.

106. Hans Pütz, *Dokumente kommunistischer Führungskorruption. Die KPD im Dienste der russischen Aussenpolitik* (Leipzig: Kurt Wildeis, 1931), 30.

107. Hans Mommsen, *Alternatives to Hitler: German Resistance Under the Nazis* (Princeton, NJ: Princeton University Press, 2003), 10.

108. George L. Mosse, *Fallen Soldiers: Reshaping the Memory of the World Wars* (New York: Oxford University Press, 1990), 7.

109. Karen Hagemann and Stefanie Schüler-Springorum eds., *Home/Front: The Military, War, and Gender in Twentieth-Century Germany* (New York: Berg, 2002), 69–73.

110. James M. Diehl, *Paramilitary Politics in Weimar Germany* (Bloomington: Indiana University Press, 1977), 94.

111. Mosse, *Fallen Soldiers*, 183. The classic study of the *Stahlhelm* is Volker R. Berghahn, *Der Stahlhelm. Bund der Frontsoldaten 1918–1935* (Düsseldorf: Droste, 1966).

112. On the relationship between the *Stahlhelm* and the *Wehrwolf*, see Diehl, *Paramilitary Politics*, 119–20.

113. Ibid., 94–99.

114. Ken Post, *Communists and National Socialists: The Foundations of a Century, 1914–1939* (New York: St. Martin's Press, 1997), 100.

115. Richard Bessel, *Germany After the First World War* (Oxford: Oxford University Press, 1995).

116. On the *Freikorps* see Robert G. L. Waite, *Vanguard of Nazism: The Free Corps Movement in Postwar Germany, 1918–1923* (Cambridge, MA: Harvard University Press, 1970).

117. Ibid.

118. Irmtraud Götz von Olenhusen, "Vom Jungstahlhelm zur SA: Die junge Nachkriegsgeneration in den paramilitärischen Verbänden der Weimarer Republik," in Wolfgang R. Krabbe, ed., *Politische Jugend in der Weimarer Republik* (Bochum: Universitätsverlag Dr. N. Brockmeyer, 1993), 178.

119. Stanley G. Payne, *Fascism: Comparison and Definition* (Madison: University of Wisconsin Press, 1980).

120. Philip Selznick, *The Organizational Weapon: A Study of Bolshevik Strategy and Tactics* (New York: McGraw-Hill, 1952), 43.

121. Eric D. Weitz, *Creating German Communism, 1890–1990: From Popular Protests to Socialist State* (Princeton, NJ: Princeton University Press, 1997), 196. See also Mallmann, *Kommunisten in der Weimarer Republik*, 109–17.

122. Diehl, *Paramilitary Politics*, 188. For a detailed discussion of the military aspects of the RFB's early development see Gruppe MAGMA, *… denn Angriff ist die beste Verteidigung." Die KPD zwischen Revolution und Faschismus* (Bonn: Pahl Rugenstein-Verlag, 2001), 85–89, 93–96.

123. "Zusammenfassende Darstellung über die Rote Frontkämpferbund (R.F.B.) und der Rote Jungsturm (R.J.)," 2. MA 100418, Bayerisches Hauptstaatsarchiv (BHStA).

124. Ibid. The *Rote Jungsturm* was founded in Jena on 22 August 1924; its name was changed to *Rote Jungfront* in January, 1925.

125. See Ward, "Revolution in the Revolution?"

126. A reference to the acronym of the Soviet Union's secret police—GPU—changed to OGPU in 1923.

127. Viktor Gilensen, "Die Komintern und die 'paramilitarischen Formationen' der Kommunist-ischen Partei Deutschlands (1926–1932)," *Forum für osteuropäische Ideen- und Zeitgeschichte* 5, no. 1 (2001): 15.

128. Weitz, *Creating German Communism*, 196. See also Gilensen, "Komintern," 16.

129. Helmut Schelsky, Die skeptische Generation. Eine Soziologie der deutschen Jugend (Düssel-dorf-Köln: Diederichs 1957).

130. Plessner, *Limits of Community*, 75, 83.

131. Ibid., 47.

132. Ibid., 131.

133. See Bernd Hüppauf, "The Birth of Fascist Man from the Spirit of the Front," in John Milfull, ed., *The Attractions of Fascism: Social Psychology and Aesthetics of the "Triumph of the Right"* (New York: Berg, 1990), 47; Bernd Hüppauf, "Langemarck, Verdun, and the Myth of a New Man in Germany after the First World War," *War & Society* 6, no. 2 (September 1988): 103; Mosse, *Fallen Soldiers*, 71; Reinhard Dithmar, *Der Langemarck-Mythos in Dichtung und Unter-richt* (Neuwied: Luchterhand, 1992).

134. See Walter Laqueur, *Young Germany: A History of the German Youth Movement* (New Bruns-wick, NJ: Transaction Books, 1984).

135. On this myth see Robert Wohl, *The Generation of 1914* (Cambridge, MA: Harvard University Press, 1983), 2.

136. Hans-Christian Brandenberg, *Die Geschichte der HJ. Wege und Irrwege einer Generation* (Co-logne: Verlag Wissenschaft, 1968), 17.

137. Ibid., 16.

138. Ibid., 90.

139. Hans Mommsen, *From Weimar to Auschwitz* (Princeton, NJ: Princeton University Press, 1991), 32.

140. Götz von Olenhusen, "Vom Jungstahlhelm zur SA," 146; Brandenberg, *Geschichte der HJ*, 20.

141. Harald Schultz-Hencke, quoted in Mommsen, *From Weimar to Auschwitz*, 33.

142. Ibid., 156.

143. Jünger had begun to publish in the journal *Arminius* in January 1926, and he never returned to *Die Standarte* after the lifting of the ban placed on it in August for publishing an article celebrating the murderers of Erzberger and Rathenau. See Thomas Nevin, *Ernst Jünger and Germany: Into the Abyss, 1914–1945* (Durham, NC: Duke University Press, 1996), 94–96.

144. The *Reichsbanner*'s youth wing, the *Jungbanner*, had almost half a million members ages 18–25 in 1928 and an additional 220,000 members ages 14–18. See Götz von Olenhusen, "Vom Jungstahlhelm zur SA," 40; Brandenberg, *Geschichte der HJ*, 88.

145. Götz von Olenhusen, "Vom Jungstahlhelm zur SA," 155.

146. Birgit Retzlaff, *Arbeiterjugend gegen Hitler. Der Widerstand ehemaliger Angehöriger der Sozialis-tischen Arbeiterjugendbewegung gegen das Dritte Reich* (Bielefeld: Paegelit, 1993), 43.

147. Quoted in Frank Bajohr, "In doppelter Isolation. Zum Widerstand der Arbeiterjugendbewe-gung gegen den Nationalsozialismus," in Wilfried Breyvogel, ed., *Piraten, Swings und Junge Garde. Jugendwiderstand im Nationalsozialismus* (Bonn: Dietz, 1991), 17.

148. Ibid.

149. Ernst Erich Noth, *Die Tragödie der deutschen Jugend* (Frankfurt am Main: Glotzi Verlag, 2002), 110.

150. Götz von Olenhusen, "Vom Jungstahlhelm zur SA," 178.

151. Bajohr, "In doppelter Isolation," 18.

152. Götz von Olenhusen, "Vom Jungstahlhelm zur SA," 177.

153. Otto Strasser, "The Fourteen Theses of the German Revolution," in Barbara Miller Lane and Leila J. Rupp, eds., *Nazi Ideology Before 1933: A Documentation* (Austin: University of Texas Press, 1978), 110.

154. *Der Angriff,* 14 April 1933. On Nazism and the mythology of heroic youth in the Great War, see Jay W. Baird, *To Die for Germany: Heroes in the Nazi Pantheon* (Bloomington: Indiana University Press, 1990), chapter 1.

155. Birgit Rätsch-Langejürgen, *Das Prinzip Widerstand. Leben und Wirken von Ernst Niekisch* (Bonn: Bouvier Verlag, 1997), 133.

156. Brandenberg, *Geschichte der HJ,* 16; on the roots of the idea of the *Volksgemeinschaft* in the war experience, see Gunther Mai, "'Verteidigungskrieg' und 'Volksgemeinschaft.' Staatliche Selbstbehauptung, nationale Solidarität und soziale Befreiung in Deutschland in der Zeit des Ersten Weltkriegs (1900–1925)," in Wolfgang Michalka, ed., *Der Erste Weltkrieg. Wirklichkeit, Wahrnehmung, Analyse* (Munich: Piper, 1994), 583–602.

157. Bruce Campbell, "The Schilljugend: From Wehrjugend to Luftschutz," in Wolfgang R. Krabbe, ed., *Politische Jugend in der Weimarer Republik* (Bochum: Universitätsverlag Dr. N. Brockmeyer, 1993), 183–201.

158. Götz von Olenhusen, "Vom Jungstahlhelm zur SA," 151.

159. Richard Bessel, "The 'Front Generation' and the Politics of Weimar Germany," in Mark Roseman, ed., *Generations in Conflict: Youth Revolt and Generational Formation in Germany, 1770–1968* (Cambridge: Cambridge University Press, 1995), 134. See also Sven Reichardt, "Totalitäre Gewaltpolitik? Überlegungen zum Verhältnis von nationalsozialistischer und kommunistischer Gewalt in der Weimarer Republik," in Wolfgang Hardtwig, ed., *Ordnungen in der Krise. Zur politischen Kulturgeschichte Deutschlands 1900–1933* (Munich: R. Oldenbourg Verlag, 2007), 399.

160. Susanne Meinl, *Nationalsozialisten gegen Hitler. Die nationalrevolutionäre Opposition um Friedrich Wilhelm Heinz* (Berlin: Siedler, 2000), 175–77.

161. F. L. Carsten, *The Rise of Fascism* (Berkeley: University of California Press, 1982), 136. On the boycott of the film see Martin Broszat, *Hitler and the Collapse of Weimar Germany* (Leamington Spa, UK: Berg, 1987), 32–36. At the premiere, in December 1930, in the *Kino Mozartsaal* on the Nollendorfplatz, Nazis interrupted the film by releasing white mice in the theater; see Sven Felix Kellerhoff, *Hitler's Berlin. Geschichte einer Hassliebe* (Berlin: be.bra Verlag, 2005).

162. Meinl, *Nationalsozialisten gegen Hitler,* 179–80. On Ewer's role in the propaganda campaign around another Nazi obsession, the martyrdom of the SA leader Horst Wessel, see Andreas Mix, "Er liebte eine Prostituierte. Wie der Student und Propagandamusiker Horst Wessel zum Vorzeige-Märtyrer der Nazis wurde," *Berliner Zeitung,* 9 October 2007.

163. Mosse, *Fallen Soldiers,* 187. Pamela Swett is absolutely correct to note that the youth of the late 1920s had had no direct experience of war and that their revolt oriented itself against adult tutelage and gender uncertainties; but it was precisely the time lag that allowed "war" to become so entrenched in the minds of German youth. See Swett, *Neighbors and Enemies,* 295.

164. Guido Grünewald, "Friedenssicherung durch radikale Kriegsdienstgegnerschaft: Der Bund der Kriegsdienstgegner (BdK) 1919–1933," in K. Holl and W. Wette, eds., *Pazifismus in der Weimarer Republik* (Paderborn: Ferdinand Schöningh, 1981), 76.

165. See Timothy S. Brown, "Subcultures, Pop Music and Politics: 'Skinheads' and 'Nazi Rock' in England and Germany," *Journal of Social History* 38, no. 1 (Fall 2004): 157–78.

166. Schüddekopf, *National-bolshewismus,* 303.

167. See Mathias von Hellfeld, *Bündische Jugend und Hitlerjugend. Zur Geschichte von Anpassung und Widerstand 1930–1939* (Cologne: Verlag Wissenschaft und Politik, 1987).

168. Ibid., 76. The *Bündisch* groups encompassed some sixty thousand youth in about thirty groups; the youth affiliates of the major *Wehrverbände* supplied another 250,000 members. See Schüddekopf, *National-bolshewismus,* 228.

169. See Felix Raabe, *Die Bündische Jugend. Ein Beitrag zur Geschichte der Weimarer Republic* (Stuttgart: Brentano Verlag, 1961); Alexander Bahar, *Sozialrevolutionärer Nationalismus zwischen Konservativer Revolution und Sozialismus. Harro Schulze-Boyson und der "Gegner"-Kreis* (Koblenz: Verlag Dietmar Fölbach, 1992); Campbell, "Schilljugend"; Detlev Peukert, *Jugend zwischen Krieg und Krise. Lebenswelten von Arbeiterjungen in der Weimarer Republik* (Cologne: Bund Verlag, 1987); Mathias von Hellfeld, *Die betrogene Generation. Jugend im Faschismus* (Cologne: Pahl-Rugenstein, 1985).

170. See James Ward, "Pipe Dreams or Revolutionary Politics: The Group of Social Revolutionary Nationalists in Weimar Germany," *Journal of Contemporary History* 15, no. 3 (July 1980): 513–32; Paetel, *Versuchung oder Chance?* See also the documents in Werner Kindt, ed., *Die deutsche Jugendbewegung 1920 bis 1933. Die bündische Zeit* (Munich: Eugen Diederichs Verlag, 1974), 1002–9.

171. Hermand Jost and Frank Trommler, *Die Kultur der Weimar Republik* (Frankfurt: Fischer, 1988), 105.

172. Rätsch-Langejürgen, *Das Prinzip Widerstand*, 137–40.

173. According to Koebel, the *Jungenschaft* had ninety groups with 1,200 young people in 1931; BA NS/23, 111: *Bündische Jugend* "An Heinrich Lüger, Reichsjugendführung/Personalamt."

174. von Hellfeld, *Bündische Jugend*, 77.

175. BA NS/23, 111: *Bündische Jugend* "An Heinrich Lüger, Reichsjugendführung/Personalamt."

176. Quoted in von Hellfeld, *Bündische Jugend*, 85.

177. Ibid., 42.

178. Laqueur, *Young Germany*. On Tusk and the militaristic aspect of the *Bündisch* idea as practiced in the *Jungenschaft*, see Silvia Klein and Bernhard Stelmaszyk, "Eberhard Köbel, 'Tusk.' Ein biographisches Porträt über die Jahre 1907–1945," in Wilfried Breyvogel, ed., *Piraten, Swings und Junge Garde. Jungendwiderstand im Nationalsozialismus* (Bonn: Dietz, 1991), 116.

179. Griffin, *Nature of Fascism*.

180. See Zeev Sternhell, "Fascist Ideology," in Walter Laqueur, ed., *Fascism: A Reader's Guide. Analyses, Interpretations, Bibliography* (Berkeley: University of California Press, 1976), 315–76.

181. Plessner, *Limits of Community*, 75.

182. Noth, *Die Tragödie*, 130. Ernst Erich Noth was the pseudonym of Paul Krantz (1909–83). He is best known for *Die Mietskaserne* (1931), a fictional depiction of interwar Berlin's working-class tenements. The book was among those burned by the Nazis on the night of 19 May 1933. Krantz had already fled into exile on 5 March.

183. Rätsch-Langejürgen, *Das Prinzip Widerstand*, 137.

184. See chapter 5.

185. Karl Rohe, *Das Reichsbanner Schwarz Rot Gold. Ein Beitrag zur Geschichte und Struktur der politischen Kampfverbände zur Zeit der Weimarer Republik* (Düsseldorf: Droste Verlag, 1966), 100.

186. Swett, *Neighbors and Enemies*, 17.

187. Götz von Olenhusen, "Vom Jungstahlhelm zur SA," 151.

188. Ibid., 155.

189. Swett, *Neighbors and Enemies*, 143–44.

190. *Neue Blätter für den Sozialismus* 2 (1931): 212.

191. Cited in ibid., 19.

192. Bajohr, "In doppelter Isolation," 32.

193. As Pamela Swett observes, "the political culture that emerged out of [the] rebellion [of young men] was similar on the extreme right and left." See *Neighbors and Enemies*, 295.

194. Campbell, "Schilljugend," 185.

195. Quoted in ibid., 187.

196. Ibid., 192.

197. Mommsen, *From Weimar to Auschwitz*, 35.

198. GStA PK Rep 77 Tit 4043 Nr. 94, "Freischar junger Nation."

199. von Hellfeld, *Bündische Jugend*, 83.
200. *Die Kommenden*, no. 31, 31 July 1932.
201. Franz Matzke, *Jugend bekennt: So sind wir!* (Leipzig: 1930).
202. Noth, *Die Tragödie*, 157. Noth identified precisely this dichotomy when he noted the way in which ideas of military discipline were intertwined with longings for social emancipation in the minds of the young generation.
203. Jünger's postwar writings tried to come to grips with this development, first by celebrating the spiritual content of the combat experience, later by reconfiguring the warrior into a "worker." See Ernst Jünger, *Der Arbeiter. Herrschaft und Gestalt* (Stuttgart: Klett-Cotta, 1982).
204. George L. Mosse, *Nationalism and Sexuality: Respectability and Abnormal Sexuality in Modern Europe* (New York: Howard Fertig, 1985); Tamar Mayer, *Gender Ironies of Nationalism: Sexing the Nation* (London: Routledge, 2000), 14.
205. Mosse, *Fallen Soldiers*, 165.
206. Quoted in ibid.
207. Ibid., 166.
208. Ibid., 60.
209. Wolfgang Lindner, *Jugendbewegung als Äußerung lebensideologischer Mentalität. Die mentalitätsgeschichtlichen Präferenzen der deutschen Jugendbewegung im Spiegel ihrer Liedertexte* (Hamburg: Verlag Dr. Kovac, 2003).
210. Mosse, *Fallen Soldiers*, 61. For an appreciation of the significance of the work of George Mosse for students of fascism, see Roger Griffin, "Withstanding the Rush of Time: The Prescience of G. L. Mosse's Anthropological Approach to Fascism," in Stanley Payne, ed., *What History Tells: George L. Mosse's Study of Modern Europe* (Madison: University of Wisconsin Press, 2003).
211. Mosse, *Fallen Soldiers*, 72.
212. Hagemann and Schüler-Springorum, *Home/Front: The Military, War, and Gender in Twentieth-Century Germany* (New York: Berg, 2002). "These positive images of German soldiers and comrades," write Hagemann and Schüler-Springorum, "were contrasted with the negative depiction of 'shirkers'. The men who had not entered the military were featured in the soldier newspapers as weak, cowardly and feminine. A good example was the sketch in the 28 April 1915 issue of the *Liller Kriegszeitung* which portrayed a rather 'womanly' man, thin with fine clothing, strolling through town with all passers-by staring at him. The caption read 'exempt from military duty.'"
213. Mosse, *Fallen Soldiers*, 168.
214. Waite, *Vanguard of Nazism*.
215. Wolfgang Lindner, *Jugendbewegung*; Noth, *Die Tragödie*, 130–31.
216. Laqueur, *Young Germany*.
217. Mosse, *Fallen Soldiers*, 167.
218. Bessel, *Political Violence*, 153. See also Schumann, *Politische*, 255–61.
219. See the sketch on Röhm in Conan Fischer, "Ernst Julius Röhm: Chief of Staff of the SA and Indispensable Outsider," in Ronald Smelser and Rainer Zitelmann, *The Nazi Elite* (New York: New York University Press, 1993), 173–82.
220. Cited in George L. Mosse, *Nazi Culture: Intellectual, Cultural and Social Life in the Third Reich* (New York: Schocken Books, 1981), 102.
221. "The taming of the activism through an 'embourgeoisement' of the SA," writes George Mosse, "was accompanied by stressing the importance of founding a family—the wife must be regarded as a 'comrade.'" See ibid., 19.
222. "When a stormtrooper put on his uniform and went to do his 'service,'" writes Peter Merkl, "he literally stripped off his humdrum worker's life, or meek bourgeois habit, and became a heroic superman to himself and his comrades. Marching and fighting in closed formation, in particular, he felt powerful and masculine beyond compare." See *Making of a Stormtrooper*, 231; see also Swett, *Neighbors and Enemies*, 17.
223. Swett, *Neighbors and Enemies*, 17.

224. See Weitz, *Creating German Communism*; Swett, *Neighbors and Enemies*. See also Eve Rosenhaft, "Links gleich rechts? Militante Straßengewalt um 1930," in Thomas Lindenberger and Alf Lüdtke, eds., *Physische Gewalt* (Frankfurt am Main: Suhrkamp, 1995).
225. Scheringer, *Das Grosse Los,* 479.
226. Götz von Olenhusen, "Vom Jungstahlhelm zur SA," 149–50.
227. Laqueur, *Young Germany,* 151.
228. Schüddekopf, *Linke Leute von Rechts.*
229. WAP Szczecin, PP Stettin, 7.10.31.
230. As Hans Coppi writes, it was the "attitude" (*Haltung*) of the Communists that appealed most to Scheringer; see "'Aufbruch,'" 30.
231. On the prison deliberations of Scheringer and his comrades, see *Das Grosse Los,* 227.
232. See the disturbing documentary film by Ludin's son Malte Ludin, *Two or Three Things I Know About Him* (2005). In a similar vein, see Alexandra Senfft, *Schweigen tut weh. Eine deutsche Familiengeschichte* (Berlin: Claassen Verlag, 2007).
233. HA 17/315, *"Pg. SA – Kameraden!",* Berlin, 1 September 1930.
234. *Frankfurter Zeitung,* no. 248, 2 April 1931, BA, R1501, 26073.
235. See WAP Szczecin, PP Stettin to OP Pommern, "Betrifft Kampfgemeinschaft revolutionärer Nationalsozialisten," 9 December 1930, and OP Hessen-Nassau to IM, 23 January 1931, "Betrifft Kampfgemeinschaft revolutionärer Nationalsozialisten," 121.
236. GStA PK, Rep. 77, Tit. 4043, Nr. 302, "Rundschreiben Nr. 4 der Sektion Geneisenau Sept. 1930."
237. This fact was readily acknowledged by the KPD; see Paul, *Aufstand der Bilder,* 88.
238. Linz, "Notes," 4–5.
239. Sternhell, *Neither Right nor Left: Fascist Ideology in France* (Princeton, NJ: Princeton University Press, 1996); David D. Robert, *The Syndicalist Tradition and Italian Fascism* (Chapel Hill: University of North Carolina Press, 1979).
240. Ernst Bloch, "Inventory of Revolutionary Appearance," 64–67.
241. Schoenbaum, *Hitler's Social Revolution.*
242. Paul, *Aufstand der Bilder,* 240, 165.
243. Those fascist groups that did foreground race did so mostly under the influence of National Socialism; see Payne, *Fascism.*
244. For an example of the former, see Sternhell, "Fascist Ideology"; for the latter, see Griffin, *Nature of Fascism.*
245. George L. Mosse, *The Nationalization of the Masses. Political Symbolism and Mass Movements in Germany from the Napoleonic Wars through the Third Reich* (Ithaca, NY: Cornell University Press, 1975).
246. The Frenchman Maurice Barrés wrote of a "Socialist Nationalism" as early as 1898, while the Italian Enrico Corradini posited a "National Socialism" in relation to the nationalist turn taken by revolutionary syndicalism.
247. Griffin defines "proto-fascism" as the phase during which fascist ideas are propagated by radical publicists but have not yet become connected with a concrete political movement; see *Nature of Fascism,* 50–51.
248. Mann, *Fascists,* 7.
249. The KPD "recognized the significance of the lower-middle-class issue from an early stage. Once the NSDAP began to dominate sections of this class, Communist concern was to increase and the struggle between the KPD and the NSDAP was to involve a battle for lower-middle-class, as well as working-class, support." See Fischer, *German Communists,* 21.
250. Abraham Ascher and Guenther Lewy, "National Bolshevism in Weimar Germany—Alliance of Political Extremes Against Democracy," *Social Research* 23, no. 4 (Winter 1956): 459.
251. Karl Radek, "Das machtlose Deutschland," *Internationale Presse-Korrespondenz,* vol. 3 (1923): 389.
252. See David Brandenberger, *National Bolshevism. Stalinist Mass Culture and the Formation of*

Modern Russian National Identity, 1931–1956 (Cambridge, MA: Harvard University Press, 2002); see also Erik Van Ree, *The Political Thought of Joseph Stalin: A Study in Twentieth-Century Revolutionary Patriotism* (New York: Routledge, 2002).

253. Ascher and Lewy, "National Bolshevism in Weimar Germany"; Furet, *Passing of an Illusion.*

254. Rätsch-Langejürgen, *Das Prinzip Widerstand,* 106.

255. Furet, *Passing of an Illusion,* 199.

256. On Bolshevism and the idea of "hardness," see Martin Amis, *Koba the Dread: Laughter and the Twenty Million* (New York: Vintage, 2002).

257. "Bourgeois behavior, as Hitler saw it, included nationalist hypocrisy while fellow citizens were in misery, exploitation of labor, class snobbery, the climactic subversion of the war effort in 1918 by support for democratic reforms, an unholy respect for formal academic qualifications, a tendency toward syphilis, defined further as willingness to marry the daughters of rich Jews, cowardice, indifference to the realities of race, exclusive preoccupation with money and personal affairs, and identification of the nation with the interests of the bourgeoisie." See Schoenbaum, *Hitler's Social Revolution,* 19.

258. William Sheridan Allen, *The Seizure of Power: The Experience of a Single German Town, 1930–1935* (New York: Franklin Watts, 1984). See also Paul, *Aufstand der Bilder.*

259. On the *Einwohnerwehren* see David Clay Large, *The Politics of Law and Order: A History of the Bavarian Einwohnerwehr, 1918–1921* (Philadelphia: American Philosophical Society, 1980).

260. Waite, *Vanguard of Nazism.*

261. Walter Laqueur, *Russia and Germany: A Century of Conflict* (Boston: Little, Brown, 1965), 55. Baltic *émigrés* such as Alfred Rosenberg and Max Erwin von Scheubner-Richter played an important role in the evolution of anti-Bolshevism from a "subsidiary question" to a key propaganda focus for Hitler; see ibid., 56–57.

262. Paul, *Aufstand der Bilder,* 234–36.

263. Laqueur, *Russia and Germany,* 55.

264. Ibid., 57.

265. Furet, *Passing of an Illusion,* 134, 191; on Goebbels's National Bolshevism, see Laqueur, *Russia and Germany,* 152–53; Schoenbaum, *Hitler's Social Revolution,* 22–25. Goebbels took up the theme of the linked fate of Germany and Russia in his novel *Michael* (1929) and in many articles in the *Nationalsozialistische Briefe;* "once Russia has awakened," he wrote in the 15 November 1925, issue, "the world will witness a miracle."

266. On conservative nervousness about the potential for "Bolshevist experiments" on the part of National Socialism, see Stephan Malinowski, "From King to Führer: The German Aristocracy and the Nazi Movement," *Bulletin of the German Historical Institute* 27, no. 1 (May 2005): 15.

267. Waldemar Gurian, *The Future of Bolshevism* (New York: Sheed & Ward, 1936), 77.

268. Essential studies of the SA include Reichardt, *Faschistische Kampfbünde;* Peter Longerich, *Die Braunen Bataillone. Geschichte der SA* (Munich: Beck, 1989); Eric G. Reiche, *The Development of the SA in Nürnberg, 1922–1934* (Cambridge: Cambridge University Press, 1986); Bessel, *Political Violence;* Jamin, *Zwischen den Klassen;* Conan Fischer, *Stormtroopers. A Social, Economic and Ideological Analysis, 1929–35* (London: George Allen & Unwin, 1983); Merkl, *Making of a Stormtrooper.*

269. Paul, *Aufstand der Bilder,* 139.

270. As Conan Fischer has observed, "the mass membership of the SA marked the Nazi movement's one and ultimately very significant success in mobilizing the working-class unemployed." See Fischer, "Conclusion," in Fischer, ed., *The Rise of National Socialism and the Working Classes in Weimar Germany* (Providence and Oxford: Berghahn, 1996), 239.

271. Paul, *Aufstand der Bilder,* 26.

272. Ibid., 134, 135.

273. See Ward, "'Smash the Fascists'"; Rosenhaft, *Beating the Fascists?*

274. Bloch, "Inventory of Revolutionary Appearance," 64–67.

275. Daniel Guérin, *The Brown Plague: Travels in Late Weimar and Early Nazi Germany* (Durham, NC: Duke University Press, 1994), 97.

276. See Reichardt, *Faschistische Kampfbünde*, 523.

277. Schoenbaum, *Hitler's Social Revolution*, 18.

278. "Empty-handed, despairing in the SA Command's policies, faith in the Third Reich lost, homeless and penniless elements will, like the peasants of the Thirty Years' War, roam the countryside. The impoverished villages and farms can no more help these people than can the remote central authorities. Has the authoritarian Reich government taken precautions? There is one that Bavaria, patriotic and with its picturesque villages, can take: the strengthening of the Bavarian Guard to a degree at which it can prevent robbery and arson. For behind the despairing SA men grins the MASK OF MOSCOW!" *Regensburger Anzeiger*, no. 270, 30 September 1932, p. 2, reprinted in Conan Fischer, *The Rise of the Nazis* (Manchester: Manchester University Press, 1995).

279. See, for example, Mommsen, *Alternatives to Hitler*, 10.

280. Laqueur, *Russia and Germany*, 56. On the use of this concept in the context of SA radicalism, see Reichardt, *Faschistische Kampfbünde*, 635–36.

281. See Adolf Hitler, *Mein Kampf* (Boston: Houghton Mifflin, 1999), 209–21.

282. See Mühlberger, *Hitler's Voice, 1:* 109.

283. Point 11, which includes the phrase "The common interest before self-interest," was constructed in opposition to what Feder called the "spiritual foundations of the present Jewish supremacy: 'Individual interest before common interest.'" See Feder, *Hitler's Official Program*, 57.

284. Barbara Miller Lane, "Nazi Ideology: Some Unfinished Business," *Central European History 7*, no. 1 (March 1974): 10–11, 19.

285. They were published before Strasser's break with Hitler. These, too, exploited the anti-Semitic aspect of Nazi economic theory, referring to "unique racial character" and so on; see Lane, "Nazi Ideology," 25. On the other hand, the program revision submitted by the northern faction was rejected by Hitler in February 1926 (ibid., 20). On the Fourteen Theses, see Bartsch, *Zwischen drei Stühlen*, 90–92.

286. Eight hundred, to be exact. A year later, there were some six thousand members in some ninety local groups, a not entirely insignificant figure if we consider that the NSDAP itself possessed only two thousand members more than a year after its founding. See Kellerhoff, *Hitler's Berlin*.

287. See Striefler, *Kampf um die Macht*, 59; see also Swett, *Neighbors and Enemies*, 211.

288. Striefler cites the use of phrases such as "Freiheit und Brot" in the *Völkischer Beobachter* and "For the oppressed, against the exploiters" in *Der Angriff*; see *Kampf um die Macht* 41–45.

289. Paul, *Aufstand der Bilder*, 255. See chapter 5.

290. As Karl O. Paetel noted, both the left and the right accused the NSDAP of having no program, but the national revolutionary groups were hardly better. Discussing the various programs on offer, Paetel observed that although Ernst Niekisch had some good ideas, his program was not really usable: "one tries to imagine someone going before a proletarian assembly with [it]." See GStA PK, Rep. 77, Tit. 4043, Nr. 395 (GSRN), "4. Rundschreiben, June 1930," p. 8.

291. See Striefler, *Kampf um die Macht*, 79–81.

292. Peter Fritzsche, *Germans into Nazis* (Cambridge, MA: Harvard University Press, 1998).

293. The term *Die Kommune* appears to have originated with Hitler and then passed into general usage in the movement; see Paul, *Aufstand der Bilder*, 144.

294. Ibid., 227–30.

295. According to Gerhard Paul, close to a third of Nazi propaganda in the Weimar Republic was aimed at criticizing the system. See ibid., 21. On the Nazi understanding of the system, see Mühlberger, *Hitler's Voice*, 21–26.

296. Meinl, *Nationalsozialisten gegen Hitler*, 159.

297. Paul, *Aufstand der Bilder*, 223.

298. The RFS was founded on June 1 as an umbrella organization for a number of local leadership schools already founded by various SA groups. Plans for the RFS had been laid before the

outbreak of the Stennes crisis in April, but the pace of the school's establishment was accelerated in the wake of the revolt. See Dietrich Orlow, *The History of the Nazi Party: 1919–1933* (Pittsburgh: University of Pittsburgh Press, 1969).

299. BA, R134/374 "Erfahrungsbericht der RFS. zum 2. Lehrgang vom 5. Juli bis 26.Juli 1931," p. 5.
300. See Fritzsche, *Germans into Nazis,* 172–83; Orlow, *History of the Nazi Party,* 11.
301. Kershaw, *Hitler, Hubris.*
302. See Orlow, *History of the Nazi Party.*
303. A fairly in-depth treatment is to be found in Bessel, *Political Violence.*
304. See Moreau, *Nationalsozialismus von Links.* On the content of the revolt in the eastern German areas under Stennes's command, see Bessell, *Political Violence.*
305. *OSAF SABE* 1 November 1926, HA 16/302.
306. Thomas Grant, *Stormtroopers and Crisis in the Nazi Movement: Activism, Ideology and Dissolution* (New York: Routledge, 2004).
307. Mommsen, *Rise and Fall,* 338.
308. Personal aggrandizement played a role in the conflict as well; there is evidence that Stennes and other SA leaders were as disappointed by the apportionment of electoral spoils as by anything else. See HA 73/1551, PD Berlin to PD Munich, 19 September 1930; Heinrich Bennecke, *Hitler und die SA* (Munich: G. Olzog, 1962).
309. One of Stennes's lieutenants complained, no doubt partly for dramatic effect, that Nazis were having the *Stahlhelm* thrown in their faces by potential recruits who questioned the NSDAP's commitment to the fight against reaction. See BA, R1501, 26071a, "Excerpt from Staf V. Mesmer's Quartalsbericht Jan.–March 1931 in J. Veltjens, 'Liebe SA-Kameraden!'"
310. BA, R1501, 26071a, "Lagebericht 16 July 1930." On Strasser's following in the Berlin Hitler Youth, see Herbert Crüger, *Ein alter Mann erzählt. Lebensbericht eines Kommunisten* (Schleuditz: GNN Verlag, 1998), 79.
311. BA, R1501 26071b, "Betrachtung zu den Ereignisse innerhalb der NSDAP vom 1. April 1931." April 22, 1931, Krach, Standartenführer III im Gausturm Berlin. Krach had been warned by SA doctor Conti that it would take a veritable campaign of intrigue to see Hitler, but he hadn't believed it until he saw it with his own eyes; Stennes demanded the resignation of *Gaugeschäftsführer* Wilke (HA 73/1551, PP Berlin to PD Munich, 16 September 1930), an increase in funding for the SA, and a minimum of two Reichstag mandates for the SA (Krach claims the demand was for three Reichstag mandates [ibid., 3]).
312. BA, R1501, 26071b, PP Berlin to IM, 21 February 1931, "Betrifft: Durchsuchung der Geschäftsräume des Osaf Ost."
313. Ibid.
314. HA 4/83, "Wie es zur Stennes-Aktion kam!"
315. Röhm's measures provoked bitter resentment among Stennes and other SA leaders. One of Stennes's close associates complained that Röhm, absent from the movement for some years, was out of touch and failed to understand the needs of the SA (BA, R1501, 26071a, Veltjens, J. "Liebe SA-Kameraden!" 7 April 1931); another wrote somewhat melodramatically that Röhm's measures amounted to "nothing less than the destruction of the SA." The reorganization of the SA, he continued, went hand in hand with the party's mistaken commitment to legality and alliance with the Nationalists. See Krach, "Betrachtung," 8.
316. HA 56/1368, *Landeskriminalpolizeiamt* (IA) Berlin, 1 May 1931; see also Orlow, *History of the Nazi Party,* 217.
317. HA 56/1368, *Landeskriminalpolizeiamt* (IA) Berlin, 1 May 1931. "Rechtsradikale Bewegung. NSDAP 1.) Die Stennes-Revolte."
318. The exact timing is unclear; Stennes claimed that his subordinates seized the offices while he was still asleep (see ibid.), although this is not mentioned in the accounts of his lieutenants (see Krach and Veltjens accounts).
319. Letter of Stennes reprinted in *Der Angriff,* no. 69, 2 April 1931.

320. HA 56/1368, *Landeskriminalpolizeiamt* (IA) Berlin, 1 May 1931. "Rechtsradikale Bewegung. NSDAP 1.) Die Stennes-Revolte." Stennes's successor, Schulz, estimated the number even higher, at 35 percent. Goebbels *Tagebücher, Teil I, Band 1*, entry for 9 April 1931.

321. Merkl, *Making of a Stormtrooper,* 179.

322. Schüddekopf, *Linke Leute von Rechts,* 323.

323. HA 56/1368. The first issue of this biweekly news sheet appeared on 9 April in an edition of twenty to thirty thousand. *Landeskriminalpolizeiamt* (IA) Berlin, 1 May 1931. "Rechtsradikale Bewegung. NSDAP 1.) Die Stennes-Revolte."

324. HA 17/325, "Nationalsozialisten Berlins!"

325. *Niedersächsische Zeitung,* no. 15, 11 April 1931, quoted in HA 73/1551, Reichsministerium des Innern, 13 May 1931, "Gründe und Auswirkungen des Zwistes Hitler-Stennes."

326. HA 73/1551, "Das Ende der SA Revolte?" *Kölnische Zeitung,* no. 189, 8 April 1931, quoted in "Gründe und Auswirkungen des Zwistes Hitler-Stennes."

327. Ibid.

328. "Ost Express," *Pravda,* no. 80, 7 April 1931, quoted in "Gründe und Auswirkungen des Zwistes Hitler-Stennes."

329. The KPD appears, in fact, to have played a role in fomenting the tensions that led up to the revolt. See Kurt G. P. Schuster, *Der Rote Frontkämpferbund 1924–1929. Beiträge zur Geschichte und Organisationsstruktur eines politischen Kampfbundes* (Düsseldorf: Droste, 1975). Stennes also appears to have had ties to the Soviet embassy in Berlin; see "Auszugsweiser Bericht in Sachen Stennes u. Genossen," 6 June 1933, IfZ 1887/56.

330. *Welt am Abend,* No. 82, 9 April 1931, BA, 26073.

331. According to Mathilde Jamin, only 10 percent of the SA leadership were workers as compared to some 50 to 55 percent of the rank and file. See *Zwischen den Klassen,* 369–71. See also Longerich, *Die Braunen Bataillone,* 144–47.

332. *Landeskriminalpolizeiamt* (IA) Berlin, 1 May 1931, "Die Stennes Revolte."

333. *Welt am Abend,* no. 82, 9 April 1931, BA, 26073. This view was echoed by a speaker at a meeting of the KPD's propaganda apparatus in Berlin, who argued that Stennes had "the assignment, conscious or unconscious, of preventing … rebellious SA proletarians from marching into the camp of the class struggle." See IfZ München MA 644, untitled fragment, probably from "Informationsmaterial (Faschismus)."

334. IfZ München MA 644, "Bericht," Berlin, 24 March 1931.

335. "An die SA. Berlins. Brief des Leutnants a. D. Scheringer," IfZ München MA 644. The appeal appeared in *Die Rote Fahne,* no. 80, under the title "Scheringer an die Berliner SA Proleten!" 5 April 1931. Scheringer also appealed to German students in "Brief an die deutschen Studenten," *Der Rote Student,* no. 2, 20 April 1931.

336. "An die SA. Berlins."

337. IfZ MA 644, "Der Rote Angriff, auf dem Prenzlauer Berg. Kampforgen gegen den Faschismus. Harausgegeben von K.P.D. Nord-Ost." *Der Rote Angriff* portrayed the defection of Scheringer as "an act of great political significance," calling on "SA proletarians and workers of the NS-DAP" to abandon their "traitorous leaders and, with the revolutionary workers under the leadership of the KPD," to "fight for the social liberation of all workers [Werktätigen] from the capitalist exploiters."

338. "An die SA. Berlins."

339. In a clear allusion to the May Day massacre of two years earlier, in which the police had fired on an illegal Communist march in Berlin, Scheringer asked: "Can someone fight for freedom and (at the same time) shoot on workers?" Ibid.

340. Ibid.

341. IfZ MA 644, "Nicht Hitler, noch Stennes, Scheringer zeigt Euch den Weg!" "SA proletarians and workers of the NSDAP!" the flier concluded, "you have recognized that your way cannot be the way of Hitler and Goebbels; you must also recognize that the way of the police captain Walther Stennes cannot and must not be your way. Scheringer calls you! Smash the NSDAP! Here to the Communist Party!!" BA, Sammlung Schumacher 330, "Stennes oder Hitler?"

342. The gulf between Hitler and Strasser has frequently been overstated, as has the supposed conservative turn in Nazi policy that accompanied the Strasser crisis. The traditional view held that the Nazis turned away from the attempt to win over the working classes in 1928–29, moving to focus on winning bourgeois voters. The NSDAP's change away from a pro-worker to a more middle-class orientation is generally placed in 1928–29. See Childers, "Social Bases," 26; J. J. Spielvogel, *Hitler and Nazi Germany: A History* (Englewood Cliffs, NJ: Prentice Hall, 1988), 48–49; Michael Kater, *The Nazi Party: A Social Profile of Members and Leaders, 1919–1945* (Cambridge, MA: Harvard University Press, 1983), 35–38, 53–54; Peter D. Stachura, "Der Kritische Wendepunkt? Die NSDAP und die Reichstagwahlen vom 20. Mai 1928," *Vierteljahreshefte für Zeitgeschichte* 26 (1978): 66–69. Orlow cites the failure of the Nazis' "urban plan" as the reason for the shift to a "rural-nationalist" plan (*History of the Nazi Party*, 76, 119–29, 138). This shift does not now appear to have taken place. Rather, as Gerhard Paul argues in *Aufstand der Bilder*, the Nazis continued to feature workers in their propaganda even while reaching out to new groups. William Brustein has emphasized the continued Nazi commitment to winning the support of the working class after 1928, calling special attention to the prolabor programs created by the NSDAP in 1930 and 1932. According to Brustein, "Hitler's chastisement of the Strassers and Goebbels had probably less to do with their insistence upon a pro–working class orientation and more to do with the former's insistence that the NSDAP must promote the interests of the *German* working class rather than those of the international working class—especially the Soviet Union's working class." See "Blue-Collar Nazism: The German Working Class and the Nazi Party," in Conan Fischer, ed., *The Rise of National Socialism and the Working Classes in Weimar Germany* (Providence and Oxford: Berghahn, 1996), 154. Falter ("How Likely") has noted the NSDAP's "particular efforts to mobilize workers" in the period 1928–33.
343. See "Der Kampf der SA gegen die Bonzakratie," in *Die Deutsche Revolution*, 12 April 1931.
344. *Deutsche Revolution*, 5 April 1931.
345. BA, Sammlung Schumacher 278, *Der Staat Seid Ihr*.
346. As Patrick Moreau notes in *Nationalsozialismus von Links*, Strasser and others ascribed to the SA the same reasons for their own split with the party, but they overlooked other issues—money, personal disagreements, the issue of Röhm's leadership—that played an important role in the outbreak of the revolt.
347. BA, Sammlung Schumacher 278, *Der Staat Seid Ihr*.
348. On Gregor Strasser's 1932 Reichstag speech see Malinowski, "From King to Führer," 14.
349. *Völkischer Beobachter*, 4 April 1931.
350. HA 17/325, "Nationalsozialisten Berlin!" See also HA 4/83, "Wie es zur Stennes-Aktion kam!"
351. HA 17/325, "Nationalsozialisten Berlin!"
352. HA 4/83, "Wie es zur Stennes-Aktion kam!" On the highly loaded quality of calling the NSDAP a "club" instead of a "party," see Roger Chickering, "Political Mobilization and Associational Life: Some Thoughts on the National Socialist German Workers' Club (e.V.)," in Larry Eugene Jones and James Retallack, eds., *Elections, Mass Politics, and Social Change in Modern Germany: New Perspectives* (New York: Cambridge University Press, 1992), 307–28.
353. HA 17/325, "Erklärung und Aufruf."
354. Bullock, *Hitler*, 149.
355. On the NSBO see Volker Kratzenberg-Annies, *Arbeiter auf dem Weg zu Hitler? Die Nationalsozialistische Betriebszellen-Organisation. Ihre Entstehung, ihre Programmatik, ihr Scheitern. 1927–1934* (Frankfurt am Main: Peter Lang, 1989); see also Gunther Mai, "National Socialist Factory Cell Organization and the German Labour Front: National Socialist Labour Policy and Organizations," in Conan Fischer, ed., *The Rise of National Socialism and the Working Classes in Weimar Germany* (Providence and Oxford: Berghahn, 1996), 117–36.
356. The Brown House was considered explosive enough an issue to receive a lecture of its own in the curriculum of the *Reichsführerschule;* see Orlow, *History of the Nazi Party*, 225.
357. Scheringer, *Das Grosse Los*, 237; Krach, "Betrachtung," 8. Goebbels mentions the trip in his

diary, observing of Scheringer: "He's concerned above all with the social question." *Goebbels Tagebücher, Teil I, Band 1,* entry for 26 February 1931.

358. Krach, "Betrachtung," 8. The issue in question was the participation of the SA in the *Grenzschutz,* the border defense organization set up by the Reichswehr to protect Germany's frontier with Poland (BA, R1501, 26071b, PP Berlin to IM, 21 February 1931, "Betrifft: Durchsuchung der Geschäftsräume des Osaf Ost."). The stormtroopers had become increasingly involved in this organization, with nationalist and militaristic motives overriding ideological objections to cooperation with the Weimar government. At the November meeting Hitler forbade SA participation in the *Grenzschutz* on precisely this latter ground, leading Kurt Kremser, the commander of the Silesian SA, to accuse him of treason to his face (IfZ ZS 177 Bd I, "Mitschreiben Gespräch Tyrell-Pfeffer von 20.2.68"). The meeting left both sides uneasy. The main topic—the SA as the basis of a future mass army—undoubtedly made Hitler nervous, while Hitler's objection to SA participation in border defense made it obvious to Stennes and others that Hitler intended to limit the independence of the SA as much as possible (IfZ 1147 Bd. I, Stennes to Vogelsang, 16 February 1957).

359. HA 17/325, "Nationalsozialisten Berlin!"

360. *Vossische Zeitung,* 5 April 1931.

361. *Vossische Zeitung,* 10 April 1931.

362. BLHA, Nachrichtenblatt Nr. 1, Nachrichtenabteilung der NS-Bewegung Stennes, 11 April 1931.

363. GStA PK, Rep. 77, Tit. 4043, Gruppenführung Silesien. Gruppenbefehl Nr. 1. Breslau, 6 June 1931.

364. BA, R1501, 26082, "Nachrichtenblatt Nr. 6," 13 July 1931.

365. *Vossische Zeitung,* 5 April 1931.

366. BA, R1501, 26071a, "SA Kameraden!"

367. HA 17/315, "Pg. SA—Kameraden!" Berlin, 1 September 1930.

368. According to Stennes, all the OSAF deputies were financially independent. Stennes's sister had high society connections, and Stennes himself had good contacts in government (IfZ, 1147 Bd. I, Stennes to Krausnick, 12 November 1956).

369. See Fischer, *Stormtroopers,* 145–46; see also Swett, *Neighbors and Enemies.*

370. *Vossische Zeitung,* 7 April 1931.

371. HA 56/1368. *Landeskriminalpolizeiamt* (IA) Berlin, 1 May 1931. "Rechtsradikale Bewegung. NSDAP 1.) Die Stennes-Revolte."

372. "Politische Schulung der SA," *Nachrichtenblatt,* no. 6, 13 July 1931.

373. "Was wir Fordern," *Nationalsozialistische Montagsblatt,* 20 July 1931. "Even if Stennes might have dreamed of a coup d'etat," writes Patrick Moreau, "he had for a long time been no revolutionary." See *Nationalsozialismus von Links,* 298.

374. HA 17/325, "Erklärung und Aufruf." Stennes's supporter in the Pomeranian SA, Hans Lustig, published an article by Dr. Ludwig Harp casting the revolt as one "between reaction and revolution, or between Rome and Germanness, which is the same thing; between the roman idea of spiritual slavery [*Gewissensknechtung*] and the German idea of freedom of conscience" (PP Stettin 16.5.31). Lustig adds at the end, "Overcome the *Bonzen!* Let them utter empty words. We are moving on to the deed. And the deed is silent!"

375. *Der Jungdeutsche,* 12 August 1931.

376. HA 56/1368, *Landeskriminalpolizeiamt* (IA) Berlin, 1 May 1931. "Rechtsradikale Bewegung. NSDAP 1.) Die Stennes-Revolte."

377. Schüddekopf, *Linke Leute von Rechts,* 323.

378. *Berliner Tageblatt,* 9 April 1931. One of the decisive factors in containing the initial phase of the revolt was the way in which the entire party organization reacted together against it; see Donald M. McKale, *The Nazi Party Courts: Hitler's Management of Conflict in His Movement, 1921–1945* (Lawrence: University Press of Kansas, 1974), 91. Hermann Göring was appointed Politischer Kommissar Oberost to oversee the expulsions of Stennes's supporters

(*Politischer Kommissar Oberost.* "Anordnung III," 17 April 1931, HA 17/325). The party's Uschla system (Investigation and Conciliation Committees) was brought into play to give legal backing to the measures, and local party leaders willingly pitched in to supply the names of suspect SA men.

379. McKale, *Nazi Party Courts*, 91.

380. The position of OSAF-Stellvertreter was abolished (IfZ 1147 Bd. I, Stennes to Vogelsang, 16 February 1957). Paul Schulz was appointed to take over Stennes's command as Kommissarischer Gruppenführer-Ost. Kurt Daluege became his adjutant. HA 6/1368, *Landeskriminalpolizeiamt* (IA) Berlin, 1 May 1931. "Rechtsradikale Bewegung. NSDAP 1.) Die Stennes-Revolte."

381. The official amalgamation of Stennes's NSKD and Strasser's KGRNS took place on 3 June 1931 (BA, R1501, 26082, "III. Die Schwarze Front").

382. When, after the failure of the alliance some months later, Strasser was criticized by Hans Wendt for going in with the SA leader in the first place (Wendt had by then come to see Stennes as a failure), Strasser excused himself with the explanation that he had only done it in order to establish better connections to the SA; WAP Szczecin, PP Stettin to OP Pommern, 10 July 1931.

383. According to Patrick Moreau, Ehrhardt hoped to use Stennes to permanently detach the SA from Hitler and bind it into a new right-wing united front with the backing of the Reichswehr. Ehrhardt appears to have hoped that an alliance with Otto Strasser would supply Stennes with the revolutionary credibility necessary to mount a serious challenge to Hitler; see Moreau, *Nationalsozialismus von Links*, 85.

384. Ehrhardt offered to help Stennes by funding a pro-rebel newspaper, the *Nationalsozialistische Montagsblatt*. Patrick Moreau speculates that Ehrhardt proposed to Stennes a coalition made up of the *Wehrwolf, Stahlhelm, Bund Oberland,* Ehrhardt's people and Strasser's KGRNS, backed by financing from heavy industry, although whether or not Ehrhardt possessed the ability to create such a wide coalition is unclear. In any case, the expansion of power represented by this arrangement must have been attractive to Stennes even if the taking on of a political organization was not. See Moreau, *Nationalsozialismus von Links*, 85. Ehrhardt managed the joining and obtained credit for the new organization from a private source (GStA PK, Rep. 77, Tit. 4043, PP Berlin, 3 June 1931).

385. BA, R1501, 26082, "National-sozialistische Kampfgemeinschaft Deutschlands," Berlin, 4 June 1931.

386. The *Kampfgemeinschaft* was composed of three main groups: Stennes's SA, centered mainly in Berlin-Brandenburg; elements of the SA and the Hitler Youth from the Rheinland and Pomerania; and many former activists from the traditional basis of the National Socialist left in Halle-Merseberg, Saxony, Silesia, and the Grenzmark; see Moreau, *Nationalsozialismus von Links*, 217, n. 276.

387. Ibid., 217.

388. Strasser recognized the danger of the split between the Stennes SA and his own party organization, and instituted ideological training on topics such as "What separates us from the NSDAP?" See ibid.

389. *Rundschreiben,* Nr. 1 der PL, 25.6.31.

390. HA 4/83, *Die Front der Arbeiter, Bauern, Soldaten,* 15 September 1931.

391. "Kampfaufruf aus dem Kerker! Brief des Oberleutnant Wendt an seine SA-Kameraden," *Die Deutsche Revolution,* no. 15, 2 April 1931.

392. *Vorwärtz,* 5 April 1931.

393. Ibid.

394. "Oberleutnant Wendt in Berlin," *Vossische Zeitung,* no. 454, 26 September 1931.

395. GStA PK, Rep. 77, Tit. 4043, Nr. 1, Ministerium des Innern, IA, Mitteilungen Nr. 18, 15 September 1931. The *Vossische Zeitung* reported that when Wendt was released from prison toward the end of 1931, he was greeted at the Friedrichstrasse train station by a crowd of some sixty Communists and National Socialists, who accompanied him in triumph down the street. See "Oberleutnant Wendt in Berlin," *Vossische Zeitung,* no. 454, 26 September 1931.

396. One of Strasser's young supporters in the Berlin Hitler Youth writes in his memoir that Stennes was suspected of being in the pay of the Reichswehr. See Crüger, *Ein alter Mann,* 86.

397. Moreau, *Nationalsozialismus von Links.*

398. It was rumored that negotiations were taking place regarding Stennes's reentry into the Nazi movement at this time, but the evidence is inconclusive (GStA PK, Rep. 77, Tit. 4043, Nr. 189, PP Berlin to IM, 14 July 1931, "Betrifft: Korvettenkapitän a.D. Ehrhardt.")

399. Moreau, *Nationalsozialismus von Links,* 89.

400. Ibid., 91.

401. A number of activists who left the NSDAP in 1929–30 later went to the KPD. They included the Nazi fellow traveler Bodo Uhse, a writer associated with the *Landvolkbewegung* in Schleswig-Holstein; Rudolf Renn, acting *Gauführer* of the NSDAP in Berlin-Brandenburg; and Wilhelm Korn, a leader of the National Socialist *Reichsführerschule;* on the latter see "'Genosse Korn.' Nationalsozialist fordert die KPD zur Revolution auf," *Der Jungdeutsche,* 23 August 1930. A number of intellectuals had gone over to the KPD even earlier, including the writer and Baltic *Freikorps* veteran Alexander Graf Stenbock-Fermor, and the (future) writer Ludwig Renn. See Coppi, "'Aufbruch,'" 24.

402. The declaration was published in the 22 November 1931, issue *of Die junge Garde: Zeitung d. Werktätigen Jugend in Stadt und Land.* Zentralorgan der Kommunistischen Jugendverbandes Deutschlands Sektion K.J.I.: "Strasser-Jugend kommt zur Roten Front. Ehemalige Hitler-Angänger an die SA-Kameraden und Hitlerjugend"; BA, ZD 279. It was also published in *Aufbruch,* no. 5, December 1931. The five signatories were "Tommy Crüger" (aka Herbert Crüger), Friedrich Kopp, Richard Schmidt, Eugen Hartmann, and Edith Noack. Crüger describes his experiences in *Ein alter Mann.*

403. Crüger, *Ein alter Mann,* 88. On Strasser's political development, see Bartsch, *Zwischen drei Stühlen.* Similar reasoning may have been behind the reluctance of many stormtroopers to join the Stennes/Strasser movement, which many dismissed, according to police authorities in Stettin, as a "monastery column" (*Kloster Kolonne*); see PP Stettin, 19 September 1931, re NSKD meeting on 3 September 1931.

404. One of Stennes's first acts in the revolt was to "depose" Goebbels as *Gauleiter* "for breech of faith." See "Nationalsozialisten Berlin!" HA 17/325.

405. BA, R 1501, 26073, "Aus Lagebericht München Nr. 99 v. April 1931." At the time of the crisis in Berlin in September 1930, Stennes's southern counterpart, August Schneidhuber, had written to the party leadership expressing many of the same complaints made by Stennes. See Reiche, *Development of the SA,* 134–35. See also "Meuterei in der Hitlergarde. Die unzufriedene SA," *Münchener Post,* no. 197, 2 June 1932; IfZ 73/1550.

406. Albert Krebs, *The Infancy of Nazism. The Memoirs of Ex-Gauleiter Albert Krebs, 1923–1933,* ed. William Sheridan Allen (New York: New Viewpoints, 1976), x.

407. See BA, R1501, 26071b, *CV Archiv Blätter,* Nr. 43 (1931), "NSDAP Gau Mecklenburg-Lübeck in Zersetzung"; *BVZ,* 12 March 1932, "Hitler schickt einen Sonderkommissar. Parteimeuterei in Kiel," BA, R1501, 26071a; BA, R1501, 26071b, RP Hannover, 29 September 1932; *FZ* (date illegible), "1600 Austritte in Hessen," BA, R1501, 26071b; GStA PK, Rep. 77, Tit. 4043, Nr. 312, Standartenbefehl vom 5.9.32 in PP Köln to RP Köln, 17 October 1932; BA SAPMO, I 2/706/13, "Der Gegner Information und Pressedienst No. 1."

408. On the Stegmann Revolt see Reiche, *Development of the SA,* 146–72; Geoffrey Pridham, *Hitler's Rise to Power: The Nazi Movement in Bavaria, 1923–1933* (London: Hart-Davis, MacGibbon, 1973), 291–94.

409. HA 17/A 1882, *Das Freikorps. Kampfblatt für Sauberkeit und Reinheit der Nationalsozialistischen Idee,* Nr. 1, Jahrgang 1933.

410. The opposition to Streicher's leadership was crystallized around the *Nazi Spiegel,* edited by a former local official of the NSDAP; see Reiche, *Development of the SA in Nürnberg, 276.*

411. The phrase was a play on the masthead of Streicher's paper, *Der Stürmer:* "The Jews are our Misfortune." See Pridham, *Hitler's Rise to Power,* 291–94.

412. BA R1501, "Aus Lagebericht Nürnberg vom 31.10.32."
413. A KPD leaflet—"SA Proletarians! Open Your Eyes! Finish the Job!"—sought, like the leaflets released in connection with the earlier Stennes Revolt, to convince the stormtroopers that they had nothing to gain by following anti-Nazi rebels but must take their revolt to its logical conclusion by joining the KPD. See BLHA, Pr Br Rep. 30 Berlin C *Polizeipräsidium Berlin,* Tit. 95, Sekt 9, Teil 2, Nr. 185.
414. *Frankfurter Zeitung,* no. 68/69, 26 January 1933. Like Stennes, Stegmann was unwilling to completely renounce Hitler. Franconian SA leaders released a statement, only a few weeks before Hitler's appointment as Reich Chancellor, noting that they did not want to rebel but that nevertheless they remained opposed to local party *Bonzen (Der Jungdeutsche,* 18 January 1933, "Zersetzung in SA und SS"). An affiliated *Freikorps Ruhr* was formed around the same time (*Vossische Zeitung,* 26 January 1933). Stegmann is reported to have died in a concentration camp (*Der Lagerspiegel,* no. 17/1948, 15 April 1948; IfZ Sp 2/2).
415. *Der Jungdeutsche,* 18 January 1933, "Zersetzung in SA und SS."
416. *Berliner Tageblatt,* 14 January 1933.
417. "Treason! Treason! Treason! It rings through the ranks! Yes, it was treason." Rep. 77, Tit. 4043, Nr. 368 (KgdF); PP Hannover to RP Hannover, 28 October 1932.
418. GStA PK, Rep. 77, Tit. 4043, Nr. 368 (KgdF); PP Hannover to RP Hannover, 28 October 1932.
419. BA Koblenz, Zsg 2/194, "Kurzer Bericht über die Grundung der G.S.R.N. (Gruppe Sozialrevolutionärer Nationalisten) in der Zeit vom 28.-31.5.1930 abgehaltenen Tagung in Berlin."
420. PP Hannover to RP Berlin, "Betr: Absplitterungsbestrebungen innerhalb der NSDAP," 22 October 1932.
421. Paul, *Aufstand der Bilder,* 103.
422. See Swett, *Neighbors and Enemies,* 208; Striefler, *Kampf um die Macht.*
423. On the strike see Swett, *Neighbors and Enemies,* 209–10; Klaus Ranier Röhl, "Fünf Tage im November. Kommunisten, Sozialdemokraten und Nationalsozialisten und der BVG-Streik vom November 1932 in Berlin," in Diethart Kerbs and Henrick Stahr, eds., *Berlin 1932. Das letzte Jahr der ersten deutschen Republik. Politik, Symbole, Medien* (Berlin: Edition Hentrich, 1992), 161–78; Klaus Ranier Röhl, *Nähe zum Gegner. Die Zusammenarbeit von Kommunisten und Nationalsozialisten beim Berliner BVG-Streik von 1932* (Frankfurt am Main: Campus Verlag, 1992).
424. The strike harmed the Nazis, as Gerhard Paul points (*Aufstand der Bilder,* 107); but Pamela Swett is probably correct that it hurt the Communists worse (*Neighbors and Enemies,* 209).
425. Swett, *Neighbors and Enemies.* Both the NSDAP and the KPD worried openly about defections to the enemy, the KPD even founding, in at least one instance, a "fluctuation committee" charged with the task of tracing membership losses to the NSDAP. See Swett, *Neighbors and Enemies,* 212. See also Wilfried Böhnke, *Die NSDAP in Ruhrgebiet 1920–1933* (Bonn: Verlag Neue Gesellschaft, 1974), 157. Böhnke notes the multisided discussions taking place in the cities of the Ruhr in the latter half of 1932 between Communists, activists from the Strasser group, and members of the SA and SS. See also Eve Rosenhaft, *Beating the Fascists?* and Conan Fischer, *German Communists.*
426. GStA PK, Rep. 77, Tit. 4043, Nr. 312, PP Köln to RP Köln, 17 October 1932. The police president noted that yet another National Socialist opposition group, the *Deutsche Jugendwehr,* had been formed, and was made up entirely of former SA and Hitler Youth members.
427. On Kayser's criticism of the NSDAP, see "Krach im Kölner Naziladen," *Rheinische Zeitung,* no. 88, 13 April 1932.
428. OP Rheinprovinz to Prussian IM, 22 October 1931.
429. At a KgdF meeting in Cologne on 10 October 31; PP Köln to RP Köln, 13 October 1931.
430. GStA PK, Rep. 77, Tit. 4043, Nr. 302, "Rundschreiben Nr. 4 der Sektion Geneisenau Sept. 1930."

174 | Notes

431. The police noted that Krause was broke and that he might be engaging in political activity for material motives. See GStA PK, Rep. 77, Tit. 4043, Nr. 368 (KgdF); PP Hannover to RP Hannover, 28 October 1932.

432. Wendt estimated that there were some three thousand members in Germany as a whole; WAP Szczecin, PP Stettin, 7.10.31.

433. See Jay W. Baird, "From Berlin to Neubabelsberg: Nazi Film Propaganda and Hitler Youth Quex," *Journal of Contemporary History* 18, no. 3 (July 1983): 495–515.

434. Swett, *Neighbors and Enemies,* 207–13.

435. Meinl, *Nationalsozialisten gegen Hitler,* 180.

436. Richard J. Golsan, "Introduction to the English-Language Edition. The Politics of History and Memory in France in the 1990s," in Rousso, ed., *Stalinism and Nazism,* xi.

437. On Bolshevik repression against anarchist, Social Revolutionary, and other leftist radicals, see Grigori Maximov, *The Guillotine at Work in Russia* (Chicago: Berkman Fund, 1940); see also Paul Avrich, *The Russian Anarchists* (Princeton, NJ: Princeton University Press, 1967). For a scholarly treatment of Western anarchist views of the Bolshevik regime, see Harold Goldberg, "Goldman and Berkman View the Bolshevik Regime," *Slavic and East European Review* 53, no. 131 (April 1975): 272–76.

438. The classic work is Maurice Brinton, *The Bolsheviks and Workers' Control, 1917–1921: The State and Counter-Revolution* (London: Solidarity, 1970); see also Silvana Malle, *The Economic Organisation of War Communism, 1918–1921* (Cambridge: Cambridge University Press, 2002).

439. In November 1917. See Martin Malia, *The Soviet Tragedy: A History of Socialism in Russia, 1917–1991* (New York: Free Press, 1994).

440. See Paul Avrich, "Nestor Makhno: The Man and the Myth," in Paul Avrich, *Anarchist Portraits* (Princeton, NJ: Princeton University Press, 1990). Two highly partisan accounts are Peter Arshinov, *The History of the Makhnovist Movement* (Detroit: Black and Red, 1974); and Voline, *The Unknown Revolution* (London: Freedom Press, 1955).

441. See Delano Dugarm, "Peasant Wars in Tambov Province," in Vladimir N. Brovkin, ed., *The Bolsheviks in Russian Society: The Revolution and the Civil Wars* (New Haven, CT: Yale University Press, 1997).

442. On the Kronstadt uprising see Israel Getzler, *Kronstadt 1917–1921: The Fate of a Soviet Democracy* (Cambridge: Cambridge University Press, 1983); Paul Avrich, *Kronstadt 1921* (Princeton, NJ: Princeton University Press, 1970). For accounts from the anarchist perspective, see Ida Mett, *The Kronstadt Uprising* (London: Solidarity, 1967); Emma Goldman, *Trotsky Protests Too Much* (Glasgow: The Anarchist Communist Federation, 1938); Alexander Berkman, "The Kronstadt Rebellion," in *Der Sindikalist* (Berlin, 1922). For an account sympathetic to the Bolsheviks, see Victor Serge, *Memoirs of a Revolutionary, 1901–41* (Oxford: Oxford University Press, 1963).

443. The same pattern of audacious mendacity and destruction of allies was repeated in the Spanish civil war. See Noam Chomsky, *Objectivity and Liberal Scholarship* (New York: New Press, 2003); the classic account is George Orwell, *Homage to Catalonia* (New York: Harcourt, 1969).

444. Stéphane Courtois et al., *The Black Book of Communism: Crimes, Terror, Repression* (Cambridge, MA: Harvard University Press, 1999); on the debate around the Black Book, see Golsan, "Introduction to the English-Language Edition. The Politics of History and Memory in France in the 1990s,." in Henry Rousso ed., *Stalinism and Nazism. History and Memory Compared* (Lincoln & London: University of Nebraska Press, 1999).

445. Ernst Nolte, "Die Vergangenheit, die nicht vergehen will," in Ernst Piper, ed., *"Historikerstreit": Die Dokumentation der Kontroverse um die Einzigartigkeit der nationalsozialistschen Judenvernichtung* (Munich: Piper, 1987); see also Ernst Nolte, *Der europäische Bürgerkrieg, 1917–1945. Nationalsozialismus und Bolschewismus* (Frankfurt: Proyläen, 1987).

446. See the summary in Furet, *Passing of an Illusion,* 159.

447. Furet, *Passing of an Illusion,* 28.

448. Bertrand Russell, *The Theory and Practice of Bolshevism* (London: George Allen & Unwin, 1920), 9. Many Western intellectuals, of course, embraced Bolshevism, among them H.G. Wells and George Bernard Shaw; see Furet, *Passing of an Illusion,* 150–55. See also the discussion in Michael Burleigh, *The Third Reich. A New History* (New York : Hill and Wang, 2000), 4, 15.

449. See Emma Goldman, *My Disillusionment in Russia* (New York: Doubleday, Page & Company, 1923).

450. "Apart from criticizing Lenin's agrarian policy and the dissolution of the constituent assembly by the Bolsheviks," writes Werner T. Angress, "[Luxemburg] raised her strongest objections against the use of terror and the curtailment of democracy and freedom. While conceding that democratic institutions had their shortcomings, she charged that to cure such institutions by abolishing them altogether was worse than the disease itself." See *Stillborn Revolution: The Communist Bid for Power in Germany, 1921–1923* (Princeton, NJ: Princeton University Press, 1963), 12.

451. See Vladimir N. Brovkin and Robert Hessen, *Dear Comrades: Menshevik Reports on the Bolshevik Revolution and the Civil War* (Stanford, CA: Hoover Institute Press, 1991).

452. Among the more important attempts to publicize the antidemocratic nature of the Bolshevik revolution from a left-radical perspective are Voline, *Unknown Revolution;* Maximov, *Guillotine at Work.* A writer for the anarchist paper *Golos Truda* ("The Voice of Labor"), Maximov was sentenced to death by the Bolsheviks and was only saved through the intervention of the steelworkers' union. He eventually made his way to Berlin, where, in cooperation with the German anarchist Rudolf Rocker and others, he participated in the founding of an international anarchist umbrella organization and a "Committee of Defense of the Revolutionists Imprisoned in Russia."

453. GSTA PK, Rep. 77, Tit. 4043, Nr. 257, "Prussian Innenministerium re Anarchistische Bewegung."

454. GSTA PK, Rep. 77, Tit. 1809, Nr. 9 (KPD 1923), IA, "Lagebericht vom 27. April 1923." Speakers at the meeting cited 10,638 deported and 48,810 political prisoners.

455. GSTA PK, Rep. 77, Tit. 1809, Nr. 9 (KPD 1923), IA, "Lagebericht vom 16. April 1923." See the piece published by Alexander Berkman in a German anarchist periodical: "Die Pariser Kommune und Kronstadt. 1871–1921–1931," *Der Syndikalist* 13, no. 11 (March 1931). German anarchism was by no means uniformly opposed to cooperation with the KPD in the early years. Erich Mühsam, in particular, invested great hopes in the Soviet experiment and attempted to work together with the KPD, before souring on the party's lack of rank-and-file democracy; see Riccardo Bavaj, *Von links gegen Weimar. Linkes antiparlamentarisches Denken in der Weimarer Republik* (Bonn: Verlag J. H. W. Dietz Nachfolger, 2005), 350–69.

456. For recent scholarly work documenting the early history of Bolshevik repression, see Eric D. Weitz, *A Century of Genocide: Utopias of Race and Nation* (Princeton, NJ: Princeton University Press, 2005); see also Anne Applebaum, *Gulag: A History* (New York: Doubleday, 2003).

457. Mallmann, *Kommunisten in der Weimarer Republik.*

458. Selznick, *Organizational Weapon,* 74.

459. Fitzpatrick, *Tear Off the Mask!* chapters 1 and 2; Fitzpatrick demonstrates how the mythological-political characteristics of class trumped socioeconomic realities at every stage.

460. Ibid., 4, 37.

461. Fischer, *German Communists,* 91; Franz Borkenau, a keen observer of the policies of the Comintern, wrote that referring to "the social-democrats [as] a *bourgeois* party was dangerously misleading. For although the social-democratic parties of the mid-twenties certainly did not stand for radical change, their membership was overwhelmingly proletarian, much more so than that of the communists." See *World Communism: A History of the Communist International* (London: George Allen & Unwin, 1938), 124.

462. Sebastian Haffner, *Failure of a Revolution: Germany, 1918–1919* (Chicago: Banner Press, 1969).

463. Chris Bowlby, "Blutmai 1929: Police, Parties and Proletarians in a Berlin Confrontation," *Historical Journal* 29, no. 1 (March 1986): 137–58.

464. Zinoviev branded Social Democracy a "wing of fascism" at the Fifth Comintern Congress in June–July 1924; Stalin spoke of fascism and Social Democracy being "twin brothers." See Klaus Hildebrand, *The Third Reich* (London and Boston: Allen & Unwin, 1984), 106. Social Democracy and fascism were compared as early as 1924; see Coppi, "'Aufbruch,'" 17.

465. Borkenau, *World Communism,* 124.

466. Quoted in Anton Kaes, Martin Jay, Edward Dimendberg eds., *The Weimar Republic Sourcebook* (Berkeley: University of California Press, 1994), 327.

467. Mallmann, *Kommunisten in der Weimarer Republik.*

468. The party leadership acknowledged, for example, the difficulty of making a convincing case within the party regarding the nationalist program, noting that "the program is seen by parts of the party as an electoral maneuver, and so far has not really been made into a foundation of our political work." See GSTA PK, Rep. 77, Tit. 4043, Nr. 367 (KgdF), "Volksrevolution gegen die faschistische Diktatur! Rededisposition für die Versammlungen zur Vorbereitung des Kampfbundkongresses am 21. Dezember."

469. Hans Putz, *Dokumente kommunistischer Führungskorruption. Die KPD im Dienste der russischen Außenpolitik* (Leipzig: Kurt Wildeis, 1931). For a revealing account of a Communist activist's frustrations with the party's strictures against cooperation with the SPD against fascism, see Josef Dünner, "Mein Auschluß aus der KPD," *Die Weltbühne,* no. 34, 23 August 1932.

470. Erich Wollenberg, *The Red Army* (London: Secker & Warburg, 1938).

471. "The news went off like a bomb in the party *Zentrale,*" writes Wollenberg; "Ernst Thaelmann was furious." Ibid., 716–17.

472. Ibid., 718–19.

473. Ibid., 723.

474. Jan Foitzik, *Zwischen den Fronten. Zur Politik, Organisation und Funktion linker politischer Klein-organisationen im Widerstand 1933 bis 1939/40* (Bonn: Verlag Neue Gesellschaft, 1986), 23.

475. For a cogent analysis of the SAPD's founding and activity see Gruppe MAGMA, *"... denn Angriff,"* 154–62.

476. OP Provinz Westfalen, 7 November 1931, "Betrifft: KPD.-Rundschreiben der Bezirksleitung Ruhrgebiet, Abtl. Agitprop-Oktober 1931, betitelt: 'Die neue Partei! Ihre Argumente—unsere Antworten!'" GSTA PK, Rep. 77, Tit. 4043, Nr. 237. On the SAPD see Hanno Drechsler, *Die Sozialistische Arbeiterpartei Deutschlands (SAPD): Ein Beitrag zur Geschichte der Deutschen Arbeiterbewegung am Ende der Weimarer Republik* (Meisenheim am Glan: Verlag Anton Hain, 1966).

477. Anna Siemsen, quoted in ibid., 241.

478. GStA PK, Rep. 77, Tit. 4043, Nr. 94, "Aufruf zur Einheitsfront!"

479. GSTA PK, Rep. 77, Tit. 4043, Nr. 237, OP Provinz Westfalen, 7 November 1931, "Betrifft: KPD.-Rundschreiben der Bezirksleitung Ruhrgebiet, Abtl. Agitprop-Oktober 1931, betitelt: 'Die neue Partei! Ihre Argumente—unsere Antworten!'"

480. Ibid.

481. This interpretation is reinforced by the KPD's renewed appeals for a "united front" after 1945, appeals that preceded the forcible integration of the SPD in the Soviet zone into a "Social-ist Unity Party," and with which the KPD continued to badger the SPD in West Germany; on the KPD's renewed use of the United Front from Below and nationalism strategies in the Federal Republic, see Patrick Major, *The Death of the KPD: Communism and Anti-Communism in West Germany, 1945–1956* (New York: Clarendon Press, 1997); see also Brown, "Richard Scheringer."

482. GSTA PK, Rep. 77, Tit. 4043, Nr. 237, OP Provinz Westfalen, 18 March 1932, "Betrifft: Rundschreiben der KPD., Berzirksleitung Ruhrgebiet, Abt. Agitprop." The KPD's aggressive tactics to win over SPD workers and sabotage the SAP<u>D</u> were not without success; a meeting in Cologne on 6 October aimed at winning SPD splitters attracted five thousand attendees,

ninety-five of whom went over to the KPD after the meeting; GStA PK, Rep. 77 Tit. 4043 Nr. 23, OP Rheinprovinz to PIM, 2 November 1931, "Betrifft: KPD und Absplitterungsbestrebungen innerhalb der S.P.D."

483. Foitzik, *Zwischen den Fronten,* 24.

484. Expelled from the KPD at the Sixth World Congress of Comintern at end of 1928, the KPD-O had between 3,500 and 6,000 members. Opposing tendencies in the leadership led eventually to a split, with one thousand members going over to the SAPD between December 1931 and early 1932. See ibid., 24–25.

485. See *Berichte über die Lage in Deutschland. Die Lagemeldungen der Gruppe Neu Beginnen aus dem Dritten Reich 1933–1936* (Bonn: Verlag J. H. W. Dietz Nachfolger, 1996), 27.

486. Prior to 1933 the membership came largely from the political leadership schools of the SPD and KPD. *Neu Beginnen* drew on sympathizers at universities in Hamburg, Frankfurt, Heidelberg, and Berlin; see Foitzik, *Zwischen den Fronten,* 28.

487. The idea of a "spiritual elite" was also active in the *Internationale Sozialistische Kampfbund* (International Socialist Fighting League). Founded in 1925, the ISK drew on a system of Kantian ethical socialism with roots in the early Youth Movement. Its stringent ethical demands reached even into the private lives of its members. It had hardly two hundred members in the late Weimar Republic, along with 600 to 1,000 close sympathizers; see ibid., 29.

488. Ibid., 25. Significantly, the SAPD was itself victim to severe factionalism among its Social Democratic, Communist, pacifist, and other elements. See Drechsler, *Die Sozialistische Arbeiterpartei Deutschlands.*

489. Swett, *Neighbors and Enemies,* 142–45; see also Karl Rohe, *Das Reichsbanner Schwarz Rot Gold.*

490. Jost and Trommler, *Die Kultur der Weimar Republik,* 98; see also Coppi, "'Aufbruch,'" 49–50.

491. Fischer, *German Communists,* 161.

492. Aumann, "From Legality to Illegality," 289.

493. See Weitz, *Creating German Communism.*

494. The major Communist papers were the creation of Willi Münzenberg, the KPD's propaganda expert; on Münzenberg, see Stephan Koch, *Double Lives: Stalin, Willi Münzenberg and the Seduction of the Intellectuals* (New York: Enigma, 2004); Sean McMeekin, *The Red Millionaire: A Political Biography of Willy Münzenberg, Moscow's Secret Propaganda Tsar in the West, 1917–1940* (New Haven, CT: Yale University Press, 2004).

495. GStA PK, Rep. 77, Tit. 4043, Nr. 1, Ministerium des Innern, IA, Mitteilungen Nr. 18, 15 September 1931, Rundschreiben des Z.K., Agitprop der KPD, July 1931.

496. On the RFB see Kurt G. P. Schuster, *Der Rote Frontkämpferbund 1924–1929. Beiträge zur Geschichte und Organisationsstruktur eines politischen Kampfbundes* (Düsseldorf: Droste, 1975).

497. "Zusammenfassende Darstellung über die Rote Frontkämpferbund (R.F.B.) und der Rote Jungsturm (R.J.)," p. 2; HstA, MA 100418.

498. BA, R134/69, "Wir führen das Volk durch rote Einheit zum Sieg!"

499. *Die Rote Fahne,* no. 92, 10 August 1924.

500. Bayerische HstA, MA 100418, Reichsministerium des Innerns to Bay Staatsministerium des Innerns, 25 June 1928, Betrifft: Roten Frontkämpferbund, p. 12.

501. Ministerialsitzung, 11 July 1929, "Auflösung des Roten Frontkämpferbund," Verbot 22 July 1929 (based on articles 177, 178 of the Versailles treaty, 23.3.1921); Bay HstA, MA 100418.

502. GSTA PK—Rep. 77, Tit. 4043, Nr. 360: RFB.

503. PP Köln to RP Köln, 24 October 1930, GSTA PK, Rep. 77, Tit. 4043, Nr. 367 (KgdF).

504. *Die Rote Fahne,* 25 December 1930.

505. James J. Ward, "'Smash the Fascists,'" 55–56.

506. PP Köln to RP, 11 November 1930, GSTA PK, Rep. 77, Tit. 4043, Nr. 367 (KgdF).

507. GStA PK, Rep. 77, Tit. 4043, Nr. 367 (KgdF), PP Düsseldorf, 29 December 1930, "Volksrevolution gegen die faschistische Diktatur! Rededisposition für die Versammlungen zur Vorbereitung des Kampfbundkongresses am 21. Dezember."

508. GSTA PK, Rep. 77, Tit. 4043, Nr. 367 (KgdF), PP Köln to RP, 31 October 1930, Z.K. des KJVD, Berlin, 15 October 1930, Jugendstaffeln of KgdF.

509. GSTA PK, Rep. 77, Tit. 4043, Nr. 367 (KgdF), PP Köln to RP, 11 November 1930.

510. Coppi, "'Aufbruch,'" 27; Schüddekopf, *National-bolshewismus,* 293.

511. The SPD also pointed out that, technically, a united front already existed in the form of the Iron Front; Christine Fischer-Defoy, *Arbeiterwiderstand in der Provinz. Arbeiterbewegung und Faschismus in Kassel und Nordhessen 1933–1945. Eine Fallstudie* (West Berlin: Verlag für Ausbildung und Studium in der Elefanten Press, 1982), 54.

512. GSTA PK, Rep. 77, Tit 4043 Nr. 225 (Antifa), "An alle Ortsgruppen, Stadtteile und Unterbezirke," 26 March 1932.

513. "The KPD had created a witches' brew of grassroots political action," writes Conan Fischer, "which, as the weakest of the three main non-confessional popular parties, it was worst placed to exploit" (*German Communists,* 161).

514. "The press reports daily … about bloody clashes between 'Nazis' and 'Communists.' First one, then the other, is declared 'guilty.'" GSAPKB—Rep 77 Tit 4043 Nr. 237, OP Provinz Westfalen, 4 January 1932.

515. "KPD in nationalistischen Kostüm"—*Vossische Zeitung,* 27 October 1932.

516. GSTA PK, Rep. 77, Tit. 4043, Nr. 225 (Antifa), "An alle Ortsgruppen, Stadtteile und Unterbezirke," 26 March 1932, Innenministerium: "b. Antifaschistische Aktion."

517. "The classless nation has no interest in imperialist conquest, since it cannot tolerate the exploitation of foreign countries. Politically it will therefore always remain on the defensive, but, of course, this does not rule out the use of a military offensive for purposes of protection." Heinrich Laufenberg and Fritz Wolffheim, *Das revolutionäre Heer* (Hamburg, 1920), 27.

518. Ascher and Lewy, "National Bolshevism," 451–52.

519. Lenin rejected their views, but only because it would be a crime to "accept battle at a time when it is obviously advantageous to the enemy and not to us." V. I. Lenin, *Left-Wing Communism, an Infantile Disorder: A Popular Essay in Marxian Strategy and Tactics* (Honolulu: University Press of the Pacific, 2001).

520. They went on to found the KAPD in 1920.

521. BA-SAPMO I 2/3/22.

522. BA, R134/69, "Wir führen das Volk durch rote Einheit zum Sieg!"

523. Georgi Dimitrov, *Against Fascism and War* (New York: International Publishers, 1986), 2.

524. *Die Junge Garde,* Nr. 56, 11 September 1932.

525. *Der Rote Frontsoldat. Organ für Proletarische Wehrpolitik Nr. 5, September 1932* Bundesarchiv T-Z-F 3515.

526. The Fifth Reich Congress of the *Rotfrontkämpferbund* in Hamburg criticized the campaign for refusal of military service (Unterschriftensammlung für "Kriegsdienstverweigerung") as a "pazifistischen Betrugsmanöver"; GSTA PK, Rep. 77, Tit. 4043, Nr. 353a (RFB 1928–29), "Richtlinien für den Wehrsport im Roten-Frontkämpfer Bund."

527. Ibid.

528. "Technichscher Arbeitsplan der Bundesleitung von 1.11.24," quoted in "Zusammenfassende Darstellung über die Rote Frontkämpferbund (R.F.B.) und der Rote Jungsturm (R.J.)"; HstA, MA 100418. Members of the RFB were trained in Moscow in chemical warfare against the police; see Gilensen, "Die Komintern," 26.

529. Coppi, "'Aufbruch,'" 31. Among the signatories to the Scheringer campaign were Georg Ledebour, Ernst Toller, Kurt Hiller, Veit Valentin, the renegade Nazi Otto Strasser, and Scheringer's former commander in the *Freikorps* days, Major Buchrucker. All of them belonged either to no party or two small splinter groups; no Communists, Nazis, or Social Democrats were represented. See Istvan Deak, *Weimar Germany's Left-wing Intellectuals: A Political History of the Weltbühne and Its Circle* (Berkeley: University of California Press, 1968), 194.

530. See the excellent discussions in Coppi, "'Aufbruch'" and Schüddekopf, *National-bolshewismus,* 298–302.

531. These included the writer Bodo Uhse of the Schleswig-Holstein *Landvolkbewegung;* Wilhelm Korn, former leader of the NSDAP *Reichsführerschule;* former acting *Gauführer* of the NSDAP for Berlin-Brandenburg, Rudolf Rehm, and the former *Gaupropagandaleiter* Lorf. See Coppi, "Aufbruch,'" 24.
532. Indeed, it is striking the extent to which the content of *Aufbruch* paralleled that in Stennes's *Arbeiter, Bauern, Soldaten.*
533. These included Walther Stennes, who, after a narrow escape from the clutches of the Gestapo after Hitler's seizure of power, became head of Chiang Kai-shek's bodyguard; see Alan Bullock, ed., *The Labyrinth: Memoirs of Walter Schellenberg, Hitler's Chief of Counterintelligence* (Cambridge, MA: Da Capo Press, 1984), 159.
534. Coppi, "'Aufbruch,'" 37–38.
535. Peter Steinbach, "Vorwart," in Susanne Römer and Hans Coppi, eds., *Aufbruch. Dokumentation einer Zeitschrift zwischen den Fronten* (Koblenz: Verlag Dietmar Fölbach, 2001), 8.
536. Susanne Römer, "'Aufbruch'—fast 70 Jahre danach," in Susanne Römer and Hans Coppi, eds., *Aufbruch. Dokumentation einer Zeitschrift zwischen den Fronten* (Koblenz: Verlag Dietmar Fölbach, 2001), 12.
537. Coppi, "'Aufbruch,'" 46.
538. Ibid., 46–47.
539. Ibid., 43, 40.
540. BA-SAPMO, I 2/705/6, "Entwurf des Programs der militärpolitischen Kurse."
541. BA, R134/69, p. 6, "Richtlinien für Aufbau und Tätigkeit des Spezialressorts zur Arbeit unter den bewaffneten Kräften," October 1931.
542. Ibid. Each department was broken down into four sections: (1) "Direction" (responsible for the overall guidance of propaganda and cell activity); (2) "Contacts and Cell Organization" (responsible for oversight of cell activities); (3) "Editorial Staff–Propaganda–Propaganda Technique" (responsible for the publication of "special literature"—newspapers, fliers, stickers—for use by the cells); (4) "Intelligence" (responsible for collecting information on the morale of the target troops, and the collection and dissemination of other valuable information).
543. Kaufmann et al, *Der Nachrichtendienst der KPD,* 209. Erich Wollenberg makes a similar claim; see *Red Army,* 408.
544. Among these were *Der Rote Gummiknüppel* (Berlin), *Der Gute Konrad* (Berlin-East), *Rund um den Tschako* (Leipzig), and *Der Schupo* (Bavaria). Kaufmann et al., *Der Nachrichtendienst der KPD,* 209. See also Gilensen, "Die Komintern," in 30–31. Nancy Aumann lists some twenty-nine different papers produced for the *Schutzpolizei* and army that had appeared already by 1929 ("From Legality to Illegality," 283).
545. See the "Entschließung der I. Reichskonferenz der Roten Schupozellen" in "Was Fordert Die Opposition in den Polizeibeamten-Verbänden?" SAPMO BA I 2/8/11-12 FBS 308/13058. At the conference, a Reich leader of the Red Schupo cells was elected and a resolution adopted calling on *Schutzpolizisten* not to allow themselves to be misused for the oppression of the workers. See Kaufmann et al., *Der Nachrichtendienst der KPD,* 209–10; Aumann, "From Legality to Illegality," 268.
546. Each formation disposed of its own "enemy department" (*Gegenapparat*), which was responsible for assigning propaganda troops to areas where the nationalist *Verbände* were particularly strong. See BA-SAPMO, I 2/705/6, "Die Zersetzungsarbeit," 1926, p. 48.
547. See, for example, *Die junge Garde. Zeitung d. Werktätigen Jugend in Stadt und Land. Zentralorgan der Kommunistischen Jugendverbandes Deutschlands Sektion K.J.I.,* various issues in the spring and autumn of 1931.
548. IfZ MA 644, "Der Rote Angriff, auf dem Prenzlauer Berg. Kampforgen gegen den Faschismus. Harausgegeben von K.P.D. Nord-Ost."
549. *Der Rote Angriff,* no. 2.
550. On Communist anti-Semitism in the Weimar Republic, see Mario Kessler, "Die KPD unter der Antisemitismus in der Weimarer Republik," *UTOPIE Kreativ* 173 (March 2005): 223–32;

Thomas Haury, *Antisemitismus von Links: Kommunistische Ideologie, Nationalismus und Anti-zionismus in der frühen DDR* (Hamburg: Hamburger Ed, 2002), chapter on Weimar; Gruppe MAGMA, *"... denn Angriff ist die beste Verteidigung,"* 203–25; D. W. Daycock, "The KPD and the NSDAP: A Study of the Relationship Between Political Extremes in Weimar Germany, 1923–1933" (Ph.D. dissertation, London School of Economics, 1980), 103. "The Communists tried hard to convince their Nazi audience that the racial question was irrelevant to their real [class] concerns. What went unnoticed ... was that too much was conceded. ... As [Communists] borrowed some of the worst images from the anti-Semitic vocabulary, one has to wonder just who was influencing whom." Quoted in Fischer, *German Communists*, 61.

551. NWHStA "Essen, den 8. November 1933." The top of the master copy of the flier bears a note from the district leadership of the KPD advising activists to see that the flier came into the possession of SA and SS men; NWHStA, "An alle UBL. Anfang Oktober 1933."
552. GStA PK, Rep. 77, Tit. 4043, Nr. 302, "Rundschreiben Nr. 4 der Sektion Geneisenau Sept. 1930."
553. NS/23—431; Der Oberste SA—Führer, den 8.12.1932, Betreff: "Obergruppe V (Dresden) meldet." "These Communist agents," the report continues, "are distributed as follows in the SA: In Dresden—26; Leipzig—28; Chemnitz—42; Plauen—11; Zwickau—18; Berlin—164."
554. HA 71/1553, "Richtlinien für den Auf- und Ausbau des Nachrichtendienstes," November 1931, pp. 2–3,
555. Propaganda-Abteilung, Gau München—Oberbayern, 13 October 1931, HA 71/1553.
556. "Ausbau des Nachrichtendienstes."
557. Ibid.
558. The SA appears to have spied on meetings of Stennes supporters as well; see, for example, the report in "An die Untergruppe H.G.," Sturmbann I/45, Hamburg, 29 September 1932. BA Sammlung Schumacher 330.
559. BLHA, Pr Br Rep. 30 Berlin C *Polizeipräsidium*, Tit. 95, Sekt 9, Teil 2, Nr. 183, "NSDAP Wochenberichte Nr. 3," 4 August 1932.
560. An SA *Sturmführer* by the name of Bassler personally saw to the creation and printing of *Der Freiheitskämpfer* while wearing the uniform of the SA; see HA 17/325, SA Gruppe Nord-West to OSAF, 16 June 1931.
561. BA, Sammlung Schumacher 278, "Die Strasser + Opposition in Gau Hamburg," 10 August 1932, re meeting of 3 August 1932. A *Sturmbannführer* warned his superiors about *Die Sturm-fahne* later in the year, noting that a local SA man had been found with one in his apartment; Sturmbann II/15: Abt-1c, Wandsbek, 12 December 1932. BA Sammlung Schumacher 330.
562. Organs of the "SA opposition groups" listed in *Aufbruch* include, by city: *Sturm, Freiheitsadler, Freiheitsarmee* (Berlin); *Kameradenbriefe* (Saxony); *Roter Sturm* (Anhalt-Dessau); *Sturmfahne, Sturmbriefe* (Hamburg); *Sturm über Essen* (Essen); *Sturmsignale, Alarm* (Düsseldorf); *SA-Kamerad* (Cologne); *Sturmsoldat* (Düren); *SA-Revolution* (Bonn); *SA-Post* (Frankfurt am Main); *Nation und Revolution* (Stuttgart); *Der revolutionäre Freiheitskämpfer* (Nuremberg); *Revolutionäre Freiheit* (Würzburg); *Sturmbanner, Front-Appell* (Munich). See *Aufbruch*, 2. Jg., Nr. 9, December 1932, p. 6.
563. BA Sammlung Schumacher 330, *Die Sturmfahne*, Jahrgang 1932, Nr. 8.
564. BA Sammlung Schumacher 330, *Die Sturmfahne*, Jahrgang 1932, Nr. 7.
565. BA Sammlung Schumacher 330, *Die Sturmfahne*, Jahrgang 1932, Nr. 11.
566. See chapter 5.
567. *Der SA Kamerad*, August 1933, Barch M 5070. A similar theme is taken up in *Alarm. Kampf-blatt der Revolutionäre SA-Leute Der Standarte 39*, May 1933, Barch M 5072.
568. *Der Freiheitskämpfer*, June 1931, HA 17/325.
569. *Die Sturmfahne* (n.d.), BA Sammlung Schumacher 330.
570. *Das Sprachrohr*, December 1930, IfZ MA 644. The political police in Berlin identified *Das Sprachrohr* as a "known Communist *Zersetzungsschrift* for the NSDAP and SA" (I.A.II., Berlin, 13 June 1931; IfZ MA 644). See also the discussion in Aumann, "From Legality to Illegality," 292–94.

571. Ibid.
572. *Das Sprachrohr,* April 1931, no. 3, BLHA, Pr Br Rep. 30 Berlin C *Polizeipräsidium,* Tit. 95, Sekt 9, Teil 2, Nr. 185.
573. Ibid.
574. Ibid.
575. *Die Sturmfahne,* 1931, BA Sammlung Schumacher 330.
576. "Her zu uns!" *Aufbruch* 2, no. 7 (September 1932): 1–2.
577. One article hailing the growing unrest in the SA cited as evidence the "SA opposition" papers appearing all over Germany, without mentioning that the overwhelming majority of these were themselves the product of the KPD's *M-Apparat.* See Dr. Falkenstein, "Sturmzeichen in der SA!" *Aufbruch* 2, no. 8 (October/November 1932): 4–7.
578. Fischer, *Stormtroopers,* 151. This may have been the "Hitler Internationale" ("we are the real German working men, we want a free fatherland") referred to by Striefler in *Kampf um die Macht,* 79–81.
579. *Die Sturmfahne* was "published by a few soldiers of the German revolution. The oppositional SA comrades from Hamburg" and signed by the "Circle of oppositional SA comrades of Standarten 9, 15, 45, 76."
580. GStA PK, Rep. 77, Tit. 4043, Nr. 312, Standartenbefehl vom 5.9.32 in PP Köln to RP Köln, 17 October 1932.
581. Paul Heider, *Antifaschistischer Kampf und revolutionäre Militärpolitik* (Berlin: Militärverlag der Deutschen Demokratischen Republik, 1976), 109.
582. Microfilm collection *Widerstand als "Hochverrat." Die Verfahren gegen deutsche Reichsangehörige vor dem Reichsgericht, dem Volksgerichtshof und dem Reichskriegsgericht,* Munich, 1998 (hereafter WaH), 0226, 8 J 438/ 35 g, p. 17.
583. See Fischer, *Stormtroopers,* chapters 6–8, and Swett, *Neighbors and Enemies,* especially chapter 4.
584. GStA PK, Rep. 77, Tit. 4043, Nr. 237, "Befehl an alle Führungen" (14.10.32), OP Provinz Westfalen, 17 February 1932.
585. The guidelines laid out recommendations for topics of discussion based on current conditions within the Nazi movement. See BLHA, Pr Br Rep. 30 Berlin C *Polizeipräsidium,* Tit. 95, Sekt 9, Teil 2, Nr. 183, "Anleitung für Diskussionen mit Kameraden der SA."
586. BLHA, Pr Br Rep. 30 Berlin C *Polizeipräsidium,* Tit. 95, Sekt. 9, Teil 2, Nr. 183, "SA Kameraden!"
587. Swett, *Neighbors and Enemies;* see the section on "Discussion with the Enemy and Membership Fluctuation," 207–13.
588. See Bartsch, *Zwischen drei Stühlen.*
589. The lyrics read in part: "Oh Potempkin, you proud Soviet ornament, At your mast, yes mast, waves the red flag, And a Red Front, Red Front, of brave comrades, Full steam ahead to the red homeland…; make way for the red battalions, make way for the red storm troops, Comrades shot by the Nazi-Stahlhelm, march in spirit with us in our ranks." See "Antifaschistischen-Lied," GSTA PK, Rep. 77, Tit. 4043, Nr. 361 (RFB Ausbildung).
590. Staatsministerium des Innerns to Reichsinnenministerium, 12 December 1928; Bay HstA, MA 100418; for more on KPD and NSDAP songs, see Bartsch, *Zwischen drei Stühlen,* 121.
591. Gilensen, "Die Komintern," 19.
592. They demanded, according to the political police, either a thoroughgoing purge of the RFB or the founding of a new organization to which only the better members of the RFB and the KgdF would be admitted (*Landeskriminalpolizeiamts* (IA) Berlin, January 1932, 1, 11–12).
593. "Rundschreiben Befehl, RFB Schulungskurse (October 1930)," GSTA PK, Rep. 77, Tit. 4043, Nr. 94.
594. There were rarely more than eight participants in one of these courses. Former soldiers were recruited to oversee weapons training. Courses in jujitsu were offered to enable members to win street fights against the police or the SA. See Rundschreiben "Befehl, RFB Schulungskurse (October 1930)," GSTA PK, Rep. 77, Tit. 4043, Nr. 94.

595. "Befehl an alle Führungen" (14.10.32); OP Provinz Westfalen, 17 February 1932; GSTA PK, Rep. 77, Tit. 4043, Nr. 237.

596. "Antifaschistischen-Lied," GSTA PK, Rep. 77, Tit. 4043, Nr. 361.

597. Fischer, *German Communists,* 161; on the phenomenon of KgdF members going over to the SA, see Conan Fischer, "The SA of the NSDAP: Social Background and Ideology of the Rank and File in the Early 1930s," *Journal of Contemporary History* 17 (1982): 659.

598. See "Scheringer an die Scheringer SA-Staffel, Ulm—Schluß mit Hitler! Vorwärtz mit der K.P.D.!" *Süddeutschen Arbeiterzeitung,* 10 April 1931.

599. A police agent's report on the KPD's attempt to found a *Schutzstaffel Scheringer* in Berlin just two weeks before the Nazi seizure of power illustrates well the dubious nature of the undertaking. *Schutzstaffel* members were to appear at meetings throughout Berlin wearing SA uniforms with a Soviet armband replacing the swastika. Franz Lange of the *Bundesleitung* was to speak at the founding meeting scheduled for 18 January—disaffected stormtroopers were to be found to appear at the founding meeting "if possible." See "Bericht über die Sitzung der Nazibearbeiter im Bereich des UB. 5," 17 January 1933; IfZ München, MA 644, frame 867 110. *Scheringer Staffeln* existed also in Hannover, Hamburg, and Cologne, composed largely or completely of RFB men; see Striefler, *Kampf um die macht,* 140–41.

600. See Reichardt, *Faschistische Kampfbünde.*

601. In the second half of 1931, for example, only 454 National Socialists—.03 percent of all new recruits—went to the KPD; see Mallmann, *Kommunisten in der Weimarer Republik,* 120. See also Fischer, "Class Enemies."

602. Less than .05 percent of new KPD members in late 1931 came from the NSDAP; Coppi, "'Aufbruch,'" 24.

603. For a view of the KPD's *Zersetzungsarbeit* among the Nazis from the perspective of the German Democratic Republic, see Heider, *Antifaschistischer Kampf.*

604. Borkenau, *World Communism.*

605. GSTA PK, OP Provinz Westfalen, 12 October 1932.

606. GSTA PK, Rep. 77, Tit. 4043, Nr. 362 (KgdF), PP Berlin, 24 June 1931.

607. *Sopade,* August 1935, 940.

608. Ibid., 946.

609. Ibid., 941.

610. Ibid., 941–42.

611. Ibid., 944.

612. Ibid., 942–43.

613. Ibid., 938.

614. Paul, *Aufstand der Bilder,* 139.

615. See Claudia Koonz, *The Nazi Conscience* (Cambridge, MA: The Belknap Press of Harvard University Press, 2003).

616. Noth, *Die Tragödie+,* 139.

617. Ibid., 203.

618. Ibid., 219.

619. Tusk, "Aus Gruppen und Bünden," in *Die Kiefer. Monatsschrift für eine junge Gesinnung* 3 (May 1933): 16.

620. For a very useful collection of documents on the activity of the *Bündische* in the Weimar Republic and in the transition to National Socialism, see Kindt, *Die deutsche Jugendbewegung.*

621. First as minister without portfolio, subsequently as minister of aviation, acting interior minister, and ultimately prime minister of Prussia.

622. Rudolf Diels, *Lucifer ante Portas. Zwischen Severing und Heydrich* (Zurich: Interverlag, 1949), 158.

623. Detlev Peukert, *Die KPD in Widerstand. Verfolgung und Untergrundarbeit an Rhein und Ruhr 1933 bis 1945* (Wuppertal: Hammer, 1980), 88.

624. Gordon A. Craig, *Germany 1866–1945* (New York: Oxford University Press, 1978), 574.

625. Kellerhoff, *Hitler's Berlin*, 95.

626. Diels, the chief of the Prussian Gestapo, called it the "uprising of the Berlin SA" (*Lucifer ante Portas*, 142).

627. Noth, *Die Tragödie*, 136.

628. Willi Münzenberg, *Propaganda als Waffe* (Paris: Éditions du Carrefour, 1937), 164. After months of violence with the onset of the regime, argued Münzenberg, the "little man" who had wanted socialism was "happy to come away with his life" (158).

629. Herbert Crüger, *Verschwiegene Zeiten. Vom geheimen Apparat der KPD ins Gefängnis der Staatssicherheit* (Berlin: LinksDruck Verlag, 1990), 58.

630. Guérin, *Brown Plague*, 118.

631. Ibid., 199–20.

632. Ibid.

633. Joseph Nyomarkay, *Charisma and Factionalism in the Nazi Party* (Minneapolis: University of Minnesota Press, 1967), 124.

634. The idea of a Second Revolution, which became so closely linked with the idea of socialism propagated by the SA and other radical sectors of the Nazi movement, appears to have originated—in a somewhat different iteration—with Gregor Strasser in 1925, who against the first revolution (of 1918) posited a "spiritual revolution" or "revolution of the soul." See Lane, "Nazi Ideology," 23–24. In a slightly different iteration, his brother Otto defined the war itself as the first revolution (ibid., 24). Ernst Röhm first used the term to refer to a follow-up to the *Machtergreifung* in April 1933; see Nyomarkay, *Charisma and*, 124.

635. Noth, *Die Tragödie*, 213.

636. BA-SAPMO, I 2/705/25, Betr. SA (15.6.34).

637. BA-SAPMO I 2/706/13.

638. "I'm an old SA man, you can talk to me," he allegedly said, "but watch out for the *Märzgefallene*, they're informers." BA-SAPMO, I 2/705/25, "Betr. SA, 1.8.34."

639. BA-SAPMO, I 2/705/25, "Betr. SA ,11.4.34." Another Communist spy records the following conversation with an SA worker. Drawn into a discussion on "the battle between capital and labor," the stormtrooper replied, "The decision will come. … But I still don't see that Communism has enough strength. Certainly, the people work, heroically risk their lives, but because of the terror they don't have any outward success. But it can come quickly to resistance, to an uprising. The first time one or more large concerns go over to resistance because of the worsening situation in the factories, it can come very fast to that. Whether the Communists then can succeed in taking over leadership, I doubt. It would be nice [Zu wünschen wäre es]. If a revolutionary crisis occurred, at least a third of my *Sturm* would fight on the side of the Communists. … When it comes to a fight, I'll be on the side of the Commune." BA-SAPMO, I 2/705/25, 2–3, "Lagebericht Nr. 7 vom 6.IV–19.IV.34."

640. BA-SAPMO, I 2/705/25, "Stimmung der SA-Männer. Abteilung Ie." From "Betr. SA-Lagebericht" (10.11.34).

641. *Sopade,* June/July 1934, p. 206.

642. *Sopade,* May/June 1934, p.145.

643. *Sopade,* April/May 1934, p. 22.

644. "Hitler's Private Armies Clash. Storm Troops Fight Steel Helmets. Nazi Minister Waylaid and Shot At," *Daily Express,* 12 June 1934.

645. *Sopade,* May/June 1934, 144–45.

646. Cited in the *New York Post,* 29 June 1934.

647. Klaus Mlynek, ed., *Gestapo Hannover Meldet … Polizei- und Regierungsberichte für das mittlere uns südliche Niedersachsen zwischen 1933 und 1937* (Hildesheim, 1986), 121.

648. Klaus-Michael Mallmann and Gerhard Paul, "Omniscient, Omnipotent, Omnipresent? Gestapo, Society and Resistance," in David Crew, ed., *Nazism and German Society, 1933–45* (London: Routledge, 1994), 186.

649. Fischer, *Stormtroopers*, 6.

650. Longerich, *Die Braunen Bataillone,* 184.
651. Bessel, *Political Violence,* 96.
652. BA Sammlung Schumacher 278.
653. Diels, *Lucifer ante Portas,* 234. The Communist intelligence apparatus complained in June 1934 that units of the Department Ie were being built within every SA unit. See "Zur Revolutionäre Arbeit in den NS-Organisationen Anfang Juni, 1934," BA-SAPMO, I 2/705/25.
654. *Sopade,* May/June 1934, 146. In Berlin, the *Feldpolizei* helped control the worst excesses of the SA, but in a manner hardly consistent with the principles of law and order. In its detention center in Berlin, wrote Rudolf Diels, were imprisoned "SA men, Communists, and entirely innocent citizens, whom the *Feldpolizei* had beaten up without distinction" (*Lucifer ante Portas,* 189).
655. *Vossische Zeitung,* 18 July 1933.
656. BA-SAPMO, I 2/705/25, "Betr. Differenzen und Stimmungsbilder aus den fasch. Organisationen" (21.2.34).
657. Ulrich Herbert, *Best. Biographische Studien über Radikalismus, Weltanschauung und Vernuft, 1903–1989* (Bonn: Dietz, 1996), 141, 142.
658. Longerich, *Die Braunen Bataillone.*
659. Herbert, *Best,* 143–45.
660. Quoted in Longerich, *Die Braunen Bataillone,* 181.
661. BA-SAPMO, I 2/706/13, "NSDAP Wochenberichte No. 22," 22.2.33.
662. Paul, *Aufstand der Bilder,* 138.
663. George L. Mosse, *The Crisis of German Ideology: Intellectual Origins of the Third Reich* (New York: Schocken Books, 1981).
664. *Vossische Zeitung,* no. 119, 11 March 1933.
665. *Vossische Zeitung,* no. 230, 15 May 1933.
666. Ibid.
667. *Vossische Zeitung,* no. 71, 11 February 1933.
668. *Vossische Zeitung,* no. 195, 25 April 1933.
669. *Vossische Zeitung,* no. 242, 22 May 1933.
670. *Vossische Zeitung,* no. 560, 16 December 1933.
671. *Vossische Zeitung,* no. 71, 11 February 1933.
672. *Vossische Zeitung,* no. 313, 2 July 1933.
673. Leni Riefenstahl, *Triumph of the Will* (1934).
674. See Baird, "From Berlin to Neubabelsberg."
675. Joseph Goebbels, *Communism with the Mask Off* (Berlin: M. Mueller, 1934).
676. On the role of *Hitler Youth Quex* in the Nazi attempt to control the meaning of the revolution, see Paul, *Aufstand der Bilder,* 139.
677. Campbell, "Schilljugend," 199–200.
678. von Hellfeld, *Bündische Jugend und Hitlerjugend,* 88–92.
679. Ibid.
680. Tusk, "Aus Gruppen und Bünden."
681. Ibid.
682. Cited in Arno Klönne, *Jugend im Dritten Reich. Die Hitler-Jugend und ihre Gegner. Dokumente und Analyse* (Düsseldorf: Eugen Diederichs Verlag, 1982), 201.
683. Paetel continued to try to exercise influence in the Hitler Youth from exile in Paris; see von Hellfeld, *Bündische Jugend und Hitlerjugend,* 99.
684. Ibid., 52–54.
685. BA NS/23, 111: *Bündische Jugend,* "An Heinrich Lüger, Reichsjugendführung/Personalamt," 23–25.
686. Hans-Ranier Sandvoß, *Widerstand 1933–1945. Widerstand in Kreuzberg* (Berlin: Gedenkstätte Deutscher Widerstand, 1996), 165.
687. von Hellfeld, *Bündische Jugend und Hitlerjugend,* 42. Danzig was a League of Nations protectorate.

688. Ibid., 95–99; see also Michael H. Kater, *Hitler Youth* (Cambridge, MA: Harvard University Press, 2004).
689. Noth, *Die Tragödie,* 138.
690. Mathias von Hellfeld has conceptualized the degree of *Bündisch* acceptance of the National Socialist regime on a scale ranging from "total conformity and identification," to "partial integration," to "articulated autonomy" (*Bündische Jugend und Hitlerjugend,* 100–101).
691. Weitz, *Creating German Communism,* 280.
692. Those losses left the party, officials estimated, with an average membership of some one hundred thousand in the same period. See Allan Merson, *Communist Resistance in Nazi Germany* (London: Lawrence & Wishart, 1985), 35.
693. WaH 0496, 15 J 126/34, p. 11.
694. NWHStA, "Zu Befehl D124 vom 31. August 1933."
695. WaH 0017, 14c/8 J 1547/31, p. 22.
696. WaH 0094, Kratsch, p. 5.
697. Merson, *Communist Resistance,* 126.
698. *Zersetzungsschriften* noted in a report of early 1935 included *Der Rote Stoßtrupp* (sent through the mail to Nazi officials in Potsdam and addressed to "all honest party comrades, comrades of the SA, SS, and HJ") and in Berlin, *Der Rote Angriff,* no. 12, "Organ der revolutionäre SA-Brigade 32"; Bericht Nr. 20, Der Oberste SA-Führer. Stabsabteilung. February 22, 1934, BA Sammlung Schumacher 330. Another report noted, among other incidents, that an "Open letter to the HJ" had appeared in Hannover, designed to look like the work of an SA man; Bericht Nr. 11, Der Oberste SA-Führer. Stabsabteilung. September 21, 1934, BA Sammlung Schumacher 330.
699. NWHStA, Essen, 8 November 1933.
700. BLHA, Pr Br Rep. 30 Berlin C *Polizeipräsidium Berlin,* Tit. 95, Sekt 9, Teil 2, Nr. 185.
701. *SA Sturmbanner,* IfZ MA 644.
702. WaH 0017, 14c/8 J 1547/31, pp. 27–28.
703. Merson, *Communist Resistance,* 122–27. On the resistance activity of the KPD in Western Germany, see Peukert, *Die KPD in Widerstand.*
704. An official in Düsseldorf reported in August 1933 that since the end of April, the following KPD papers had been found in his area of administration since the end of April: "Der Revolutionär" (Wuppertal, March/April 1933), "Mit Sichel und Hammer" (Wuppertal, March/April 1933), "An Arbeiter und Bauern," "Gewerkschaftszeitung," "Spartakus," "Ruhr-Echo," "Die Freiheit," "Die rote Fahne," "Kruppscher Jungproleten," "Die Solidarität," "Das Tribunal," "Rot-Sport"; Regierungs-Präsident Düsseldorf to Preuß InnenMin, 30.8.33.
705. Sandvoß, *Widerstand,* 101.
706. Diels, *Lucifer ante Portas,* 153. Diels's contention is supported by Erich Wollenberg. *Red Army,* 708; Joachim Fest makes a similar claim in *The Face of the Third Reich* (London: Wiedenfeld & Nicolson, 1970), 220.
707. Longerich, *Die Braunen Bataillone,* 193.
708. Gisevius, *To the Bitter End,* 105. Waite echoes this figure; R. G. L. Waite, *Vanguard of Nazism,* 274. Conan Fischer doubts that the percentage was so high for Germany as a whole but acknowledges that the number was still significant (*German Communists,* 190).
709. Sandvoß, *Widerstand,* 103.
710. Reichardt, *Faschistische Kampfbünde,* 524.
711. Albert Grzesinski, head of the Berlin police force in 1930–32, said that 30 percent of the Berlin SA was made up of Communists already in 1932; Reichardt, *Faschistische Kampfbünde,* 524.
712. They are collected in BA, NS/23—9.
713. NWHStA, Düsseldorf, 6 April 1933. Peter Kramer, the former leader of a KPD *Ortsgruppe* in the Ruhr, joined the SA to protect himself from arrest; NWHStA, Dü 21231, Kramer, Peter. Werner Kraus went a step further, passing himself off as a junior officer, even though he was only a simple SA man; NWHStA, D 34045, Kraus, Werner.

714. BA-SAPMO, I 2/705/25, 16.3.34, p. 4.
715. National Archives, German Documents, Reel 85, cited in Nyomarkay, *Charisma and Faction-alism*. For a justificatory treatment of the KPD's activity within the SA and other Nazi orga-nizations after 1933 from the perspective of the GDR, see Heider, *Antifaschistischer Kampf*, 93–114.
716. Merson, *Communist Resistance*.
717. Crüger, *Verschwiegene Zeiten*, 58.
718. These included "SA opposition" papers *Der Rote Sturm* (The Red Storm) and *Die Rote Stan-darte* (The Red Standard).
719. Crüger, *Verschwiegene Zeiten*, 61. According to Crüger, the leader of the home knew that Crüger had left the Hitler Youth to join the Strasser movement, but not of his activity for the KPD. Crüger's radical posture provoked no opposition from the leader of the home, who was quite forthright in proclaiming the goal of the school to be the preparation of students for the coming Second Revolution.
720. BA-SAPMO, I 2/705/25, "Lagebericht Nr. 7 vom 6.IV - 19.IV.34." The activist estimated that the *Sturm* was comprised of two-thirds workers, the remainder being made up of white-collar workers (*Angestellte*) and the sons of small tradesmen (*Söhne Kleingewerbetreibender*).
721. SAPMO, BA, I 2/705/4, "… der Gestapomethoden und Konspiration. Beispiels und Lehren für den unterirdischen Kampf."
722. *Weissbuch über die Erschiessungen des 30. Juni* (Paris, 1935), 154.
723. BLHA, Pr Br Rep. 30 Berlin C *Polizeipräsidium*, Tit. 95, Sekt 9, Teil 2, Nr. 188, "Unser revolu-tionäre Arbeit innerhalb der SA," Sonder-Informationsdienst der RL der RSG. "These 'Com-mune-cells,'" the guidelines continued, "otherwise known as the 'Opposition,' must draw up a program of demands and work together in the closest association with RFB (to be hastily rebuilt) and its revolutionary *Sturms*. They must publish opposition leaflets and newspapers for the *Sturms* and *Standarten*." BLHA, Pr Br Rep. 30 Berlin C *Polizeipräsidium*, Tit. 95, Sekt 9, Teil 2, Nr.188, "Unser revolutionäre Arbeit innerhalb der SA," Sonder-Informationsdienst der RL der RSG." The demands appeared in the flier *SA-Mann Erwache!* distributed by the KPD in the Rheinland; NWHStA, "Essen, 8 November 1933."
724. BA-SAPMO, I 2/705/13, "An den Gegner, über den Gegner, vom Gegner, Nr. 1, Februar 1935."
725. The Black Front addressed the affair in its series titled "*Huttenbriefe*. The Black Front speaks to the German People." An article titled "Hitler's Betrayal of the SA" closed with the slogans: "Down with the reaction! Long live the socialist revolution! Down with Hitler! Hail Ger-many." Otto Strasser—whose brother Gregor had been among the victims of the SS murder squads—called for continued struggle in an uncharacteristically bloodthirsty tone: "The Sec-ond Revolution is on the march—over the corpses of Goebbels, Göring, and Hitler—to a new Germany of socialist justice and national freedom." WaH 0038, 17 J 94/34, p. 14.
726. WaH 0718, 8 J 444/35, p. 10.
727. An invaluable source for the study of the Strasser opposition after 1933, and of the *Alltagsge-schichte* of resistance in Berlin under the Nazis generally, is the series *Widerstand 1933–1945*, edited by Hans-Ranier Sandvoß. The work's volumes on the various city districts combine rich firsthand accounts with concise and helpful essays.
728. WaH 0718, 8 J 444/35, p. 10.
729. Ibid., 7.
730. Ibid., 21.
731. Copies of these fliers are, unfortunately, not extant.
732. WaH 0718, 8 J 444/35, p. 22–28.
733. WaH 0222, 8 J 381/34, pp. 4, 19. "Hitler's only strength," Simon wrote, "is the trust [of the people]. Everything else is bluff or force. These factors still exist today; but for how long? A revolutionary has time."

734. Rätsch-Langejürgen, *Das Prinzip Widerstand*, 117.
735. Noth, *Die Tragödie*, 215–19.
736. BA-SAPMO, (I 2/705/25), "Betr. Miles - Bericht," 2.3.34, p. 4.
737. Quoted in the introduction to *Berichte über die Lage in Deutschland*, li.
738. Gisevius, *To the Bitter End*, 94.
739. Münzenberg, *Propaganda als Waffe*, 157.
740. NWHStA, Dü 21231, Kramer, Peter.
741. NWHStA, D 6615, Wankum, Konrad, 29.10.86. The incident took place in 1935; the authorities decided that Wankum had done his duty and let him off.
742. Silvia Rodgers, *Red Saint, Pink Daughter: A Communist Childhood in Berlin and London* (Manchester: A. Deutsch, 1997), 97. The speaker is Rodger's mother, paraphrased by Rodgers.
743. Ibid., 97. "Fritz Walter was one of many to cross over to the Nazis," writes Rodgers, "but others were less open about it and gave pretexts: we are joining the Nazis in order to spy, in order to sabotage, in order to persuade people they are in the wrong place—'to enlighten them!'" (98).
744. See Fischer, *German Communists*, 113.
745. NWHStA, Ge 12594. K.M., Düsseldorf-Gerresheim, 31.8.1933. "An den Herrn Standartenführer Hauptmann a.D. Lohbeck."
746. NWHStA, D 24480 Hess, Adolf; PP Duisberg-Hamborn (24 March 1934).
747. NWHStA , Stapo Duisberg-Hamborn to Stapo Düss (15 July 1935).
748. BA-SAPMO, I 2/705/25, "Betr. Miles - Bericht," 2.3.34, p. 4. Work in the SA for these Communists consisted mainly of meetings in apartments in groups of four, where "schoolwork" was carried out. Every ten days a small newspaper, *Der Rote Kämpfer*, was published, but was mainly intended for the activists themselves.
749. "Bericht des Hannoverschen Polizeipräsident an den Regierungspräsidenten über den Stand der kommunistischen Bewegung," 7 June 1933, in Mlynek, *Gestapo Hannover meldet*, 47.
750. It had not actually been he but another activist who had advised the young man to enter the SA. BA-SAPMO, I 2/705/25, 16.3.34, p. 3.
751. Ibid., 4.
752. BA-SAPMO, I 2/705/25, Betr. Miles Bericht 28.4.34.
753. BA-SAPMO, I 2/705/25, "Lagebericht Nr. 7 vom 6.IV–19.IV.34."
754. *Sopade*, November/December 1934, 764.
755. BA-SAPMO, I 2/705/25, "Betr. Rundschreiben der SA-Reserve I Landesverband Berlin-Brandenburg (16.3.34)."
756. Longerich, *Die Braunen Bataillone*, 191–92.
757. *Sopade*, April/May 1934, 19.
758. BA-SAPMO, I 2/705/25, "Betr. SA-Lagebericht (10.11.34)."
759. *Sopade*, April/May 1934, 18–19.
760. *Sopade*, June/July 1934, 187.
761. *Sopade*, April/May 1934, 19.
762. *Sopade*, August 1935, 947.
763. The recommendations of the Berlin party organization published in June included "the maintenance and buildup of the SA newspapers that have appeared up until now … and the use of all opportunities yielded by the SA to penetrate the other military organizations or units"; see BA-SAPMO I 2/705/4, "Über die antimilitärische Arbeit (Berliner Vorschläge) June 1935." Further recommendations published in August read: "In the center of [our] antimilitary tasks stands the work within the SA. … The goals of this work are the creation of (a) a network of strongholds in the SA throughout the entire Reich; (b) firm groups and cells in the most important storm battalions and special formations (NSKK, Pioneer *Sturms*); (c) the revolutionizing of entire *Sturms;* (d) regular publication of SA opposition newspapers and fliers through opposition groups in the SA." See BA-SAPMO I 2/705/4, "Vorschläge zur Verbesserung der mil.pol. Arbeit," 26 August 1935.

764. The Kayser group in Cologne continued to publish leaflets and hold discussion groups through December 1935. An affiliated group in Essen held out until 1936 before it was uncovered and broken by the Gestapo.

765. Gisevius, *To the Bitter End*, 94.

766. Ibid., 96.

767. Richard Scheringer was rumored to have been killed in the purge. He was released from prison through the intervention of his friend Hanns Ludin and General von Reichenau; see Ernst Niekisch, *Gewagtes Leben. Errinerungen eines deutschen Revolutionärs, 1889–1945* (Cologne: Verlag Wissenschaft und Politik Berend von Nottbeck, 1974), 185. After the war, Scheringer placed himself at the forefront of Communist politics in southern Germany, accepting the post of state secretary for agriculture in Bavaria. Scheringer's tenure there ended abruptly when the American occupation authorities found his name on the Nazi Party rolls in Berlin and sentenced him to two weeks' imprisonment for falsifying his denazification questionnaire; see Scheringer, *Das Grosse Los,* 498. In a pamphlet subsequently published by the KPD to clear him, Scheringer claimed that his name was entered on the NSDAP's rolls without his consent during his imprisonment in fortress Gollnow, and he argued that his role as figurehead for the KPD's campaign of subversion against the Nazis had actually been a form of "resistance" that had born fruit in the increasing disorganization of the NSDAP in 1932. His infatuation with the stormtroopers of the SA—and the KPD's role in subverting Weimar democracy through its "social fascism" strategy—received no mention. See Scheringer to Plaum, 23 August 1947, in Hugo Erlich, *Der Fall Scheringer* (München: Franz Verlag, 1948), 9.

768. See Robert Gellately, *The Gestapo and German Society: Enforcing Racial Policy, 1933–1945* (Oxford: Clarendon Press, 1991); see also Mallmann and Paul, "Omniscient, Omnipotent, Omnipresent?"

769. See Bahar, *Sozialrevolutionärer Nationalismus;* Rätsch-Langejürgen, *Das Prinzip Widerstand;* Oswald Bindrich and Susanne Römer, *Beppo Römer. Ein Leben zwischen Revolution und Nation* (Berlin: Edition Hentrich, 1991).

770. Koebel came back to East Berlin in 1948 and joined East Germany's ruling party, the SED (Socialist Unity Party). He was expelled in 1951 and died in 1955. See Sandvoß, *Widerstand,* 166.

771. Brown, "Richard Scheringer." The Black Front tried unsuccessfully to arrange Scheringer's escape to Prague; see the trial records of Herbert Blank and Walter Schreck (8J306/35 and 2H 30/35) in the microfilm collection WaH.

772. Portions of Ludin's correspondence pertaining to the Final Solution in Slovakia appear in the records of the Adolf Eichmann trial. Addressing the fallout from a pastoral letter from the Slovakian Church alerting the faithful to the murderous realities of Jewish deportation, Ludin wrote reassuringly to the Foreign Office in Berlin that "the anti-Semitism of the Slovakian people, founded in experience, as well as the anti-Semitic propaganda being carried out by us, has created an atmosphere that appears to be no longer favorable for such [interventions]." Ludin ordered the propaganda office to ignore the pastoral letter and continue with its anti-Semitic propaganda. See Hanns Ludin to Auswärtige Amt Berlin, 13 April 1943, Institute für Zeitgeschichte, Eich 1016.

773. Mosse, *Crisis of German Ideology,* 279. "The mass enthusiasm which over a half a century of *Völkisch* agitation had made explosive, and which, if not resolved, could become dangerous to its own creators," writes Mosse, "was shifted away from the real social and economic grievances and channeled into anti-Semitism. The Jew was made to bear the brunt and, although this too had been standard in the *Völkisch* movement, Hitler made it stick" (292).

774. HA 17/325, SA Gruppe Nord-West to OSAF, 16 June 1931.

775. Roger Eatwell, *Fascism: A History* (New York: Allen Lane, 1996), 39.

776. For an elaboration of the concept of "working toward the Führer," see Kershaw, *Hitler, Hubris,* chapter 13.

777. See Roger Griffin, "Last Rights?" Afterward to S. Ramet, ed., *The Radical Right in Central and Eastern Europe* (University Park, PA: Penn State University Press, 1999), 297–321.
778. Holger Jenrich, *Anarchistische Presse in Deutschland 1945–1985* (Grafenau-Döffingen: Trozdem Verlag, 1988), 76–87.
779. See the comments of Peter Steinbach, "Vorwart," in Susanne Römer and Hans Coppi, eds., *Aufbruch. Dokumentation einer Zeitschrift zwischen den Fronten* (Koblenz: Verlag Dietmar Fölbach, 2001).
780. See Brown, "Richard Scheringer"; for a discussion of this phenomenon in France, see Jeffrey M. Bale, "'National Revolutionary' Groupuscules and the Resurgence of 'Left Wing' Fascism: The Case of France's Nouvelle Résistance," *Institute for Jewish Policy Research* 36, no. 2 (2002): 24–49. See also Roger Griffin, "From Slime Mould to Rhizome: An Introduction to the Groupuscular Right," *Patterns of Prejudice* 37, no. 1 (March 2003): 27–50.
781. A prominent part of the right-wing effort to co-opt left-wing positions has revolved around environmental issues. For a politically engaged discussion of this issue, see Janet Biehl, "'Ecology' and the Modernization of Fascism in the German Ultra-Right," in Janet Biehl and Peter Staudenmaier, ed., *Ecofascism: Lessons from the German Experience* (Edinburgh: AK Press, 1995). National Revolutionaries were active in the Green Party until their expulsion in the early 1980s. See Hans-Georg Betz, "On the German Question: Left, Right, and the Politics of National Identity," *Radical America* 20, no. 1 (1987): 45–46; Oliver Geden, "Die Ökologische Rechte," in *Antifa Reader. Antifaschistisches Handbuch und Ratgeber* (Berlin: Elefanten Press, 1996), 227–34. On the connections between other environmental organizations and the radical right, see Volkmar Wölk, "Neue Trends im ökofaschistischen Netzwerk: Am Beispiel der Anthroposophen, dem Weltbund zum Schutz des Lebens und der ÖDP," in Raimund Hethey and Peter Kratz, eds., *In bester Gesellschaft: Antifa-Recherche zwischen Konservativismus und Neo-Faschismus* (Göttingen: Verlag Die Werkstatt, 1991). There is also a strong strain of mystical, New Age thought associated with right-wing environmentalism, above all in the work of Rudolf Bahro; see Roger Niedenführ, "New Age: Die spirituelle Rehabilitierung der Nationalsozialisten durch Rudolf Bahro, Rainer Langhans und J. Kirchoff," in Raimund Hethey and Peter Kratz, eds., *In bester Gesellschaft: Antifa-Recherche zwischen Konservatismus und Neo-faschismus,* (Göttingen: Verlag die Werkstatt, 1991), 141–54.
782. See Diethelm Prowe, "Fascism, Neo-Fascism, New Radical Right?" in Roger Griffin, ed., *International Fascism: Theories, Causes, and the New Consensus* (London: Arnold, 1998), 305–24.
783. See Wolfgang Benz, *Jahrbuch für Antisemitismus-forschung 10* (Frankfurt am Main: Campus-Verlag, 2001).

BIBLIOGRAPHY

Archival Sources

Bundesarchiv Berlin, Berlin-Lichterfelde:
  Nachlass Scheringer
  Reichsministerium des Innern (15.01)
  R58
  R134
  NS22
  NS23
  NS26
  ZD279
  Zsg2/194
  Sammlung Schumacher
  ZB (Library)

Stiftung Archiv der Parteien und Massenorganisationen der DDR (SAPMO-BA)
  Flugblattsammlung

Bundesarchiv Koblenz
  BAK Zsg 2/192
  Zsg 2/194

Geheimes Staatsarchiv, Preussischer Kulturbesitz (GStA PK)
  Ministerium des Innern
  Nachlaß Daluege

Brandenburgisches Landeshauptarchiv
  Pr Br Rep 30 Berlin C *Polizeipräsidium*

Institut für Zeitgeschichte Munich (IfZ)
  Eich

F7
Fa 3
Fa 70
Fa 88
Fa 701
Fa 230
MA 133
MA 644
MA 747
Sp 2/2
ZS 177 Bd I
ZS 1147 Bd I-II
ZS 2443

NSDAP Hauptarchiv (Hoover Institute Microfilm Collection)

Bayerisches Hauptstaatsarchiv München (BHStA)
    Staatsministerium des Innern

Nordrhein-Westfälisches Hauptstaatsarchiv Düsseldorf-Mauerstrasse:
    RW34 (Stapostelle Köln)
    RW36 (Stapostelle Düsseldorf, Aussenstellen)
    RW58 (Gestapo-Personalakten)

Newspapers and Periodicals

Arbeiter, Bauern, Soldaten
Arbeiter Illustrierte Zeitung
Aufbruch
Basiler Vorwarts
Berliner Tageblatt
Berliner Volkszeitung
C.V.-Archiv-Blätter
Daily Express
Das Freikorps
Demokratische Zeitungsdienst
Der Angriff
Der Freiheitskämpfer
Der Jungdeutsche
Der Junge Antifaschist
Der Rote Angriff
Der Rote Angriff. Kampfblatt der proletar. Revolution!
Der Rote Frontsoldat. Organ für proletarische Wehrpolitik
Der Rote Student
Der SA-Kamerad
Der SA-Mann
Der Samstags-Beobachter

Der Staat Seid Ihr
Der Sturmbanner
Der Völkischer Beobachter
Deutsche Nachrichten
Die Brennessel
Die Deutsche Revolution
Die Junge Garde. Zeitung d. werktätigen Jugend in Stadt und Land.
Die Kiefer. Monatsschrift für eine junge Gesinnung.
Die Kommenden
Die Rote Fahne
Die Sturmfahne
Frankfurter Zeitung
Front-Appell
Kameraden Briefe
Kölnische Zeitung
Rheinische Zeitung
Rote Jungfront
Rotes Sturmbanner
SA-Revolution
Sturm
Sturm. Organ der Revolutionären SA an der Saar
Sturmbereit
Sturmbanner. Funktionäreorgan des Kampfbundes gegen den Faschismus
Sturmfahne. Von Arbeitern für Arbeiter
Sturmfahne. Organ der Werktätigen Südbayerns
Süddeutschen Arbeiterzeitung
Vorwärtz
Vossische Zeitung
Welt am Abend

Published Primary Sources

Crüger, Herbert, *Ein alter Mann erzählt. Lebensbericht eines Kommunisten.* Schleuditz: GNN Verlag, 1998.
———. *Verschwiegene Zeiten. Vom geheimen Apparat der KPD ins Gefängnis der Staatssicherheit.* Berlin: LinksDruck Verlag, 1990.
Feder, Gottfried. *Hitler's Official Program and Its Fundamental Ideas.* 1920; (New York: Howard Fertig, 1971).
Gisevius, Hans Bernd. *To the Bitter End.* Boston: Houghton Mifflin Company, 1947.
Goebbels, Joseph. *Communism with the Mask Off.* Berlin: M. Mueller, 1934.
———. *Die Tagebücher von Joseph Goebbels. Sämtliche Fragmente. Teil I. Aufzeichnungen 1924–1941.* 2 vols. Edited by Elke Fröhlich. Munich: K. G. Sauer, 1987.
Gäbler, Fritz. "Erinnerungen an meine Festungshaft in Gollnow und meine erste Bekanntschaft mit Richard Scheringer." *Beiträge zur Geschichte der deutschen Arbeiterbewegung,* vols. 1–4. 1961.
Guérin, Daniel. *The Brown Plague: Travels in Late Weimar and Early Nazi Germany.* Durham, NC: Duke University Press, 1994.

Hitler, Adolf. *Mein Kampf.* Boston: Houghton Mifflin, 1999.

Krebs, Albert. *The Infancy of Nazism: The Memoirs of Ex-Gauleiter Albert Krebs, 1923–1933.* Edited by William Sheridan Allen. New York: New Viewpoints, 1976.

Münzenberg, Willi. *Propaganda als Waffe.* Paris: Éditions du Carrefour, 1937.

Niekisch, Ernst. *Gewagtes Leben. Errinerungen eines deutschen Revolutionärs, 1889–1945.* Cologne: Verlag Wissenschaft und Politik Berend von Nottbeck, 1974.

Noth, Ernst Erich. *Die Tragödie der deutschen Jugend.* Frankfurt am Main: Glotzi Verlag, 2002.

Ossietzky, Carl von. *Sämtliche Schriften. Band VI. 1931–1933. Texte 969–1082.* Edited by Gerhard Kraiker, Gunther Nickel, Renke Siems, and Elke Suhr. Reibeck bei Hamburg: Rohwolt, 1994.

Pütz, Hans. *Dokumente kommunistischer Führungskorruption. Die KPD im Dienste der russischen Aussenpolitik.* Leipzig: Kurt Wildeis, 1931.

Rodgers, Silvia. *Red Saint, Pink Daughter: A Communist Childhood in Berlin and London* (Manchester: A. Deutsch, 1997).

Scheringer, Richard. *Das Grosse Los. Unter Soldaten, Bauern und Rebellen.* Hamburg: Rohwolt, 1959.

Strasser, Otto. *Mein Kampf. Eine Politische Autobiographie.* Frankfurt: Streit-Zeit-Bucher 1969.

Documentary Collections

Berichte über die Lage in Deutschland. Die Lagemeldungen der Gruppe Neu Beginnen aus dem Dritten Reich 1933–1936 (Bonn: Verlag J. H. W. Dietz Nachfolger, 1996).

Deutschland-Bericht der Sopade. 2 vols. Frankfurt am Main, 1980.

Kindt, Werner, ed. *Die deutsche Jugendbewegung 1920 bis 1933. Die bündische Zeit.* Munich: Eugen Diederichs Verlag, 1974.

Lane, Barbara Miller, and Leila J. Rupp, eds. *Nazi Ideology Before 1933: A Documentation.* Austin: University of Texas Press, 1978.

Langkau-Alex, Ursula. *Deutsche Volksfront 1932–1939. Zwischen Berlin, Paris, Prag und Moskau.* 3 vols. Berlin: Akademie Verlag, 2004.

Mlynek, Klaus, ed. *Gestapo Hannover Meldet … Polizei- und Regierungsberichte für das mittlere uns südliche Niedersachsen zwischen 1933 und 1937.* Hildesheim: Veröffentlichungen der historischen Kommission für Niedersachsen und Bremen, 1986.

Mühlberger, Detlef, ed. *Hitler's Voice: The Völkischer Beobachter, 1920–1933.* 2 vols. Bern: Peter Lang, 2004.

Pikarski, Margot, and Elke Warning, eds. *Gestapo-Berichte über den antifaschistischen Widerstandskampf der KPD 1933–1945.* 3 vols. Berlin: Dietz, 1989.

Weber, Hermann, ed. *Der deutsche Kommunismus. Dokumente.* Cologne: Kiepenheuer & Witsch, 1963.

Secondary Sources

Allen, William Sheridan. *The Seizure of Power: The Experience of a Single German Town. 1930–1935.* New York: Franklin Watts, 1984.

Aly, Götz. *Hitler's Volksstaat. Raub, Rassenkrieg und nationaler Sozialismus.* Frankfurt: Fischer, 2005.

Amis, Martin. *Koba the Dread: Laughter and the Twenty Million.* New York: Vintage, 2002.

Angress, Werner T. *Stillborn Revolution: The Communist Bid for Power in Germany, 1921–1923.* Princeton, NJ: Princeton University Press, 1963.

Ascher, Abraham, and Guenther Lewy. "National Bolshevism in Weimar Germany— Alliance of Political Extremes Against Democracy." *Social Research* 23, no. 4 (Winter 1956): 450–80.

Aumann, Nancy. "From Legality to Illegality: The Communist Party of Germany in Transition, 1930–1933." Ph.D. dissertation, University of Wisconsin–Madison, 1982.

Avrich, Paul. *The Russian Anarchists.* Princeton, NJ: Princeton University Press, 1967.
———. *Kronstadt 1921.* Princeton, NJ: Princeton University Press, 1970.

Bahar, Alexander. *Sozialrevolutionärer Nationalismus zwischen Konservativer Revolution und Sozialismus. Harro Schulze-Boyson und der "Gegner"-Kreis.* Koblenz: Verlag Dietmar Fölbach, 1992.

Bahne, Siegfried. "Die Kommunistische Partei Deutschlands." In Erich Matthias and Rudolf Morsey, eds., *Das Ende der Parteien 1933.* Düsseldorf: Droste, 1960.
———. *Die KPD und das Ende von Weimar. Das Scheitern einer Politik 1932–1935.* Frankfurt am Main: Campus Verlag, 1976.

Baird, Jay W. "From Berlin to Neubabelsberg: Nazi Film Propaganda and Hitler Youth Quex." *Journal of Contemporary History* 18, no. 3 (July 1983): 495–515.
———. *To Die for Germany: Heroes in the Nazi Pantheon.* Bloomington: Indiana University Press, 1990.

Bajohr, Frank. "In doppelter Isolation. Zum Widerstand der Arbeiterjugendbewegung gegen den Nationalsozialismus." In Wilfried Breyvogel, ed., *Piraten, Swings und Junge Garde. Jugendwiderstand im Nationalsozialismus,* 17–35. Bonn: Dietz, 1991.

Baldwin, Peter. "Social Interpretations of Nazism: Renewing a Tradition." *Journal of Contemporary History* 25, no. 1 (January 1990): 5–37.

Bale, Jeffrey M. "'National Revolutionary' Groupuscules and the Resurgence of 'Left Wing' Fascism: The Case of France's Nouvelle Résistance." *Institute for Jewish Policy Research* 36, no. 2 (2002): 24–49.

Bartsch, Günther. *Zwischen drei Stühlen. Otto Strasser. Eine Biographie.* Koblenz: Verlag Siegfried Bublies, 1990.

Bassler, Gerhard P. "The Communist Movement in the German Revolution, 1918–1919: A Problem of Historical Typology?" *Central European History* 6, no. 3 (September 1973): 233–79.

Bavaj, Riccardo. *Von links gegen Weimar. Linkes antiparlamentarisches Denken in der Weimarer Republik.* Bonn: Verlag J. H. W. Dietz Nachfolger, 2005.

Bavaj, Riccardo, and Florentine Fritzen. *Deutschland—Ein Land ohne revolutionäre Traditionen? Revolutionen im Deutschland des 19. und 20. Jahrhunderts im lichte neuerer geistes- und kulturgeschichtlicher Erkenntnisse.* Frankfurt am Main: Peter Lang, 2005.

Benjamin, Walter. "The Work of Art in the Age of Mechanical Reproduction." In *Illuminations,* 217–51. New York: Schocken Books, 1968.

Bennecke, Heinrich. *Hitler und die SA.* Munich: G. Olzog, 1962.

Berghahn, Volker R. *Der Stahlhelm. Bund der Frontsoldaten 1918–1935.* Düsseldorf: Droste, 1966.

Bergmann, Theodor. *"Gegen den Strom." Die Geschichte der KPD (Opposition).* Hamburg: VSA-Verlag, 2000.

Bessel, Richard. "The 'Front Generation' and the Politics of Weimar Germany." In Mark Roseman, ed., *Generations in Conflict: Youth Revolt and Generational Formation in Germany, 1770–1968,* 121–36. Cambridge: Cambridge University Press, 1995.

———. *Germany After the First World War.* Oxford: Oxford University Press, 1995.

———. "The Great War in German Memory: The Soldiers of the First World War, Demobilization, and Weimar Political Culture." *German History* 6 (1988): 20–34.

———. "Kriegserfahrungen und Kriegserinnerungen: Nachwirkungen des Ersten Weltkrieges auf das politische und soziale Leben der Weimarer Republik." In Marcel van der Linden, Herman de Lange, and Gottfried Mergner, eds., *Kriegsbegeisterung und mentale Kriegsvorbereitung. Interdisziplinäre Studien.* Berlin: Duncker & Humboldt, 1991.

———. "Living with the Nazis: Some Recent Writing on the Social History of the Third Reich." *European History Quarterly* 14, no. 2 (April 1984): 211–220.

———. "Militarismus im innenpolitischen Leben der Weimarer Republik: Von den Freikorps zur SA." In Klaus-Jürgen Müller and Eckhardt Opitz, eds., *Militär und Militarismus in der Weimarer Republik,* 193–222. Düsseldorf: Droste, 1978.

———. *Political Violence and the Rise of Nazism: The Stormtroopers in Eastern Germany, 1925–1934.* New Haven, CT: Yale University Press, 1984.

———. "Politische Gewalt und die Krise der Weimarer Republik." In Lutz Niethammer, ed., *Bürgerliche Gesellschaft in Deutschland. Historische Einblicke, Fragen, Perspektiven.* Frankfurt am Main: Fischer Taschenbuch Verlag, 1990.

———. "1933: A Failed Counter-Revolution." In E. E. Rice, ed., *Revolution and Counter-Revolution.* Oxford: Blackwell, 1991.

Bessel, Richard, and Mathilde Jamin. "Nazis, Workers, and the Uses of Quantitative Evidence." *Social History* 4 (January 1979): 111–16.

Betz, Hans-Georg. "On the German Question: Left, Right, and the Politics of National Identity." *Radical America* 20, no. 1 (1987): 45–46.

Bindrich, Oswald, and Susanne Römer. *Beppo Römer. Ein Leben zwischen Revolution und Nation.* Berlin: Edition Hentrich, 1991.

Bloch, Charles. *Die SA und die Krise des NS-Regimes 1934.* Frankfurt am Main: Suhrkamp, 1970.

Bloch, Ernst. "Inventory of Revolutionary Appearance." In *Heritage of Our Times,* trans. J. Cummings. 1933. Cambridge: Polity Press, 1991, 64–67.

Boesch, Hermann. *Jugend in der Weimar Republik.* Isenbüttel: Aurora Verlag, 1986.

Böhnke, Wilfried. *Die NSDAP in Ruhrgebiet 1920–1933.* Bonn: Verlag Neue Gesellschaft, 1974.

Bowlby, Chris. "Blutmai 1929: Police, Parties and Proletarians in a Berlin Confrontation." *Historical Journal* 29, no. 1 (March 1986): 137–58.

Borkenau, Franz. *World Communism: A History of the Communist International.* London: George Allen & Unwin, 1938.

Bracher, Karl Dietrich. *The German Dictatorship: The Origins, Structure, and Effects of National Socialism.* New York: Praeger, 1970.

Brandenberg, Hans-Christian. *Die Geschichte der HJ. Wege und Irrwege einer Generation.* Cologne: Verlag Wissenschaft, 1968.

Brandenberger, David. *National Bolshevism: Stalinist Mass Culture and the Formation of Modern Russian National Identity, 1931–1956.* Cambridge, MA: Harvard University Press, 2002.

Breitman, Richard. "Nazism in the Eyes of German Social Democracy." In Michael N. Dobkowski and Isidor Wallimann, eds., *Towards the Holocaust: The Social and Economic Collapse of the Weimar Republic.* Westport, CT: Greenwood Press, 1983.

Breyvogel, Wilfried. "Einleitung." In Wilfried Breyvogel, ed., *Piraten, Swings und Junge Garde. Jungendwiderstand im Nationalsozialismus,* 9–16. Bonn: Dietz, 1991.

Broszat, Martin. *German National Socialism, 1919–1945.* Santa Barbara: Clio Press, 1966.

———. *Hitler and the Collapse of Weimar Germany.* Leamington Spa, UK: Berg, 1987.

Brown, Timothy S. "'Beefsteak Nazis' and 'Brown Bolshevists': Boundaries and Identity in the Rise of National Socialism." Paper presented at the Annual Meeting of the American Historical Association, San Francisco, January 2002.

———. "Richard Scheringer, the KPD and the Politics of Class and Nation in Germany: 1922–1969." *Contemporary European History* 14, no. 1 (August 2005): 317–46.

Brustein, William. "Blue-Collar Nazism: The German Working Class and the Nazi Party." In Conan Fischer, ed., *The Rise of National Socialism and the Working Classes in Weimar Germany,* 137–62. Providence and Oxford: Berghahn, 1996.

Bucher, Peter. *Der Reichswehrprozeß. Der Hochverrat der Ulmer Reichswehroffiziere 1929/30.* Boppard am Rhein: H. Boldt, 1967.

Buchloh, Ingrid. *Die Nationalsozialistische Machtergreifung in Duisberg. Eine Fallstudie.* Duisberg: Duisburger Forschungen, 1980.

Bullock, Alan. *Hitler: A Study in Tyranny.* New York: Bantam, 1953.

Burleigh, Michael, *The Third Reich. A New History.* New York : Hill and Wang, 2000.

———, ed., *The Labyrinth: Memoirs of Walter Schellenberg, Hitler's Chief of Counterintelligence.* Cambridge, MA: Da Capo Press, 1984.

Campbell, Bruce. "The SA After the Röhm Purge." *Journal of Contemporary History* 28 (1993): 659–74.

———. *The SA Generals and the Rise of Nazism.* Lexington: University Press of Kentucky, 1998.

———. "The Schilljugend: From Wehrjugend to Luftschutz." In Wolfgang R. Krabbe, ed., *Politische Jugend in der Weimarer Republik,* 183–201. Bochum: Universitätsverlag Dr. N. Brockmeyer, 1993. 183–201.

Carsten, Francis L. *Reichswehr und Politik, 1918–1933.* Cologne: Kiepenheuer & Witsch, 1965.

———. *The Rise of Fascism.* Berkeley: University of California Press, 1982.

Chickering, Roger. "Political Mobilization and Associational Life: Some Thoughts on the National Socialist German Workers' Club (e.V.)." In Larry Eugene Jones and James Retallack, eds., *Elections, Mass Politics, and Social Change in Modern Germany. New Perspectives,* 307–28. New York: Cambridge University Press, 1992.

Childers, Thomas. *The Nazi Voter: The Social Foundations of Fascism in Germany, 1919–1933.* Chapel Hill: University of North Carolina Press, 1983.

———. "The Social Bases of the National Socialist Vote." *Journal of Contemporary History* 11 (1976): 17–42.

Coppi, Hans. "'Aufbruch' im Spannungsfeld von Nationalismus und Kommunismus— eine Zeitschrift für Grenzgänger." In Susanne Römer und Hans Coppi, eds.,

Aufbruch. Dokumentation einer Zeitschrift zwischen den Fronten, 50. Koblenz: Verlag Dietmar Fölbach, 2001.

———. "Die nationalsozialistischen Bäume im sozialdemokratischen Wald. Die KPD im antifaschistischen Zweifrontenkrieg" (Teil 1). *UTOPIE kreativ.* 96 (October 1998): 5–12.

Courtois, Stéphane, et al. *The Black Book of Communism: Crimes, Terror, Repression.* Cambridge, MA: Harvard University Press, 1999.

Craig, Gordon A. *Germany, 1866–1945.* New York: Oxford University Press, 1978.

———. *The Politics of the Prussian Army, 1640–1945.* Oxford: Clarendon Press, 1955.

Deak, Istvan. *Weimar Germany's Left-Wing Intellectuals: A Political History of the Weltbühne and Its Circle.* Berkeley: University of California Press, 1968.

Diehl, James M. *Paramilitary Politics in Weimar Germany.* Bloomington: Indiana University Press, 1977.

Diels, Rudolf. *Lucifer ante Portas. Zwischen Severing und Heydrich.* Zurich: Interverlag, 1949.

Dithmar, Reinhard. *Der Langemarck-Mythos in Dichtung und Unterricht.* Neuwied: Luchterhand, 1992.

Doehler, Edgar, and Egbert Fischer. *Revolutionäre Militärpolitik gegen faschistische Gefahr. Militärpolitische Probleme des Antifaschistische Kampfes der KPD von 1929 bis 1933.* Berlin: Militärverlag der Deutschen Demokratischen Republik, 1982.

Drechsler, Hanno. *Die Sozialistische Arbeiterpartei Deutschlands (SAPD): Ein Beitrag zur Geschichte der Deutschen Arbeiterbewegung am Ende der Weimarer Republik.* Meisenheim am Glan: Verlag Anton Hain, 1966.

Dupeux, Louis. *Nationalbolshewismus in Deutschland 1919–1933. Kommunistische Strategie und konservative Dynamik.* Munich: Verlag C. H. Beck, 1985.

Eatwell, Roger. *Fascism: A History.* New York: Vintage, 1995.

———. "Towards a New Model of Generic Fascism." *Journal of Theoretical Politics* 2 (1992): 161–94.

Erlich, Hugo, *Der Fall Scheringer* (München: Franz Verlag, 1948).

Falter, Jürgen. "Die Jungmitglieder der NSDAP zwischen 1925 und 1933. Ein demographisches und soziales Profil." In Wolfgang R. Krabbe, ed., *Politische Jugend in der Weimarer Republik,* 202–21. Bochum: Universitätsverlag Dr. N. Brockmeyer, 1993.

———. *Hitler's Wähler.* Munich: Beck, 1991.

———. "How Likely Were Workers to Vote for the NSDAP?" In Conan Fischer, ed., *The Rise of National Socialism and the Working Classes in Weimar Germany,* 9–45. Providence and Oxford: Berghahn, 1996.

Fest, Joachim. *The Face of the Third Reich.* London: Wiedenfeld & Nicolson, 1970.

Fischer, Conan. "Class Enemies or Class Brothers? Communist-Nazi Relations in Germany, 1929–33." *European History Review* 15, no. 3 (July 1985): 259–79.

———. *The German Communists and the Rise of Nazism.* Basingstoke, UK: Macmillan, 1991.

———. "The Occupational Background of the SA's Rank and File Membership During the Depression Years, 1929 to Mid-1934." In Peter D. Stachura, ed., *The Shaping of the Nazi State,* 131–59 (London: Croom Helm, 1978).

———. *The Rise of the Nazis.* Manchester: Manchester University Press, 1995.

———. "The SA of the NSDAP: Social Background and Ideology of the Rank and File in the Early 1930s." *Journal of Contemporary History* 17 (1982): 651–70.

————. *Stormtroopers: A Social, Economic and Ideological Analysis, 1929–35*. London: George Allen & Unwin, 1983.

Fischer, Conan, and Carolyn Hicks. "Statistics and the Historian: The Occupational Profile of the SA of the NSDAP." *Social History* 5 (January 1980): 131–38.

Fischer, Conan, and Detlef Mühlberger. "The Pattern of the SA's Social Appeal." In Conan Fischer, ed., *The Rise of National Socialism and the Working Classes in Weimar Germany*, 99–113. Providence and Oxford: Berghahn, 1996.

Fischer, Ruth. *Stalin and German Communism: A Study in the Origins of the State Party*. Cambridge, MA: Harvard University Press, 1948.

Fischer-Defoy, Christine. *Arbeiterwiderstand in der Provinz. Arbeiterbewegung und Faschismus in Kassel und Nordhessen 1933–1945. Eine Fallstudie*. West Berlin: Verlag für Ausbildung und Studium in der Elefanten Press, 1982.

Fitzpatrick, Sheila. *Tear Off the Mask! Identity and Imposture in Twentieth-Century Russia*. Princeton, NJ:: Princeton University Press, 2005.

Flechtheim, Ossip Kurt. *Die KPD in der Weimarer Republik*. Hamburg: Junius, 1986.

Foitzik, Jan. *Zwischen den Fronten. Zur Politik, Organisation und Funktion linker politischer Kleinorganisationen im Widerstand 1933 bis 1939/40*. Bonn: Verlag Neue Gesellschaft, 1986.

Fritzsche, Peter. *Germans into Nazis*. Cambridge, MA: Harvard University Press, 1998.

————. "Nazi Modern." *Modernism/Modernity* 3, no. 1 (1996): 1–22.

Furet, François. *The Passing of an Illusion: The Idea of Communism in the Twentieth Century*. Chicago: University of Chicago Press, 1995.

Furet, François, and Ernst Nolte. *Fascism and Communism*. Lincoln: University of Nebraska Press, 2001.

Geary, Dick. "Nazis and Workers: A Response to Conan Fischer's 'Class Enemies or Class Brothers.'" *European History Review* 15, no. 4 (October 1985).

Gellately, Robert. *The Gestapo and German Society: Enforcing Racial Policy, 1933–1945*. Oxford: Clarendon Press, 1991.

Gilensen, Viktor. "Die Komintern und die 'paramilitarischen Formationen' der Kommunistischen Partei Deutschlands (1926–1932)." *Forum für osteuropäische Ideen- und Zeitgeschichte* 5, no. 1 (2001): 9–50.

Gleason, Abbott. *Totalitarianism: The Inner History of the Cold War*. New York: Oxford University Press, 1995.

Goldberg, Harold. "Goldman and Berkman View the Bolshevik Regime." *Slavic and East European Review* 53, no. 131 (April 1975): 272–76.

Golsan, Richard J. "Introduction to the English-Language Edition: The Politics of History and Memory in France in the 1990s." In Henry Rousso, ed., *Stalinism and Nazism: History and Memory Compared*. Lincoln: University of Nebraska Press, 1999.

Gordon, Harold J. *Hitler and the Beer Hall Putsch*. Princeton, NJ: Princeton University Press, 1972.

Gossweiler, Kurt. *Die Strasser-Legende*. Berlin: Ed. ost/Neue Berlin, 1994.

Götz von Olenhusen, Irmtraud. "Vom Jungstahlhelm zur SA: Die junge Nachkriegsgeneration in den paramilitärischen Verbänden der Weimarer Republik," in Wolfgang R. Krabbe, ed., *Politische Jugend in der Weimarer Republik*, 146–82. Bochum: Universitätsverlag Dr. N. Brockmeyer, 1993.

Grant, Thomas. *Stormtroopers and Crisis in the Nazi Movement: Activism, Ideology and Dissolution*. New York: Routledge, 2004.

Gray, John. *Al Qaeda and What It Means to Be Modern.* New York: The New Press, 2003.

Griffin, Roger. "From Slime Mould to Rhizome: An Introduction to the Groupuscular Right." *Patterns of Prejudice* 37, no. 1 (March 2003): 27–50.

———. "Last Rights?" Afterword in S. Ramet, ed., *The Radical Right in Central and Eastern Europe,* 297–231. University Park, PA: Penn State University Press, 1999.

———. *The Nature of Fascism.* New York: Routledge, 1991.

———. "'Racism' or 'Rebirth'? The Case for Granting German Citizenship to the Alien Concept 'Generic Fascism.'" *Ethik und Sozialwissenschaften* 11, no. 2 (July 2000): 300–303.

———. "Withstanding the Rush of Time: The Prescience of G. L. Mosse's Anthropological Approach to Fascism." In Stanley Payne, ed., *What History Tells: George L. Mosse's Study of Modern Europe.* Madison: University of Wisconsin Press, 2003.

Gross, Babette. *Willy Münzenberg, Eine politische Biographie.* Stuttgart: Deutsche Verlagsanstalt, 1968.

Gruppe MAGMA. *"... denn Angriff ist die beste Verteidigung." Die KPD zwischen Revolution und Faschismus.* Bonn: Pahl Rugenstein-Verlag, 2001.

Grünewald, Guido. "Friedenssicherung durch radikale Kriegsdienstgegnerschaft: Der Bund der Kriegsdienstgegner (BdK) 1919–1933." In K. Holl and W. Wette, eds., *Pazifismus in der Weimarer Republik,* 77–90. Paderborn: Ferdinand Schöningh, 1981.

Gurian, Waldemar. *The Future of Bolshevism.* New York: Sheed & Ward, 1936.

Haffner, Sebastian. *Failure of a Revolution: Germany, 1918–1919.* Chicago: Banner Press, 1969.

Hagemann, Karen, and Stefanie Schüler-Springorum, eds. *Home/Front: The Military, War, and Gender in Twentieth-Century Germany.* New York: Berg, 2002.

Hambrecht, Ranier. *Der Aufstieg der NSDAP in Mittel- und Oberfranken, 1925–1933. Nürnberger Werkstücke zur Stadt- und Landesgeschichte,* vol. 17. Nuremberg: Korn und Berg, 1976.

Hancock, Eleanor. "Ernst Röhm and the Experience of World War I." *Journal of Military History* 60, no. 1 (January 1996): 39–60.

———. "'Only the Real, the True, the Masculine Held Its Value': Ernst Röhm, Masculinity, and Male Homosexuality." *Journal of the History of Sexuality* 8, no. 41 (1998): 616–41.

Heiden, Konrad. *A History of National Socialism.* New York: Knopf, 1935.

Heider, Paul. *Antifaschistischer Kampf und revolutionäre Militärpolitik.* Berlin: Militärverlag der Deutschen Demokratischen Republik, 1976.

Hellfeld, Mathias von. *Bündische Jugend und Hitlerjugend. Zur Geschichte von Anpassung und Widerstand 1930–1939.* Cologne: Verlag Wissenschaft und Politik, 1987.

———. *Die betrogene Generation. Jugend im Faschismus.* Cologne: Pahl Rugenstein-Verlag, 1985.

Herbert, Ulrich. *Best. Biographische Studien über Radikalismus, Weltanschauung und Vernuft, 1903–1989.* Bonn: Dietz, 1996.

Herf, Jeffrey. *Reactionary Modernism: Technology, Culture, and Politics in Weimar and the Third Reich.* Cambridge: Cambridge University Press, 1986.

Herlemann, Beatrix. "Communist Resistance Between Comintern Directives and Nazi Terror." In David E. Barclay and Eric D. Weitz, eds., *Between Reform and Revolution: German Socialism and Communism from 1840 to 1990,* 357–71. New York: Berghahn, 1998.

———. *Die Emigration als Kampfposten. Die Einleitung des kommunistischen Widerstandes in Deutschland aus Frankreich, Belgien und den Niederlanden.* Königstein im Taunus: Verlag Anton Hain, 1982.

Herzog, Dagmar. *Sex After Fascism: Memory and Morality in Twentieth-Century Germany.* Princeton, NJ: Princeton University Press, 2005.

Hoffmann, Hilmar. *The Triumph of Propaganda: Film and National Socialism, 1933–1945.* Providence: Berghahn, 1997.

Holst, Herbert. "Richard Scheringer. Ein Beitrag zur Biographie.'" Diplom-Arbeit, University of Rostock, 26 January 1976.

Hüppauf, Bernd. "The Birth of Fascist Man from the Spirit of the Front." In John Milfull, ed., *The Attractions of Fascism: Social Psychology and Aesthetics of the "Triumph of the Right."* New York: Berg, 1990.

———. "Langemarck, Verdun, and the Myth of a New Man in Germany After the First World War." *War & Society* 6, no. 2 (September 1988): 70–103.

Jamin, Mathilde. "Methodische Konzeption einer Quantitative Analyse zur sozialen Zusammensetzung der SA." In Reinhard Mann, ed., *Die Nationalsozialisten: Analysen Faschistischer Bewegungen, Historisch-sozialwissenschaftliche Forschungen* 9, 84–97. Stuttgart: Klett-Cotta, 1980.

———. "Zur Rolle der SA im nationalsozialistischen Herrschaftssystem." in G. Hirschfeld and L. Kettenacker, eds., *The "Führer State": Myth and Reality. Studies on the Structure and Politics of the Third Reich.* Stuttgart: Klett-Cotta, 1981.

———. "Zur Sozialstruktur des Nationalsozialismus." *Politische Vierteljahresschrift* 19 (1978): 88–91.

———. *Zwischen den Klassen: Zur Sozialstruktur der SA-Führerschaft* (Wuppertal: Hammer, 1984).

Jenrich, Holger. *Anarchistische Presse in Deutschland 1945–1985.* Grafenau-Döffingen: Trozdem Verlag, 1988.

Jochmann, Werner. *Nationalsozialismus und Revolution. Ursprung und Geschichte der NSDAP in Hamburg 1922–1933.* Frankfurt am Main: Europäische Verlagsanstalt, 1963.

Jost, Hermand, and Frank Trommler. *Die Kultur der Weimar Republik.* Frankfurt: Fischer, 1988.

Jarausch, Konrad H. *Students, Society, and Politics in Imperial Germany: The Rise of Academic Illiberalism.* Princeton, NJ: Princeton University Press, 1982.

Jones, Larry Eugene. "Liberalism and the Challenge of the Younger Generation: The Young Liberal Struggle for a Reform of the Weimar Party System, 1928–1930." In Wolfgang R. Krabbe, ed., *Politische Jugend in der Weimarer Republik,* 106–28. Bochum: Universitätsverlag Dr. N. Brockmeyer, 1993.

Jünger, Ernst. *Der Arbeiter. Herrschaft und Gestalt.* Stuttgart: Klett-Cotta, 1982.

Kaes, Anton, Martin Jay, and Edward Dimendberg eds., *The Weimar Republic Sourcebook.* Berkeley: University of California Press, 1994.

Kater, Michael H. "Ansätze zu einer Soziologie der SA bis zur Röhm-Krise." *Soziale Bewegungen und Politische Verfassung, Industrielle Welt: Schriftenreihe des Arbeitskreises für moderne Sozialgeschichte* 62 (1975): 339–79.

———. *Hitler Youth.* Cambridge, MA: Harvard University Press, 2004.

———. *The Nazi Party: A Social Profile of Members and Leaders, 1919–1945.* Cambridge: Harvard University Press, 1983.

————. *Studentenschaft und Rechtsradikalismus in Deutschland 1918–1933.* Hamburg: Hoffmann und Campe, 1975.

Kaufmann, Bernd, et al. *Der Nachrichtendienst der KPD 1919–1937.* Berlin: Dietz Verlag, 1993.

Kele, Max H. *Nazis and Workers: National Socialist Appeals to German Labor, 1919– 1933.* Chapel Hill: University of North Carolina Press, 1972.

Kellerhoff, Sven Felix. *Hitler's Berlin. Geschichte einer Hassliebe.* Berlin: be.bra Verlag, 2005.

Kershaw, Ian. *Hitler, 1889–1936: Hubris.* New York: Norton, 1998.

————. *Hitler, 1936–1945: Nemesis.* New York: Norton, 2001.

————. *The Nazi Dictatorship: Problems and Perspectives of Interpretation.* London: Hodder Arnold, 2000.

Kershaw, Ian, and Moshe Lewin, eds. *Stalinism and Nazism: Dictatorships in Comparison.* Cambridge: Cambridge University Press, 1997.

Klein, Silvia, and Bernhard Stelmaszyk. "Eberhard Köbel, 'Tusk.' Ein biographisches Porträt über die Jahre 1907–1945." In Wilfried Breyvogel, ed., *Piraten, Swings und Junge Garde. Jugendwiderstand im Nationalsozialismus,* 102–36. Bonn: Dietz, 1991.

Klönne, Arno. *Jugend im Dritten Reich. Die Hitler-Jugend und ihre Gegner. Dokumente und Analyse.* Düsseldorf: Eugen Diederichs Verlag, 1982.

Koch, Stephan. *Double Lives: Stalin, Willi Münzenberg and the Seduction of the Intellectuals.* New York: Enigma, 2004.

Koonz, Claudia. *The Nazi Conscience.* Cambridge, MA: The Belknap Press of Harvard University Press, 2003.

Kratzenberg-Annies, Volker. *Arbeiter auf dem Weg zu Hitler? Die Nationalsozialistische Betriebszellen-Organisation. Ihre Entstehung, ihre Programmatik, ihr Scheitern. 1927– 1934.* Frankfurt am Main: Peter Lang, 1989.

Kruppe, Bernd. "Rechtsextreme Wehrverbände in der Weimarer Republik. Die Entwicklung seit 1918 und ihre Rolle in den politischen Entscheidungen des Jahres 1932." In Diethart Kerbs and Henrick Stahr, eds., *Berlin 1932. Das letzte Jahr der ersten deutschen Republik. Politik, Symbole, Medien,* 115–30. Berlin: Edition Hentrich, 1992.

Kühnl, Reinhard. *Die nationalsozialistische Linke 1925–1930.* Meisenheim am Glan: Hain, 1966.

Lane, Barbara Miller. "Nazi Ideology: Some Unfinished Business." *Central European History* 7, no. 1 (March 1974): 3–30.

Laqueur, Walter. *Russia and Germany: A Century of Conflict.* Boston: Little, Brown, 1965.

————. *Young Germany: A History of the German Youth Movement.* New Brunswick, NJ: Transaction Books, 1984.

Lindner, Wolfgang. *Jugendbewegung als Äußerung lebensideologischer Mentalität. Die mentalitätsgeschichtlichen Präferenzen der deutschen Jugendbewegung im Spiegel ihrer Liedertexte.* Hamburg: Verlag Dr. Kovac, 2003.

Linz, Juan J. "Some Notes Toward a Comparative Study of Fascism in Sociological Historical Perspective." In Walter Laqueur, ed., *Fascism: A Reader's Guide,* 3–121. Berkeley: University of California Press, 1976.

Loewenberg, P. "The Psychohistorical Origins of the Nazi Youth Cohort." *American Historical Review* 75 (1971): 1457–1502.

Loewenheim, Walter. *Geschichte der Org [Neu Beginnen] 1929–1935. Eine zeitgenössische Analyse Herausgegeben von Jan Foitzik*. Berlin: Edition Hentrich, 1995.

Longerich, Peter. *Die Braunen Bataillone. Geschichte der SA*. Munich: Beck, 1989.

Lüpke, Reinhard. "Zwischen Jugendbewegung und Linksopposition. Die Jungsozialisten in der Weimarer Republik 1919–1931." In Wolfgang R. Krabbe, ed., *Politische Jugend in der Weimarer Republik*, 73–86. Bochum: Universitätsverlag Dr. N. Brockmeyer, 1993.

———. *Zwischen Marx und Wandervogel. Die Jungsozialisten in der Weimarer Republik 1919–1931*. Marburg: Verlag Arbeiterbewegung und Gesellschaftswissenschaft, 1984.

Lütgemeier-Davin, Reinhold. "Basismobilisierung gegen den Krieg: Die Nie-wieder-Krieg-Bewegung in der Weimarer Republik." In K. Holl and W. Wette, eds., *Pazifismus in der Weimarer Republik*, 47–76. Paderborn: Ferdinand Schöningh, 1981.

Mai, Gunther. "Arbeiterschaft und 'Volksgemeinschaft." In Winfried Speitkamp, ed., *Staat, Gesellschaft, Wissenschaft. Beiträge zur modernen hessischen Geschichte*, 211. Marburg: Elwert, 1994.

———. *Die Geislinger Metallarbeiterbewegung zwischen Klassenkampf und Volksgemeinschaft 1931–1933/34*. Düsseldorf: Droste, 1984.

———. "National Socialist Factory Cell Organization and the German Labour Front: National Socialist Labour Policy and Organizations." In Conan Fischer, ed., *The Rise of National Socialism and the Working Classes in Weimar Germany*, 117–36. Providence and Oxford: Berghahn, 1996.

———. "'Verteidigungskrieg' und 'Volksgemeinschaft.' Staatliche Selbstbehauptung, nationale Solidarität und soziale Befreiung in Deutschland in der Zeit des Ersten Weltkriegs (1900–1925)." In Wolfgang Michalka, ed., *Der Erste Weltkrieg: Wirklichkeit, Wahrnehmung, Analyse*, 583–602. Munich: Piper, 1994.

Major, Patrick. *The Death of the KPD: Communism and Anti-Communism in West Germany, 1945–1956*. New York: Clarendon Press, 1997.

Malinowski, Stephan. "From King to Führer: The German Aristocracy and the Nazi Movement." *Bulletin of the German Historical Institute* 27, no. 1 (May 2005): 5–28.

Mallmann, Klaus-Michael. *Kommunisten in der Weimarer Republik. Sozialgeschichte einer revolutionären Bewegung*. Darmstadt: Wissenschaftliche Buchgesellschaft, 1996.

———. "Kommunistischer Widerstand 1933–1945. Anmerkungen zu Forschungsstand und Forschungsdefiziten." In Peter Steinbach and Johannes Tuchel, eds., *Widerstand gegen den Nationalsozialismus*, 113–25. Bonn: Bundeszentrale fur Politische Bildung, 1994.

Mallmann, Klaus-Michael, and Gerhard Paul. "Omniscient, Omnipotent, Omnipresent? Gestapo, Society and Resistance." In David Crew, ed., *Nazism and German Society 1933–45*, 166–96. London: Routledge, 1994.

Mammach, Klaus. *Die deutsche Widerstandsbewegung, 1933–1939*. Berlin: Dietz Verlag, 1974.

Mann, Michael. "The contradictions of continuous revolution." In Ian Kershaw and Moshe Lewin, eds., *Stalinism and Nazism: Dictatorships in Comparison*, 135–57. Cambridge: Cambridge University Press, 1997.

———. *Fascists*. Cambridge: Cambridge University Press, 2004.

Maximov, Grigori. *The Guillotine at Work in Russia*. Chicago: Berkman Fund, 1940.

McKale, Donald M. *The Nazi Party Courts: Hitler's Management of Conflict in His Movement, 1921–1945.* Lawrence: University Press of Kansas, 1974.

McMeekin, Sean. *The Red Millionaire: A Political Biography of Willy Münzenberg, Moscow's Secret Propaganda Tsar in the West, 1917–1940.* New Haven, CT: Yale University Press, 2004.

Mehringer, Hartmut. "Die KPD in Bayern 1919–1945. Vorgeschichte, Verfolgung und Widerstand." In Martin Broszat and Hartmut Mehringer, eds., *Bayern in der NS-Zeit. V. Die Parteien KPD, SPD, BVP in Verfolgung und Widerstand,* 1–286. Munich: R. Oldenbourg, 1983.

Meinl, Susanne. *Nationalsozialisten gegen Hitler. Die nationalrevolutionäre Opposition um Friedrich Wilhelm Heinz.* Berlin: Siedler, 2000.

Merkl, Peter H. *The Making of a Stormtrooper.* Princeton, NJ: Princeton University Press, 1980.

———. *Political Violence Under the Swastika: 581 Early Nazis.* Princeton, NJ: Princeton University Press, 1975.).

Merson, Allan. *Communist Resistance in Nazi Germany.* London: Lawrence & Wishart, 1985.

Meyer, Thomas. *Die Inszenierung des Scheins. Voraussetzungen und Folgen symbolischer Politik.* Frankfurt am Main: Suhrkamp, 1992.

Mommsen, Hans. *Alternatives to Hitler: German Resistance Under the Nazis.* Princeton, NJ: Princeton University Press, 2003.

———. *From Weimar to Auschwitz.* Princeton, NJ: Princeton University Press, 1991.

———. "National Socialism: Continuity and Change." In Walter Laqueur, ed., *Fascism: A Reader's Guide,* 179–210. Berkeley: University of California Press, 1976.

———. *The Rise and Fall of Weimar Democracy.* Chapel Hill: University of North Carolina Press, 1989.

Moreau, Patrick. *Nationalsozialismus von Links. "Die Kampfgemeinschaft Revolutionärer Nationalsozialisten" und die "schwarze Front" Otto Strassers 1930–1935.* Stuttgart: Deutsche Verlagsanstalt, 1984.

———. "Otto Strasser: Nationalist Socialism versus National Socialism." In Ronald Smelser and Rainer Zitelmann, eds., *The Nazi Elite,* 235–44. New York: New York University Press, 1993.

Morgan, David. *The Socialist Left and the German Revolution: A History of the German Independent Social Democratic Party, 1917–1922.* Ithaca, NY: Cornell University Press, 1975.

Mosse, George L. *The Crisis of German Ideology. Intellectual Origins of the Third Reich.* New York: Schocken Books, 1981.

———. *Fallen Soldiers: Reshaping the Memory of the World Wars.* New York: Oxford University Press, 1990.

———. *The Fascist Revolution: Toward a General Theory of Fascism.* New York: Howard Fertig, 1999.

———. *Nationalism and Sexuality: Respectability and Abnormal Sexuality in Modern Europe.* New York: Howard Fertig, 1985.

———. *The Nationalization of the Masses: Political Symbolism and Mass Movements in Germany from the Napoleonic Wars through the Third Reich.* Ithaca, NY:: Cornell University Press, 1975.

———. *Nazi Culture: Intellectual, Cultural and Social Life in the Third Reich.* New York: Schocken Books, 1981.

Mühlberger, Detlef. *Hitler's Followers: Studies in the Sociology of the Nazi Movement.* London: Routledge, 1991.

———. *The Social Bases of Nazism, 1919–1933.* Cambridge: Cambridge University Press, 2003.

———. "The Sociology of the NSDAP: The Question of Working-Class Membership." *Journal of Contemporary History* 15 (July 1980): 493–512.

Nevin, Thomas. *Ernst Jünger and Germany: Into the Abyss, 1914–1945.* Durham, NC: Duke University Press, 1996.

Noakes, Jeremy. *The Nazi Party in Lower Saxony, 1921–1933.* London: Oxford University Press, 1971.

Nyomarkay, Joseph. *Charisma and Factionalism in the Nazi Party.* Minneapolis: University of Minnesota Press, 1967.

Orlow, Dietrich. *The History of the Nazi Party: 1919–1933.* Pittsburgh: University of Pittsburgh Press, 1969.

Paetel, Karl O. *Versuchung oder Chance? Zur Geschichte des Nationalbolshevismus.* Göttingen: Musterschmidt-Verlag, 1965.

Paul, Gerhard *Aufstand der Bilder. Die NS-Propaganda vor 1933.* Bonn: Dietz, 1990.

———. "Die widerspenstige "Volksgemeinschaft." Dissens und Verweigerung im Dritten Reich." In Peter Steinbach and Johannes Tuchel, eds., *Widerstand gegen den Nationalsozialismus,* 395–410. Bonn: Bundeszentrale für Politische Bildung, 1994.

Paul, Wolfgang. *Das Feldlager. Jugend zwischen Langemarck und Stalingrad.* Esslingen am Neckar: Bechtle, 1978.

Payne, Stanley G. *Fascism: Comparison and Definition.* Madison: University of Wisconsin Press, 1980.

———. *A History of Fascism, 1914–1945.* Madison: University of Wisconsin Press, 1995.

Peukert, Detlev. *Die Edelweisspiraten. Protestbewegungen jugendlicher Arbeiter im Dritten Reich. Eine Dokumentation.* Cologne: Bund Verlag, 1980.

———. *Die KPD in Widerstand. Verfolgung und Untergrundarbeit an Rhein und Ruhr 1933 bis 1945.* Wuppertal: Hammer, 1980.

———. *Jugend zwischen Krieg und Krise. Lebenswelten von Arbeiterjungen in der Weimarer Republik.* Cologne: Bund Verlag, 1987.

———. *The Weimar Republic: The Crisis of Classical Modernity.* London: Allen Lane, 1991.

Pikarski, Margot. *Jugend im Berliner Widerstand.* Berlin: Militärverlag der Deutschen Demokratischen Republik, 1984.

Plessner, Helmuth. *The Limits of Community: A Critique of Social Radicalism.* Amherst, N.Y.: Humanity Books, 1999.

Poewe, Karla. *New Religions and the Nazis.* New York: Routledge, 2006.

Post, Ken. *Communists and National Socialists: The Foundations of a Century, 1914–1939.* New York: St. Martin's Press, 1997.

Pridham, Geoffrey. *Hitler's Rise to Power: The Nazi Movement in Bavaria, 1923–1933.* London: Hart-Davis, MacGibbon, 1973.

Prowe, Diethelm. "Fascism, Neo-Fascism, New Radical Right?" In Roger Griffin, ed., *International Fascism: Theories, Causes, and the New Consensus,* 305–24. London: Arnold, 1998.

Raabe, Felix. *Die Bündische Jugend. Ein Beitrag zur Geschichte der Weimarer Republic.* Stuttgart: Brentano Verlag, 1961.

Rätsch-Langejürgen, Birgit. *Das Prinzip Widerstand. Leben und Wirken von Ernst Niekisch.* Bonn: Bouvier Verlag, 1997.

Rauschning, Hermann. *The Revolution of Nihilism: Warning to the West.* New York: Longmans, Green, 1939.

———. *The Voice of Destruction.* New York: G. P. Putnam's Sons, 1940.

Reichardt, Sven. *Faschistische Kampfbünde. Gewalt und Gemeinschaft im italienischen Squadrismus und in der deutschen SA.* Cologne: Böhlau Verlag, 2002.

———. "Gewalt, Körper, Politik. Paradoxien in der deutschen Kulturgeschichte der Zwischenkriegszeit." In Wolfgang Hardtwig, ed., *Politische Kulturgeschichte der Zwischenkriegszeit 1918–1939*, 205–39. Göttingen: Vandenhoeck & Ruprecht, 2005.

———. "Totalitäre Gewaltpolitik? Überlegungen zum Verhältnis von national-sozialistischer und kommunistischer Gewalt in der Weimarer Republik." In Wolfgang Hardtwig, ed., *Ordnungen in der Krise. Zur politischen Kulturgeschichte Deutschlands 1900–1933*, 377–402. Munich: R. Oldenbourg Verlag, 2007.

Reiche, Eric G. *The Development of the SA in Nürnberg, 1922–1934.* Cambridge: Cambridge University Press, 1986.

Reimann, Viktor. *Goebbels.* New York: Doubleday, 1976.

Rengstorf, Ernst-Viktor. *Links-Opposition in der Weimarer SPD. Die "Klassenkampf-Gruppe" 1928–1931.* Hannover: SOAK Verlag, 1978.

Retzlaff, Birgit. *Arbeiterjugend gegen Hitler. Der Widerstand ehemaliger Angehöriger der Sozialistischen Arbeiterjugendbewegung gegen das Dritte Reich.* Bielefeld: Paegelit, 1993.

Reulecke, Jürgen. "Hat die Jugendbewegung den Nationalsozialismus vorbereitet? Zum Umgang mit einer falschen Frage." In Wolfgang R. Krabbe, ed., *Politische Jugend in der Weimarer Republik*, 222–43. Bochum: Universitätsverlag Dr. N. Brockmeyer, 1993.

Reuth, Ralf Georg. *Goebbels.* Munich: Piper, 1990.

Robert, David D. *The Syndicalist Tradition and Italian Fascism.* Chapel Hill: University of North Carolina Press, 1979.

Rohe, Karl. *Das Reichsbanner Schwarz Rot Gold. Ein Beitrag zur Geschichte und Struktur der politischen Kampfverbände zur Zeit der Weimarer Republik.* Düsseldorf: Droste Verlag, 1966.

Röhl, Klaus Ranier. "Fünf Tage im November. Kommunisten, Sozialdemokraten und Nationalsozialisten und der BVG-Streik vom November 1932 in Berlin." In Diethart Kerbs und Henrick Stahr, eds., *Berlin 1932. Das letzte Jahr der ersten deutschen Republik. Politik, Symbole, Medien*, 161–78. Berlin: Edition Hentrich, 1992.

———. *Nähe zum Gegner. Die Zusammenarbeit von Kommunisten und National-sozialisten beim Berliner BVG-Streik von 1932.* Frankfurt am Main: Campus Verlag, 1992.

Römer, Susanne. "'Aufbruch'—fast 70 Jahre danach." In Susanne Römer und Hans Coppi, eds., *Aufbruch. Dokumentation einer Zeitschrift zwischen den Fronten.* Koblenz: Verlag Dietmar Fölbach, 2001.

Roseman, Mark, "Introduction: Generation Conflict and German History, 1770–1968." In Mark Roseman, ed., *Generations in Conflict: Youth Revolt and Generational Formation in Germany, 1770–1968*, 1–46. Cambridge: Cambridge University Press, 1995.

Rosenhaft, Eve. *Beating the Fascists? The German Communists and Political Violence, 1929–1933.* Cambridge: Cambridge University Press, 1983.

———. "Links gleich rechts? Militante Straßengewalt um 1930." In Thomas Lindenberger and Alf Lüdtke, eds., *Physische Gewalt.* Frankfurt am Main: Suhrkamp, 1995.

———. "Working-Class Life and Working-Class Politics: Communists, Nazis and the State in the Battle for the Streets, Berlin 1928–1932." In Richard Bessel and E.J. Feuchtwanger eds., *Social Change and Political Development in Weimar Germany,* 207–40. London: Croom Helm, 1981.

Rousso, Henry, ed. *Stalinism and Nazism: History and Memory Compared.* Lincoln: University of Nebraska Press, 1999.

Russell, Bertrand. *The Theory and Practice of Bolshevism.* London: George Allen & Unwin, 1920.

Sandvoß, Hans-Ranier. *Widerstand 1933–1945.* Berlin: Gedenkstätte Deutscher Widerstand, 1996.

Schelsky, Helmut, Die skeptische Generation. Eine Soziologie der deutschen Jugend. Düsseldorf-Köln: Diederichs, 1957.

Schneider, Michael. *Unterm Hakenkreuz. Arbeiter und Arbeiterbewegung 1933 bis 1939.* Bonn: Dietz, 1999.

Schoenbaum, David. *Hitler's Social Revolution: Class and Status in Nazi Germany, 1933–1939.* Garden City, NY: Anchor Books, 1967.

Schüddekopf, Otto-Ernst. *Linke Leute von Rechts. Die nationalrevolutionären Minderheiten und der Kommunismus in der Weimarer Republik.* Stuttgart: Kohlhammer, 1960.

———. *National-bolshewismus in Deutschland 1918–1933.* Frankfurt am Main: Ullstein, 1972.

Schumann, Dirk. *Politische Gewalt in der Weimarer Republik: Kampf um die Strasse und Furcht vor dem Bürgerkrieg.* Essen: Klartext, 2001.

Schuster, Kurt G. P. *Der Rote Frontkämpferbund 1924–1929. Beiträge zur Geschichte und Organisationsstruktur eines politischen Kampfbundes.* Düsseldorf: Droste, 1975.

Schwarz, Georg. *Völker hört die Signale. KPD bankrott.* Berlin, 1933.

Selznick, Philip. *The Organizational Weapon: A Study of Bolshevik Strategy and Tactics.* New York: McGraw-Hill, 1952.

Sewell, William H., Jr. "The Concept(s) of Culture." In Victoria E. Bonnell and Lynn Hunt, eds., *Beyond the Cultural Turn: New Directions in the Study of Society and Culture,* 35–61. Berkeley: University of California Press, 1999.

Smelser, Ronald, and Rainer Zitelmann. *The Nazi Elite.* New York: NYU Press, 1993.

Spielvogel, J. J. *Hitler and Nazi Germany: A History.* Englewood Cliffs, NJ: Prentice Hall, 1988.

Stachura, Peter D. "Der Kritische Wendepunkt? Die NSDAP und die Reichstagwahlen vom 20. Mai 1928," *Vierteljahreshefte für Zeitgeschichte,* 26, 1978, 66–69.

———. *Nazi Youth in the Weimar Republic.* Santa Barbara, CA: Clio Books, 1975.

———. "The Nazis, the Bourgeoisie and the Workers during the Kampfzeit." In Peter D. Stachura, ed., *The Nazi Machtergreifung,* 15–32. London: Allen and Unwin, 1983.

———. "Who Were the Nazis? A Socio-Political Analysis of the National Socialist Machtübernahme" *European Studies Review* 11 (July 1981): 293–324.

Stearns, Peter N. *Be a Man! Males in Modern Society.* New York: Holmes & Meier, 1990.

Stern, Fritz. *The Politics of Cultural Despair: A Study in the Rise of the Germanic Ideology.* Berkeley,: University of California Press, 1961.

Sternhell, Zeev. "Fascist Ideology." In Walter Laqueur, ed., *Fascism: A Reader's Guide. Analyses, Interpretations, Bibliography,* 315–76. Berkeley: University of California Press, 1976.

———. *Neither Right nor Left: Fascist Ideology in France.* Princeton, NJ: Princeton University Press, 1996.

Sternhell, Zeev, with Mario Sznajder and Maia Asheri. *The Birth of Fascist Ideology: From Cultural Rebellion to Political Revolution.* Princeton, NJ: Princeton University Press, 1994.

Stöver, Bernd. *Volksgemeinschaft im Dritten Reich. Die Konsensbereitschaft der Deutschen im Spiegel sozialistischer Berichte.* Düsseldorf: Droste Verlag, 1993.

Striefler, Christian. *Kampf um die Macht. Kommunisten und Nationalsozialisten am Ende der Weimarer Republik.* Berlin: Propyläen, 1993.

Suny, Ronald Grigor, "Back and Beyond: Reversing the Cultural Turn?" *American Historical Review,* December 2002, 1476–99.

Swett, Pamela. *Neighbors and Enemies: The Culture of Radicalism in Berlin, 1929–1933.* Cambridge: Cambridge University Press, 2004.

Szejnmann, Claus-Christian. *Nazism in Central Germany: The Brownshirts in "Red" Saxony.* Providence and Oxford: Berghahn, 1999.

———. "The Rise of the Nazi Party in the Working-Class Milieu of Saxony." In Conan Fischer, ed., *The Rise of National Socialism and the Working Classes in Weimar Germany,* 189–216. Providence and Oxford: Berghahn, 1996.

Taylor, Charles. *The Ethics of Authenticity.* Cambridge, MA: Harvard University Press, 1992.

Theweleit, Klaus. *Male Fantasies.* 2 vols. Minneapolis: University of Minnesota Press, 1987.

Trotsky, Leon. *The Struggle Against Fascism in Germany.* New York: Pathfinder Press, 1971.

Van Ree, Erik. *The Political Thought of Joseph Stalin: A Study in Twentieth-Century Revolutionary Patriotism.* New York: Routledge, 2002.

Van Roon, Ger. *Widerstand im Dritten Reich.* Munich: Beck'sche Reihe, 1987.

Vogelsang, Thilo. *Reichwehr, Staat und NSDAP. Beiträge zur deutschen Geschichte 1930– 1932.* Stuttgart: Deutsche Verlagsanstalt, 1962.

———. "Der Sogenannte 'Scheringer Kreis.'" In *Gutachten der Institut für Zeitge- schichte,* vol. 2, 469–70. Stuttgart: Deutsche Verlagsanstalt, 1966.

Voline, *The Unknown Revolution.* London: Freedom Press, 1955.

Waite, Robert G. L. *Vanguard of Nazism: The Free Corps Movement in Postwar Germany, 1918–1923.* Cambridge, MA: Harvard University Press, 1970.

Ward, James J. Pipe Dreams or Revolutionary Politics: The Group of Social Revo- lutionary Nationalists in Weimar Germany." *Journal of Contemporary History* 15 (1980): 513–532.

———. 'Revolution in the Revolution? Ideas of Armed Struggle in the German Communist Movement, 1929–1933." Paper presented at the History Conference of Hudson Valley Colleges and Universities, Bard College, 27 October 1983.

———. "'Smash the Fascists…'": German Communist Efforts to Counter the Nazis, 1930–31." *Central European History* 14, no. 1 (1981): 30–62.

Weber, Herman. "Einleitung." In Herman Weber, ed., *Die Generallinie. Rundschreiben des Zentralkomitees der KPD an die Bezirke 1929–1933*, vii–cxvii. Düsseldorf: Droste, 1981.

———. "Zur Politik der KPD 1929–1933." In Manfred Scharrer, ed., *Kampflose Kapitulation. Arbeiter Bewegung 1933*, 121–61. Hamburg: Rowohlt, 1984.

Weißbecker, Manfred, and Kurt Pätzold. *Geschichte der NSDAP 1920–1945*. Cologne: Papyrossa, 1981.

Weitz, Eric D. *A Century of Genocide: Utopias of Race and Nation*. Princeton, NJ: Princeton University Press, 2005.

———. *Creating German Communism, 1890–1990: From Popular Protests to Socialist State*. Princeton, NJ: Princeton University Press, 1997.

———. "Racial Politics Without the Concept of Race: Reevaluating Soviet Ethnic and National Purges." *Slavic Review* 61, no. 1 (Spring 2002): 1–29.

Wette, Wolfgang. "Einleitung: Probleme des Pazifismus in der Zwischenkriegszeit." In K. Holland W. Wette, eds., *Pazifismus in der Weimarer Republik*, 9–25. Paderborn: Ferdinand Schöningh, 1981.

Williams, Robert C. *Culture in Exile: Russian Émigrés in Germany, 1881–1941*. Ithaca, NY: Cornell University Press, 1972.

Wippermann, Wolfgang. "Die nationalsozialistische 'Machtergreifung' in Berlin." In *Stadtfront: Berlin West Berlin*, 119–23. Berlin: Elefanten Press, 1989.

———. "Falsch gedacht und nicht gehandelt. Der 20. Juli 1932 und das Scheitern des sozialdemokratischen Antifaschismus." In Diethart Kerbs and Henrick Stahr, eds., *Berlin 1932. Das letzte Jahr der ersten deutschen Republik. Politik, Symbole, Medien*, 115–30. Berlin: Edition Hentrich, 1992.

Wohl, Robert. *The Generation of 1914*. Cambridge, MA: Harvard University Press, 1983.

Wollenberg, Erich. *The Red Army*. London: Secker & Warburg, 1938.

Wurgaft, Lewis D. *Kurt Hiller and the Politics of Action on the German Left, 1914–1933*. Philadelphia: American Philosophical Society, 1977.

Ziegler, Herbert F. *Nazi Germany's New Aristocracy: The SS Leadership, 1925–1939*. Princeton, NJ: Princeton University Press, 1989.

Zorn, Wolfgang. "Student Politics in the Weimar Republic." *Journal of Contemporary History* 5, no. 1 (1970): 128–143.

INDEX

Monographs in German History

www.ingramcontent.com/pod-product-compliance
Lightning Source LLC
Chambersburg PA
CBHW060036030426
42334CB00019B/2358